Rave Culture

Tammy L. Anderson

Rave Culture

The Alteration and Decline of a
Philadelphia Music Scene

TEMPLE UNIVERSITY PRESS
Philadelphia

Temple University Press
1601 North Broad Street
Philadelphia PA 19122
www.temple.edu/tempress

Photos © Tammy L. Anderson

∞ The paper used in this publication meets the requirements of the American
National Standard for Information Sciences—Permanence of Paper for Printed Library
Materials, ANSI Z39.48-1992

*All attempts were made to locate the people in the photographs published in this book. If you believe
you may be one of them, please contact Temple University Press, and the publisher will include appropriate acknowledgment in subsequent editions of the book.*

Library of Congress Cataloging-in-Publication Data

Anderson, Tammy L., 1963–
    Rave culture : the alteration and decline of a Philadelphia music scene / Tammy L. Anderson.
      p. cm.
    Includes bibliographical references.
    ISBN 978-1-59213-933-0 (cloth : alk. paper) — ISBN 978-1-59213-934-7 (pbk. : alk. paper)
    1. Young adults—Pennsylvania—Philadelphia—Social life and culture—History—21st century.
    2. Rave culture—Pennsylvania—Philadelphia—History—21st century.   I. Title.
    HQ799.73.P55A53 2009
    306'.1097481109049—dc22

                                                                                    2008047839

2 4 6 8 9 7 5 3 1

Contents

Acknowledgments

Ethnographies are generally huge undertakings that take a lot of time, effort, support, and cooperation from many people, not just the ethnographer who launched the study. This is certainly the case with my study of rave culture. The study took several years to complete, and the book a few additional years to write. Numerous people, from diverse locations and unique positions, assisted me in completing my work. I should like to give them a "shout out" here to express my deep gratitude for their generosity in my research endeavor.

To begin, this work would not have been possible without the cooperation and kindness of the respondents and key informants included in this study. I am extremely appreciative for the time they took to tell me their stories and offer me their perspectives on rave culture and contemporary EDM scenes. I also owe thanks for the benevolence and valuable insights I received from the many EDM enthusiasts and stakeholders in Philadelphia. They took time to assist me with my fieldwork and gave me feedback on my interpretations and analyses. Foremost among them are Nigel Richards, Jamie Morris, Matt Leutwyler, Mike Pizutti, Sean O'Neal, Billy Leupold, Dave Mass, Art Cuebik, and the rest of the 611 Records staff. I am also grateful to Ben Camp, Carl Richards, Josh Wink, King Britt, Mark Butler, Jared Hupp, Stephanie Douglas, Tracy and Renee Shuron, Oronde, Deach, Ron, and Kate. I am deeply indebted to them for embracing and tolerating me and my project.

Outside of Philadelphia, many other U.S. EDM professionals, fans, and support groups also provided valuable information and useful suggestions. I am especially grateful to David Ireland, Eve Falcon, and Genghis Cohen for their perspectives on West Coast and national developments in dance music. Thanks also go to DJ Nikadeemas, Frankie Bones, and Jason from Blackkat.org for their New York City perspective. DJ Skate from Boston was also helpful early on. Noel Sanger, Lainie Capicotto, and Chris Fortier added critical national input on EDM's place in the contemporary music industry. Bill Piper, from the Drug Policy Alliance, gave inside information on political action regarding rave-related legislation.

The international focus of my project was facilitated by still other EDM stakeholders in places such as Canada, Europe, and the United Kingdom. Wes Straub from Calgary gave cultural input and technical knowledge throughout the project. Kev Hill, Kellilicious and SheJay, Robert Easter, Greg Zizique, Nigel Parkinson, and the Paul Harris Forum provided a keen understanding of and valuable recommendations for understanding the many U.K. EDM scenes, especially those located in London. Alfredo Fiorito, Amanda Sinclair, DJ Da Cat, Mark DeMark, and Medrano and the Balearic People Promotion Group afforded the same in Ibiza, Spain. Finally, CP from Belgium was helpful as well.

There are many people in various academic settings whose assistance and support also made this project possible. To begin, I would like to thank the University of Delaware (UD) and its department of sociology and criminal justice—my home. I am grateful for the substantive, editorial, and emotional support given me by all my colleagues but especially by Joel Best, Susan Miller, and Ronet Bachman. Thanks also go to our department's support staff—Judy Watson, Nancy Quillen, Vicky Becker, and Linda Keen—for their assistance in administrative and technical tasks. Finally, numerous student research assistants deserve recognition for their assistance with the ethnographic data and administrative and background work. They include Phil Kavanaugh, Gabby Mulnick, Megan Greene, Ashley Ings, Eric Best, Erin Fimble, Olivia Fredericks, Kevin Owocki, Carina Yasiejko, and my spring 2006 and 2008 undergraduate SOCI467 classes in Culture, Music, and Deviance.

The book went through several revisions. Each worked to enhance its clarity and message. These improvements were made possible by the patient, careful, and thorough reviewing of manuscript drafts by Joel Best, Susan Miller, Will Straw, Geoffrey Hunt, Fiona Measham, Phil Hadfield, Manuel Guzman, the anonymous reviewers at Temple University Press, the anonymous reviewers for my 2007 paper coauthored with Phil Kavanaugh in *Sociology Compass*, the anonymous reviewers for my 2008 paper coauthored with Phil Kavanaugh in the *Sociological Quarterly*, and Karen Cerulo and the anonymous reviewers at *Sociological Forum* for my 2009 paper.

Finally, I received essential grant support from the UD Office of Research and Sponsored Programs' General University Research program and Center for International Studies as well as from the National Institute of Justice.

1

Introduction

t is 11:30 P.M. on a hot July night in 2004, near Philadelphia's riverfront. I am walking toward the entrance of one of the city's largest electronic dance music (EDM) parties. In the weeks prior, I heard some locals call this event a rave, but most people simply referred to it by its name: Explosion! I am recalling the many contradictory opinions I have heard during my fieldwork about raves' current state. Tonight, I suppose, I will get another chance to think about that debate, since this is the only contemporary party I have heard some scene insiders call a rave.

The group that owns and promotes this party put me on the guest list, which saves me a whopping $40. As soon as I pass through front gate security (metal detector and pat-down), club staff put a yellow plastic band around my wrist, signifying that I am over twenty-one years of age. Younger than twenty-one-year-old partygoers get blue bands. I hear some complaints about the color-coded bands—mostly rants against club alcohol policies—but most objections are about the steep cover charge.

Inside the nightclub, I begin surveying the event's layout. The first room I come to is the party's "main stage" or "main room," which, judging from the reputations of the DJs posted on a list outside, is the trance music room. Eight DJs are scheduled to play here, rotating pretty much every hour.

The DJ is playing music from a booth high above the dance floor. A mostly white and Asian crowd is listening or watching. Others are chatting or dancing, some with glow sticks. I feel slightly overdressed. My shirt is fitted and feminine, not over-sized with a catchy slogan, like those on the people around me.

My pants (jeans) are tight rather than baggy, comfy, or covered with pockets. And my shoes are black leather wedges, not sneakers or trendy sports shoes.

Undeterred by my wardrobe faux pas, I start dancing beside two Asian males, who greet me with smiles and hand me glow sticks. After thirty minutes or so, I thank my sweaty and happy dancing buddies, pass my glow sticks on to a tattooed woman beside me, and move on to check out the two bars in the main room.

The first bar is elevated on a platform, level with the DJ booth. It is guarded by security. A tall, muscular man asks about my wrist band when I start climbing the stairs. He tells me I need a yellow one to enter. I raise my arm and he lets me pass. A few older heterosexual couples are standing around flirting over swanky drinks—imported beer for the men and colorful cocktails for the women. They are dressed more like me, but not much is happening here, so I drift into the other bar.

At the under-twenty-one-year-old bar, only Pepsi products are being sold. Not many people are hanging out here either, but I start talking to a young Goth couple—Craig and Eva—who look more out of place than do I. The young man intrigues me immensely because his hair is glued into a razor-thin, multicolored Mohawk stretching more than a foot above his head. His girlfriend has dyed jet-black hair; heavy, dark makeup; and a black outfit, including fishnet stockings with knee-high, platform leather boots. Silver rings and studs pierce both of their noses and tongues.

Craig and Eva are kind and talkative and I buy them Pepsis as we chat about Goth, rave, and EDM cultures. About thirty minutes into our conversation, a commotion between club security and a skinny, black, male breaks out close by. People immediately converge around us to see what is going on. Two security guards confiscate his pills and disappear into a private room, leaving the third guard behind to supervise the "suspect." A few minutes later, several other security guards push into the room and stay there about ten minutes. They emerge without the pills and tell the young "suspect" he can go back to the party.

As the commotion subsides, the crowd I am standing in disbands. Craig and Eva have slipped away during the distraction. The people around me want to know what happened, but the bouncers remain tight-lipped and the young male under suspicion has disappeared. So, I take a quick peek into the adjacent small, dank, and sweaty techno room, see a handful of people talking along its perimeter, and head outside to the drum and bass tent.

This tent is packed, mostly with white and black males dancing somewhat aggressively to very fast music. There does not seem to be any room on the dance floor, so I make my way to the bar that surrounds it, also guarded by security checking for yellow wristbands. I become frustrated because I can barely maneuver my way through this crowd and I am getting tired from being on my feet for more than two hours now. Clearly, I am wearing the wrong shoes! Thankfully, I see an outdoor chill area and nudge my way toward it to find a place to sit down and relax.

The outdoor chill area encompasses the main tent where progressive house music is being played by some of the event's most famous DJs. This is going to be a good spot for me since the air is fresh, the space comfortable, and the music fantastic. I locate a spot to sit down, a cement step near the Porto-pots, and I say hello to two white guys, Aidan and Connor, sitting next to me. They tell me they are from Cleveland and ask me where I am from. I tell them I live close by and then we start talking about the party, dance music, and DJs.

I take this opportunity to ask them if this event is a rave. My question ignites a heated discussion about how this branded party has changed over the years and what this signifies for rave culture. It also "outs" me as an academic studying the rave and EDM scenes, which both men find interesting. Aidan indulges my question by complaining that the party is more like a concert or at least costs as much as one. He says he cannot buy a proper drink because the cover charge and his "chemicals" have tapped him out. He says this means he has to refill his water bottle in the bathroom, rather than buying new ones for $5 apiece. Connor calls my attention to the "corporatism" around us. He tells me in the old days—in 1999 when he was fifteen—companies like Pepsi, Red Bull, or Sobe did not sponsor raves, but now they did. Connor told me he also was not going to pay $5 for water or Pepsi or $7 for a Red Bull or bottle of Sobe.

Just then, Aidan yells, "Yo! Check out the dude puking over by the Porto-pots." The two men look at each other and say, "Wonder what he's on?" Aidan and Connor leave me behind to go find out, unconcerned about whether event security might interfere with their euphoric plans. So, I get back up to dance. By 4:00 A.M., sweating, heaving, and altered states are more common among the remaining partygoers.

In my car on the way home, I think about the party and how different or similar it might have been to a late 1990s[2] rave in Philadelphia or elsewhere in the United States. Back then, I was a mid-thirties postdoctoral student in Chicago, socially distant from rave scenes anywhere. I wondered if raves in the past were corporate sponsored, had guest lists, cost $40 to get in, and had electronic security. Early in my project, I read that "shady" people made lots of money from raves and had often endangered ravers via overcrowding, drug selling, inadequate water and fluid supply, and exposure to theft and other crimes (Collin 1997; Hill 2002; McRobbie 1994; Redhead 1993, 1995; Reynolds 1999). While I did see some drug selling and the drum and bass tent was packed, tonight's security and event staff seemed overly concerned with safety and policy enforcement. And there was no shortage of modern comforts for attendees (ample sitting space, fresh air, fluids, bathrooms, etc.). Yes, there were Aidan and Connor's complaints, but there also were glow sticks, drug use and drug sickness, and lots of EDM, DJs, and dancing.

Maybe raves had changed, but in what ways and why? The relative infrequency of events like Explosion! in Philadelphia and their diminished attendance (Explosion! was down more than 50 percent from peak rave years, a promoter told me on the way out) certainly made me think that decline, not simply change, was occurring. Was rave culture dying? What forces were reshaping raves or helping to bring about their decline, and who were the people, groups, and institutions involved?

Historical Glimpse of Raves

After the civil rights victories, liberal social policies, and an emerging secular morality in the 1960s and 1970s, the United States entered a conservative period in the 1980s. Ronald Reagan's presidency earmarked a rightward shift toward capitalism, laissez-faire government, individualism, and religious morality. The conservative 1980s would also host the coming of age of Generation X,[3] that is, the Baby Boomers' children. While many Generation Xers grew up listening to their parents' stories about equality, freedom, war, peace, Woodstock, and debauchery, their own reality would be anchored in materialism, corporatism, alienation, equity challenges, parents groups, and War on Drugs policies. It is within this context that raves originated.

Raves, or grassroots-organized, antiestablishment,[4] unlicensed all-night dance parties featuring electronically produced dance music (EDM), emerged during the repressive Thatcher and Reagan eras in the United Kingdom and United States via Generation X's[5] efforts and actions. Many teens and young adults in the late 1980s and early 1990s responded to cultural tension by participating in raves. Raves' significance as a cultural phenomenon gained momentum during the Majors-Blair and Clinton administrations of the 1990s, even while these more liberal governments actively sought to control raves' existence through drug-related and other social policies. This law-and-order approach stemmed from concern, mostly from white middle-class parents, that their Generation X children would fall victim to drugs and lawlessness.

In the past, similar concerns about youth activities, especially those involving music and drugs (e.g., jazz and marijuana, or hippies, LSD, and cocaine), motivated government controls on drugs and the subcultures, scenes, or lifestyles that celebrated them (Cohen 1972; Goode and Ben-Yehuda 1994; Hier 2002). Thus, by the late 1990s, when raves peaked in the United States, social problems, drugs, and public health scholars were treating them as another troublesome matter to be controlled, rather than a meaningful cultural experience.

Since their emergence, aspects of rave culture have spread beyond late-night parties to other types of settings, for example, art galleries, social benefits, and chat rooms (see also Chapter 4). EDM—raves' primary cultural product—became emancipated from the rave scene and can now be found in leisure establishments, popular culture, and everyday life. For example, today you can hear dance music in upscale city restaurants, at spin and aerobic classes, or as background music on video games. The events or parties themselves have also dramatically changed in form and style, departing significantly from their original form.

Today, scholars and authorities[6] debate the current state of raves (Anderson and Kavanaugh 2007). Two perspectives tend to dominate. The first is especially favored in the United Kingdom among British scholars. They conclude that raves are over in both the United States and the United Kingdom, but they do not rule out their return. These conclusions appear at the end of a vast number of culturally oriented books and papers[7] that have done a good job documenting the origins and ascent of raves. Raves' decline or death, they argue, is largely due to both local and nationwide[8] social control policies. Today, they talk and write about "clubbing" instead (e.g., Hadfield 2006; Malbon 1999; Measham 2008; Silverstone, Hobbs, and Pearson 2009), which includes numerous EDM and other youth-based music activities.

Another viewpoint is more drugs- and deviance-oriented. It has been favored among government institutions in both the United States and United Kingdom and most clearly articulated by substance abuse and public health scholars. This viewpoint claims raves still exist in the United States and constitute a social and public health problem. Many drug researchers[9] have obtained large grants from federal agencies to study club drugs[10] problems. Those favoring this approach typically do not focus on the culture of the scene. As a result, they do not distinguish past raves from EDM parties housed in commercial club culture today, nor do they seriously consider their social significance.[11] They consider raves any extended-hour or all-night events, featuring EDM and illicit drug use; by this definition, raves are alive and well.

Objectives and Thesis

This book presents my ethnographic study of the alteration and decline of the rave scene in Philadelphia, from its high point in the mid- to late-1990s to its diminished and fragmented state today. Raves carved out an alternative, EDM lifestyle via an underground youth scene that many across the world participated in and enjoyed. However, even more quickly than their creation and ascent, perhaps, was raves' subsequent alteration and decline. Briefly stated, this is a story about the forces, institutions, and people that helped usher the once highly popular rave scene toward its death.

In Chapters 1 through 5, I lay out my argument for raves' alteration and decline in Philadelphia. In the process, I draw comparisons to other U.S. locations where raves once thrived. For example, in a 2005 post on a popular U.S.-based rave and EDM Web site, www.raves.com, journalist Shawn Wallace[12] wrote a rave obituary for Washington, D.C.:

On the heels of some long, well-fought battles by the clubbing community, we [the rave scene] made some progress. In the end though, we have seen the rave party slowly fade into a distant memory. As super-clubs began to focus theme nights around DJs and getting numbers in the doors, somewhere along the way the party became secondary to creating the next big marketing brand.

Chapter 6 reports on fieldwork I did in London and Ibiza, Spain, in the summers of 2004 and 2005. This comparison work allows a preliminary glance at the viability of the alteration and decline thesis beyond the core research site. To be perfectly clear, then, this is primarily a study of the transformation of one music scene in a northeastern U.S. city.

The study examines a few basic objectives which promise to contribute to the sociology of scenes, culture, youth, identity, deviance, and social control. A primary goal is to develop a preliminary explanation of scene alteration and decline, one that considers multiple and intersecting forces. Specifically, why has the rave scene changed and declined over time? By engaging this question, the book illustrates how cultural collectives operate in everyday life and identifies their resilience and vulnerability to forces internal and external to them. The resulting explanation may be of value for understanding change in other types of scenes and social worlds.

Before such an explanation can be offered, however, an understanding of how raves have changed over time is necessary.

Second, what do raves look like today compared to the past? Today's EDM scene differentially showcases raves' cultural elements in six different types of parties or events that can be placed on what I call a "rave–club culture continuum." Existing studies (e.g., Malbon 1999 and Thornton 1996) have shown that raves have commercialized over time, but they have neglected the important middle ground between original raves and commercial club culture. Therefore, addressing the inattention to the cultural space between authenticity and commercialism will likely inform matters pertaining to identity, alternative lifestyles, underground-mainstream tensions, and how and why certain cultural elements are carried into the future while others are left behind.

A third objective is to advance knowledge about the connections between individual and collective identities. Identity has been a central topic in studies of music collectives and the people (e.g., youth) who populate them. To date, much of the scholarly focus has been on the collective side of identity as it relates to social change (Denisoff and Peterson 1972; Eyerman and Jamison 1998; Futrell, Simi, and Gottschalk 2006; Roscigno et al. 2002), subcultural resistance (Frith 1981; Haenfler 2004a), or commoditization (Shank 1994). Much less work addresses the link between personal and collective identities. By describing the "ideal types" of people involved in the past rave and current EDM scenes, how they differentially got linked up to them, and how their involvement helped change the scene over time, I hope to contribute to the understanding of personal and collective identities within music collectives and other social worlds.

A fourth objective is to understand how everyday people engage in cultural work to restore, preserve, or adapt their scene. Such cultural work can compromise alternative lifestyles and oppositional identity or reinforce them. Resources—social, cultural, and financial capital—play an important role in the cultural work and outcomes people can accomplish. Consequently, this book offers insights into the cultural work people do to secure change within the social worlds that matter most to them.

A final objective is to further evaluate the book's major conclusions by reporting on comparative work on scenes in London and Ibiza, Spain. To date, very few studies of scenes have offered such comparisons. In addition to providing important support for the sociological contributions of the book, such comparisons add interesting information and permit a sort of cerebral voyage to other places.

Origins of the Research Project

My interest in raves and the EDM scene started a few years prior to the Explosion! party described above and accidentally in the fall of 2000. I was participating in a national craze, using a popular Internet program to download "free" music to my PC at my new university office. I immediately found that, among the available songs, there were "remixes," or extended EDM versions of popular songs I knew. While I had never heard of most of the DJs who remixed songs by famous artists (e.g., Donna Summer, Madonna, and Sara MacLachlan), I gathered they must be onto something special because there were loads of wonderful remixes and plenty of people file-sharing them. For example, early on I downloaded about fifteen different versions of Madonna's "Erotica" and noticed a huge increase in others tapping my hard drive for them.

At the beginning, it was the music itself, however, that motivated my interest in this research topic. I quickly grew to adore what I would later learn were house, trance, and techno music. I found their structure and form simultaneously energizing and soothing and I was at a point in my life when I needed that. The relative absence of lyrics and the fast beat pattern (e.g., 125–160 beats per minute) stimulated and liberated my thoughts from what seemed like constant messages of materialism, machismo, and heterosexism in commercial radio. Later, I would learn—from scene insiders and academics—that others found this music to be inspirational as well and that peace, community, and connections were often underlying messages. It also helped, of course, that the music could induce trance-like states and release endorphins.[13] The music did this for me and many others naturally, without chemical assistance, although there was no denying that the music was closely tied with drugs, including ecstasy (E), Gamma hydroxy butynate (GHB), Rohypnol, ketamine (K), and LSD.

As I began to admire some DJs' work, I moved away from remixes of popular tunes and began searching the Internet for more original tracks by the DJs themselves. I wanted underground[14] stuff, anything not commercially available. While I started looking for dance CDs at big retail stores, I used Internet radio stations to find them as well. In early 2002, I found one called www. clubradio.net. Here, DJs like Kev Hill[15] and Greg Zizique from London, DJ Chewmacca from Scotland, Wes Straub from Calgary, CP from Belgium, DJ Skate from Boston, Eve Falcon from Los Angeles, and many others from all over the United States and the world posted dance music mixshows by genre (e.g., techno, house, trance, break beat, jungle/drum and bass) that you could listen to on your computer. Single tracks were not available there. Furthermore, it was not really possible to jump track by track when listening to one of these mixshows, like you could on a typical CD. Thus, you had to listen to the entire mixshow, which was anywhere from about forty-five to seventy minutes in length.

The mixshow's fusion of EDM tracks into what sounded to me like an electronic symphony was most revelational. I found popular radio songs too short, directive, and haphazard. By contrast, the EDM mixshow was a collage of longer tracks, mixed together and at times over the top of one another, to create a new sound,[16] one that transported me to a different place. In many ways, the mixshow—the musical form showcased at raves—embodied a journey or story composed of parts (musical tracks) assembled by a DJ. Many DJs sought to navigate the listener toward a higher consciousness. Thus, the rave DJ was like a conductor, storyteller, or even a shaman.[17] Later in the project, at Josh Wink's Philadelphia monthly, guest DJ David Alvarado explained:

> Like any other person, I basically use the influences and experiences in my life. I piece them together in the mixshow that is completely different from the next guy. The fan should sit back and allow the story to be told.

Whether streamed to my computer, burned on a CD, or mixed live, I consumed these mixshows just as Alvarado, Wink, and nearly every other DJ I spoke with wanted. And my listening to their musical stories or traveling on their journeys delivered what I valued most about EDM music—enlightenment, inspiration, and connection.

I started e-mailing the virtual www.clubradio.net DJs to request their mixshows on CD so that I could listen to them outside of my office. They were mostly white males—with some exceptions—and they were from numerous cities, states, and countries as indicated above. I wrote to lots of them and got lots of responses. These virtual DJs became my first key informants and I stayed in touch with them over the course of my study.[18]

While much of our communication was about mutual tastes in music and their expertise in assembling a mixshow, it also focused on more cultural matters pertaining to the scenes and sites where EDM genres were showcased. Because of this, I soon learned about the connection between musical genres and the scenes that surround them and also about raves and rave culture.

In the summer of 2003, I discovered 611 Records, a dance music record store in Philadelphia and a central site of Philadelphia's EDM scene. The 611 store was said to be one of the best stores for EDM music south of New York City, which has birthed many, many music scenes, including EDM's predecessor: disco. From my interaction with the store's staff—who were mostly local DJs—I began learning about the Philadelphia scene. These part-time retail workers and DJs explained how the EDM scene in Philadelphia was inherently tied to neighboring cities, towns, and states and other countries[19] and communication strategies using Web sites, chat rooms, and event flyers to market music events.

My connection with the 611 DJs also proved a direct passage into the culture of the contemporary EDM scene. The guys—especially Cameron (techno/house DJ and producer), Rick (progressive DJ/producer), Tony (hard techno DJ), and Chris (techno DJ)—told me about events I "had" to attend. Typically, I did not question them. I went where they were playing or to events they recommended. In addition, my biweekly visits to the store would result in my taking home a new stack of rave or EDM event flyers. These hung on the wall inside the record store, dropped off by those involved in the scene on the East Coast. There were tons of them!

Over time, these flyers not only served to identify events for observation and recruitment but also became a source of information and amusement. For example, Chris and I developed an EDM culture game, using the flyers as our game-pieces. Each flyer was illustrated with identity markers—language, images, and color—that we attempted to place on what was emerging as a rave–club culture continuum. I'd pick up a card and attempt to categorize it, while guys like Chris, Doug, William, and Jon (all store employees and DJs) refereed. Given their expertise and insider status, I deferred to their judgments on the flyers or events until my own insider status became established. Then, we debated. I describe these cultural markers in more detail in the next chapter.

In the meantime, I was attending many dance music parties locally. My observations at EDM events exposed me live to the remnants of the rave scene and to modern club culture, where I learned that modern EDM parties were very different from one another and unlike raves in the past. For example, newer "raves"—like the one described above—featured multiple tents or rooms anchored in a specific genre (e.g., hard house versus drum and bass), with a lineup of DJs trading off every hour or so. While many attendees had their genre preferences, there existed a sense of respect and tolerance that connected them to a larger EDM collective identity at the event. However, most EDM parties I attended featured only one genre (rather than many housed together), had a "main" act (i.e., DJ), and did not possess such a physically or symbolically unified structure. Over time, it became apparent that the trend toward music fragmentation and scene specialization would fundamentally help alter rave culture and the EDM scene.

Furthermore, all of the events featured the art of live DJ-ing, but I quickly learned that the vibes of events (between and across genres) differed dramatically, thus accounting for diverse meanings for attendees. At the more rave-like events, I often found the qualities I liked about EDM music and mix-shows: enlightenment, inspiration, and connection. For example, after a visit to a nightclub in London 2004, I wrote in my journal:

> There were three-dimensional tunnels of light beckoning me to enter, pleading for me to come inside and take a journey on them to a different world! I found it mind-altering to hear the music and stand within this passage of light. I kept putting my hands up into it, trying to break it up, but its neon brilliance over-powered me. Its reach was far, out to the chill areas where those who were on synthetic trips rested.

Later that month at another London club where Philadelphia native Paul Ferris was DJ-ing, I noted:

> The club was still crowded at 5am and most people were on the dance floor paying attention to Paul. The vibe was really about the DJ and his music. Drugs took a close second with dancing not too far behind. People were positioned on the floor so they could see Ferris. It stayed like that all night. Paul is their hero. The fans stayed in tune with him all night and had an ear to his every move. This was a temporary community of sound and movement. Nothing else existed for them, no matter where they came from. And I met people from Germany, Spain, Italy, Ireland, Scotland, the Czech. Republic, South Africa, and, of course, England. The world seemed at peace and in unity here. Whether this is a stated politics or not, it seems to happen when people come together for this music.

Yet, many other EDM events, especially those in Philadelphia, lacked this type of vibe, purpose, community, and interaction. Instead, more commercial club culture themes of status and heightened sexuality dominated, with the DJ's work often being reduced to background music for courtship and other socializing rituals. Rick, a white male DJ, explained to me:

> Like nowadays, people are more about going out and getting fucked up, and trying, you know, to meet guys or girls or whatever, you know, and it's like the music is more of a background thing.

Comments like this intrigued me academically and caused me personal consternation. On the one hand, I was curious about the differences between EDM events and the people who attended or produced them. On the other, I was afraid that the music and scenes I was growing to love, and the cultural elements they celebrated, were in jeopardy. I was becoming more enmeshed in a scene that was in transition and, perhaps, decline. Consequently, I launched an "official" (i.e., university-funded and IRB-approved) study of the cultural aspects of the EDM scene in the spring of 2004.

The approach I used to gather information for this book is called an auto-ethnography. Autoethnographies are those where the investigator acts as both an observer of and participant in the social world he or she is studying. From the beginning, I was an evolving member of the scene I was investigating (Merton 1988). My dual role as a member in the EDM scene and as a researcher of it requires making myself visible throughout the book (L. Anderson 2006) via the principle of reflexivity. This means paying attention to how I interacted with people in the scene and reflecting critically on any problems I encountered. I discuss more about reflexivity and other aspects of the autoethnographic approach in the methods appendix.

The Research Site

Philadelphia is the largest city in Pennsylvania and the fifth largest in the United States (U.S. Census Bureau 2000). Its early raves were often held in abandoned warehouses or in parks and open fields in the surrounding area rather than the city proper. As raves gained popularity and moved indoors, they relocated into large nightclubs located on or near Summerfield Boulevard, which dissects the city's industrial center and ends at its riverfront. Two of these venues, Epic and The Lighthouse,[20] catered specifically to raves and the burgeoning EDM scene.

The Philadelphia rave and EDM scenes are similar to those in other major U.S. cities in at least two major ways. First, Philadelphia was home to several rave DJ pioneers, who are now superstars on the global EDM scene. A few are still based in Philadelphia and host monthly events that keep the local scene viable. Second, like nightclubs in New York and New Orleans, two of Philadelphia's major rave nightclubs were shut down for various violations, including—but not limited to—illegal drug use and sales. These closings happened before passage of the federal Rave Act: they were local law enforcement operations designed to control the rave scene.

Additional evidence of rave culture's decline in Philadelphia can be found in Table 1.1, a breakdown of DJ club events in the city. Over the course of my study, there was a decline of EDM parties (of all varieties) and a precipitous increase in hip hop parties. One obstacle for the rave scene in Philadelphia has been the dominance of hip hop in the city's leisure industry, as indicated in Table 1.1. Philadelphia's smaller size, in comparison to New York and Los Angeles (which have more prominent EDM scenes currently) and demographic profile (working class and nearly half African American) may privilege hip hop over EDM as the music of choice among local residents, especially among younger clubbers today.[21]

Philadelphia is not unique. There is additional local and national evidence that the EDM scene is struggling and that raves are over. For example, one

TABLE 1.1   A 2003–2005 COMPARISON OF DJ EVENTS LISTED IN THE
            PHILADELPHIA CITY PAPER

| Year | Primary[a] Genre Listed | | | | Total Events |
	EDM[b]	Hip Hop	Funk/Soul	Other[c]	
2003	99 (46%)	62 (29%)	18 (8%)	36 (17%)	215
2004	101 (44%)	76 (33%)	11 (5%)	41 (18%)	229
2005	79 (30%)	114 (43%)	18 (7%)	56 (21%)	267

Source: This table is compiled from Sean O'Neal's "DJ Nights" column in the *Philadelphia City Paper*, a weekly listing of who's spinning what and where within the city limits. While the column does not list every DJ-ed party, it is comprehensive and considered the best of its kind in Philadelphia. For this table, I randomly chose a week—the second week in May—for a yearly comparison. While there may be some seasonal or annual variation in events, comparing the same week each year allows for a meaningful analysis. Percentages are rounded; thus they may not total 100.

[a]*Primary* is defined as the first genre listed in the event's entry. Many events list more than one genre of music, but there is a general understanding that what is marked as the first genre is largely how the event is identified.
[b]This category includes all house, deep house, and progressive house, trance, techno, electro, and drum and bass genres—all considered within the EDM scene.
[c]This category includes world music, rock/pop, reggae, Latin, ambient, industrial/goth, and trip hop.

disappointment for dance music has come from commercial radio. Just a few years ago, Michael Paoletta (2000a) wrote in *Billboard* that dance music was getting increased airtime on mainstream and commercial radio. Yet, between 2004 and 2005, I learned that several dance music radio stations in Miami, Philadelphia, and elsewhere had closed. Today, EDM remains largely available on satellite or cable radio channels or college radio stations. Only the most commercialized pop star remixes (e.g., Top 40 songs by artists such as Madonna, Beyonce, etc.) might be in rotation on commercial radio stations.

Also, many rave support groups, alliances, and constituencies have disbanded or changed priorities since raves' peak in the mid- to late-1990s. For example, the ROAR political action group I quoted at the beginning of this chapter is now defunct. Gone too are other lobbying groups that supported the EDM scene or came to its defense when it was under scrutiny. For instance, the EM:DEF,[22] set up by the Drug Policy Alliance (DPA), the leading drug policy reform institution in the United States, to protect the national scene against federal drug laws like the Rave Act, is now fairly dormant,[23] and rave-related legislation is not currently a priority at DPA.

At a more local level, groups like the DC Nightlife Coalition (DCNC) used to combat antinightlife activities in the nation's capital. The group's Web page is no longer up and running and the group has also disbanded. The former president of DCNC, Barrett Atwood, signed off from his duties with a call for action:

> As you may know, I am the former president of the DC Nightlife Coalition (DCNC). Now defunct, DCNC was a grassroots political organization that sought to protect DC's nightlife by opposing such things as

the Rave Act and the abuse of voluntary agreements in DC's neighborhoods. In that role, I often met with DC council members and I believe
I have some insight into some of their personalities and into their views
on nightlife in DC. Therefore, I'm reaching out to you to encourage you
to elect pro-nightlife politicians here in DC (see www.buzzlife.com).

Given these developments, Philadelphia is as likely as any U.S. city to investigate the alteration and decline of the rave scene, and even though this is
primarily a study of a local music scene, findings reported here can be placed
in a broader context thanks to fieldwork I conducted in London in 2004 and
Ibiza, Spain, in 2004 and 2005. This comparative research enables me to show
that the study of local scenes can be valuable in informing our understanding
of both national and international phenomena.

Understanding Cultural Change from Music Scenes

The study of scenes, music and otherwise, is fairly new to sociology. Early on,
John Irwin (1977) defined them as expressive, leisure-oriented social worlds,[24]
most often urban, that people voluntarily joined for pleasure and gratification.
All scenes have a central activity and physical space where that activity occurs
and culture develops. Later, Will Straw (2004) described cultural scenes as
entities that cohered around clusters of social and cultural activity and a particular genre of cultural production (e.g., music).

While both Irwin and Straw viewed music scenes as types of cultural
scenes, a distinction between the two would emerge as the study of music collectives exploded in sociology in the late twentieth century.[25] For Bennett
(2000, 2001; Bennett and Peterson 2004), music scenes are geographical spaces
where cultural (e.g., music production) and social activities (music consumption)
center around a particular musical genre or set of interrelated genres. Thus,
scenes have a discernible culture (e.g., rave culture). They also feature participants, collective or group[26] identity, and distinctive cultural elements such as
identity markers (rave fashion), ideology, ethos (e.g., PLUR), and behaviors
(dancing and drug taking). These are described in more detail in Chapter 2.
Music scenes evolve from the pursuit of fan interests and practices, which help
inspire constant innovation (Bennett 2006). While music scenes are especially
likely to be found in cities (Sara Cohen 2007; Straw 2004) or other specific
localities, they may cross physical and virtual boundaries and achieve a much
broader appeal (Bennett and Peterson 2004; Straw 1991).

Notable music scenes include the English punk scene in the 1970s and
1980s, the New Orleans jazz scene in the 1930s and 1940s, and the 1980s and
1990s rave scenes in the United Kingdom and United States. Scholars have
used music scenes to articulate sociological concepts and ideas; most notably,

Howard Becker (1963) used the jazz scene to elucidate deviant identity, subculture, and social control. Scholars from the Centre for Contemporary Cultural
Studies (CCCS) used the English punk scene and the earlier mods and rockers
to examine youth resistance and countercultural identity (e.g., Hebdige 1979).
Still others have investigated collective identity (e.g., race and nationality) and
social change[27] in, for example, rock and roll (Frith 1981), white power music
(Futrell, Simi, and Gottschalk 2006), rap or hip hop (Chasteen and Shriver
1998), world music (Connell and Gibson 2004), punk (McLoone 2004), bhangra (Dudrah 2002; Huq 2003), black metal (Kahn-Harris 2004), and the punk
straightedge movement (Haenfler 2004a, 2004b).

     Currently, a debate is waging in sociology about the appropriateness of the
terms *scenes*, *subcultures*, and *tribes* to discuss music communities.[28] I prefer to
use the terms *scene* and, to a lesser extent, *tribe* to describe the subject matter
in this book. This is because the concept of scenes captures the people active
within the collective as well as the many institutions, agencies, groups, cultural
products (e.g., music), venues, media, communication outlets, and activities
that comprise a scene. Throughout the book, therefore, I use the term *rave* or
EDM scene to refer to people, activities, culture and cultural products (e.g.,
music and parties), institutions, communication outlets, and physical spaces.
My use of the term *rave* or *EDM culture* or *lifestyle* pertains to the unique culture elements and lifestyle sensibilities located in either scene.

     Early work utilized the term *subculture* to explicate raves' origins and
ascent (Knutagard 1996; McRobbie 1994; Melechi 1993; Redhead 1993,
1995; Reynolds 1999; Rietveld 1993) and more recent work on other music
collectives; for example, the White Power movement[29] (Futrell, Simi, and
Gottschalk 2006) or hardcore straightedge (Haenfler 2006; Williams 2006),
adopts the same approach. These scholars note that subcultures have ex-
plicit political goals and activities focused on social change. However, raves'
goals were focused on resistance through indifference and creating an alternative social world that opposed mainstream culture. They were not geared
toward political goals. Also, Bennett (1999, 2001, 2002) and Ben Malbon (1999)
have argued that the concept of subculture has come to imply a static social
group with a particular social class. Instead, people attending raves came from
many social classes. These are still other reasons to employ the term *scenes*
in this study.

     The terms *tribes* and *neotribes* have also appeared to describe youth groups
who populate scenes. They are fluid cliques with loose, apolitical collective
identities. Bennett (1999, 2001) and Malbon (1999) believe these terms are useful in the study of youth and popular music because membership to collectives
can be temporary, brief, and without commitment. I also believe that the scene
concept is more useful than the concepts of tribes and neotribes. While it is
true that scenes are often populated with tribes or neotribes, and that such
groups engage in activities that define and alter collectives, scenes are broader
in scope simply because they contain things external to groups and people who

are not necessarily attached to them. At certain points in this book, therefore, I refer to scenes as having tribes or to tribes as helping to shape scenes.

Book Overview

Chapter 2 provides a discussion of the cultural elements of raves and the current of the EDM scene and its event types. In other words, it details the parameters of raves' alteration: it explains what raves were in the past and what they look like today. Understanding such alteration requires a discussion of authenticity, or how to define what a real rave is. Opinions about this vary among scholars, policymakers, and scene participants. Yet, by reviewing what might constitute a real rave, we can gauge how they have changed over time.

Chapter 3 continues marking scene alteration by focusing on the content and change in scene-related collective and personal identities. The goal of Chapter 3 is not only to further describe alterations in raves' collective identity; it is also to provide understanding of the types of people involved and how they differentially get linked into the scene. To date, elaboration of the connections between these identity types has not been offered in studies of music scenes, nor has it played an important role in the more public-health or deviance-oriented work related to music scenes and other contexts of social concern.

In Chapter 4, I address questions about how and why raves changed after rapid ascent and widespread success in the 1990s. I detail intersections among five main reasons: (1) *generational schism*, or the aging out of Generation X ravers and failure to recruit younger, Generation Y participants; (2) *commercialization*, or the appropriation of rave culture and EDM events into the music industry for economic reasons; (3) *cultural hedonism and self-destruction*, that the rave lifestyle and culture were ultimately too deviant and hedonistic, leading to their demise; (4) *formal social control*, or actions by federal, state, and local government agencies to quash the rave scene; and (5) *genre specialization and the development of subscenes*. Attention to these matters fills an important gap left by past work, which has failed to comprehensively explain the reasons for raves' alteration and decline.

In Chapter 5, I discuss how people and groups negotiated the transformation using a few different methods of cultural work: restoration, preservation, and adaptation. This work has also contributed to raves' metamorphosis and, furthermore, will be important in defining the scene's future. By linking more external forces of change with these forms of individual action, the book will likely facilitate a better understanding on not only raves but also other music scenes and popular culture phenomena.

In Chapter 6, I compare what I discovered in Philadelphia with London and Ibiza, Spain. This comparative work considers the utility of the Philadelphia-based findings for other EDM sites. In the closing chapter of this book, Chapter 7, I consider the future of the EDM scene in the United States and beyond. Many believe that cultural phenomena (especially pop-culture varieties) come and go in cycles. Where will future cultural work take EDM and youth culture in the twenty-first century? Will raves come back en vogue? Will EDM music become more institutionalized? Or will both the EDM scene and genres of music fade to dust? Speculations about these matters are discussed in Chapter 7 and will also be considered for other contemporary music scenes, such as hip hop and mash-up—two dominating scenes in Philadelphia with growing national and international appeal.

2

Corporate Raves, Weeklies, Underground Parties, and More

Defining the Rave–Club Culture Continuum

This isn't a rave. If it is, it's a very corny one.
—Youseff, black male security at Philadelphia nightclub

I sell a nine-hour vacation from the world for $40.
—Conrad, white male EDM promoter

Youseff is a security guard at one of the nightclubs I visited regularly to observe EDM events. He is a fixture in Philadelphia's clubbing scene, having been a bouncer for many years. He is not a raver or dance music fan. He has told me on numerous occasions that the music was too fast and repetitive and had no lyrics.

Shortly after meeting him in 2004, I brought up the Rave Act (i.e., Illicit Drug Anti-Proliferation Act of 2003)[1] while we were standing on his club's main floor with more than four hundred others listening to 125-beats-per-minute house music mixed by a famous DJ, whom Youseff did not know or care about. He was ignorant about the new law but familiar with police surveillance of Philadelphia's clubbing district. So I explained it to him, mentioning that it might target events like this at his club. That's when he uttered his statement quoted at the beginning of this chapter, professing some knowledge of raves even while not being a fan of them.

Conrad is another stalwart on Philadelphia's clubbing scene. He is currently a leading EDM promoter with roots dating back to the early rave era. As a young man, Conrad loved EDM so much that he helped organize and market local raves. As the scene gained momentum, his resultant profits and increasing cultural and social clout enabled him to purchase a nightclub, which would later become Philadelphia's premier rave or EDM venue between 1994 and 2000, peaking in 1998. By the time I interviewed him in 2005, his nightclub had closed and people, including Conrad, were discussing the demise of raves and the current EDM scene. Yet he was still in the business of organizing and marketing large, high-profile events in the city.

Today, Conrad is the major owner of a promotional group that throws "branded"[2] EDM parties. He sees his future competition as Clear Channel, one of the leading media and entertainment companies in the country. He rejects the classification of his events as raves, mostly because the word carries serious stigma which would compromise the legitimacy of his business. Yet, he privately tells me about his love of the music and continued belief in the PLUR ethos. PLUR is a rave-era acronym meaning peace, love, unity, and respect. In addition, his events showcase DJ lineups and identity and lifestyle markers that many attribute to classic rave culture. It was when I asked him to describe his "product" or "brand" that he uttered his statement quoted at the beginning of this chapter.

What is a rave? Do any still exist? If so, how have they changed? What do they look like today? How do people define them today and describe what they were in the past? These questions form the subject matter of this chapter. It discusses the alteration of raves' form or style, something necessary to understand not only scene transformation but also how decline might have come about.

This chapter provides rich detail on what EDM events look like today and how they can be currently situated on a continuum between "authentic raves" and commercial club culture. While other studies of raves and music scenes have shown how events have commercialized over time, they have neglected the cultural and social middle-ground between authenticity and commercialism. By describing such cultural space, this chapter calls into question the authenticity/commercialism dichotomy in narratives about culture and music. Music scenes are not entirely authentic or commercial, nor are their cultural products, events, or participants. Instead, a scene and all of its components and products likely have aspects of both of these extremes and may more suitably exist in an in-between area. This may be the case especially with scenes and collectives that persist over time.

Understanding the Space between Authenticity and Commercialism

What is a real rave, real hip hop, or true punk? While such questions have garnered much attention in vast literatures on music and popular culture, there remains confusion. Why? One reason, many claim, is that authenticity does not objectively exist. If that's the case, it might be dubious to discuss raves' alteration or decline since there was never such a thing as an "authentic" rave in the first place. But how can we consider the alteration and decline of a music scene if we do not have a clear sense of what it was in the first place? Surely we need to establish some common understanding of this before we can effectively claim something is in transition or decline.

Perhaps a wiser approach would be to treat people's beliefs, ideas, viewpoints, and experiences as the basis, for example, of raves' meaningful reality. Peterson and Grazian have adopted this position in their own studies of music scenes. Instead of trying to establish what "real" country[3] or blues[4] are, for example, they investigate how people search for what they perceive as authentic versions of each and the scenes that surround them. However, even if we agree that consensus in perspective and experience allows us to effectively mark authenticity (as a so-called method of it), we still need to clarify what thing we are trying to establish as authentic or not.

Establishing music scene authenticity, by which to gauge alteration or decline, is likely to be difficult because music scenes contain many things (as indicated in Chapter 1). So, the question "what is a real rave, real hip hop or true punk" asks about two different components of music scenes—events (e.g., a rave) and music (e.g., hip hop, punk, or techno). Discussion of a scene's alteration and decline requires, therefore, addressing the relationship between its components, something also neglected by past research.

Take, for example, Mickey Hess's book *Is Hip Hop Dead?* (2007). He points out that Nas's 2006 CD *Hip Hop Is Dead* (which inspired Hess's book title) gets nostalgic for a past time when hip hop was motivated by artistic passion rather than commercialism and profit. The authenticity discussion here is about a particular cultural product—music—and those who produce or distribute it. Such works fit nicely into early Frankfurt School work by Horkheimer and Adorno. But how did hip hop's musical expansion (a type of alteration) impact other aspects of the local scenes that birthed and continue to produce the sound?

Keith Negus's (1999) delineation of two culture industry narratives helps us understand this. The "industry produces culture" perspective focuses on how, when working with artists or marketing goods to consumers, leisure companies deliver cultural goods that conform to capitalist principles and commercial criteria. In a sort of top-down fashion, corporate big shots exploit grassroots cultural products (e.g., hip hop) for exchange rather than use or artistic value (Adorno 1991). This is largely what both Hess and Nas are referring to when discussing hip hop's death. For them and others, the music industry has replaced hip hop's musical authenticity with mainstream or standardized (Adorno 1991) formats. Artists and other stakeholders who go along with this are labeled "sell-outs." Yet, this appears to have been a successful strategy since numerous forms of hip hop currently thrive in the United States and abroad.

When music, the premier music scene cultural product, is commercialized, other cultural components (e.g., ethos, identities, identity markers, norms) of the collective may be altered as well. A good example of this can be found with the Sex Pistols and the 1970s punk subculture they helped originate. At least two documentaries, including *The Great Rock and Roll Swindle* (a 1980 mockumentary) and *The Filth and the Fury* (2000), trace the sociopolitical, grassroots origins of the anti-Thatcher punk subculture of the Sex Pistols. As the band's popularity grew and punk caught on, music industry insider Malcolm McLaren transformed them into a commercial commodity. Several cultural signifiers (clothes, music, and style) were subsequently commoditized for sale in broader markets. A few years later, punk was declared dead (early 1980s; see Reynolds 2006).

Alternatively, a "culture as industry" (Negus 1999) viewpoint is more grounded in people's experiences at the local level, where music scenes provide alternative lifestyles and collective and personal identities. Here, music is believed to be more authentic at a scene's origins or if it retains a grassroots, DIY form of cultural production. This viewpoint also emphasizes economics, claiming that as scenes expand from the bottom up, commercialization takes hold and changes cultural traits (Baulch 2002; Looseley 2003; MacLeod 1999; Ryan Moore 2005). There is, of course, a reciprocal or dynamic relationship between these two approaches (Negus 1999), and rave culture and the EDM scene illustrate them both.

To sum up, there are likely degrees of authenticity, not concrete standards of it, in any music scene. The cultural space between authenticity and commercialism is vast, meaningful, and under-studied. Moreover, a scene's authenticity is manufactured and manipulated from the top down by outside professionals (industry as culture) and from the bottom up by scene participants (culture as industry). Therefore, in order to understand raves' alteration and decline, we need to first describe the cultural space between the original raves of the 1990s and modern EDM events today. Still, we should not limit our understanding of music scene transformation to commercial forces only. Others likely play an equal, if not more important, role. This is a point I return to in later chapters, especially Chapter 4.

Viewpoints on Raves

From the beginning of my research, people within and outside the EDM scene disagreed about whether raves still existed. This suggested that the scene might be in decline. Most scene insiders viewed raves as mostly something in the past, although others disagreed. Their lack of consensus is illustrated in an Internet chat room dialogue which one of my key informants, Doug, posted for me on one of Philadelphia's leading EDM chat rooms. We asked, "Do raves still exist? Your thoughts." Here are some of the answers we got:

> It's like eating your favorite food every day, eventually that shit gets old. So, no, raves don't exist around these parts any more due to overkill. But, out in the mid-west it still goes down. I suppose over-seas too, but I think those are more club based.

> Like massives [raves with huge crowds]? I went to one last Saturday. It was called *Sonic Nation* and there were about 5k people there. Candy kids and E and everything. It wasn't really underground, though. Same kind of security as a high profile concert.

I consider any event that costs as much as a concert, has as many people as a concert, and plays music just like a concert to be . . . a concert or a festival of some sort, not a rave.

Raves, as in electronic music parties that went all night thrown in illegal venues? I don't know of any in existence, and neither do any of those people who were more in touch with that sort of thing from back in the day. I guess it's possible, but seems pretty unheard of.

Actually there seems, from my understanding and what XX has told me, to be a light still shining in Detroit. We went to one that got busted a couple weeks ago and he went to another one not to long ago. So yeah, there are still raves.

Raves are a good way to get REAL underground music out there. I mean c'mon, the club scene doesn't exactly define the underground as we know it . . . not to mention there's the internet, and the becoming of bad local DJ's who all got their own club night around town.

They still hella exist. I don't know what you are all talking about.

They exist—it's just we aren't underground or young enough to know/ care.

There is Nothing.

As you can see, scene insiders were divided on raves' existence, and they expressed some disappointment and sense of concern about that. Their assessments about raves are very different than those of many U.S. academics and policymakers discussed in Chapter 1. This chat room dialogue, as well as information from respondents and informants reported in this chapter, shows that scene insiders side more so with U.K. scholars in defining raves in terms of a broader range of cultural traits.

Grounding the Rave–Club Culture Continuum

Presently, there are many kinds of EDM parties that can be differentially located onto what I call a rave–club culture continuum, with six current variations of EDM events from most to least rave-like: underground parties, corporate raves, music festivals, monthlies, weeklies, and superstar one-offs. The events are defined by their cultural elements, including ethos, organization, norms, behaviors, and identity markers. These EDM parties culturally exist somewhere between the original or authentic[5] raves of the 1980s and 1990s and more commercial club events today.[6] My work indicates this to be the case not only in Philadelphia but also in other national and international locations.

Perhaps one of the most significant stories about raves is their transition to legally owned and privately operated, commercial establishments.[7] Is this an example of a simple business move or its selling out? Is this an example of raves' and the EDM scene's success or failure, their growth or demise? Surely other music scenes or social movements with strong music elements experienced this as well. How can what we learn from the rave experience help explain what happened in these other cases?

Original rave parties were held in illegal locations, outside of the legitimate entertainment district (and often outdoors), a point I elaborate on later in this chapter. Over time and for many reasons, they moved indoors to legally operated venues, mostly clubs with liquor licenses, approved zoning standards, and insurance policies. Through my research, I have found that this transition is one of the defining factors of raves' alteration and decline, and I discuss it more in Chapter 4. Thus, raves merged with commercial club culture, or the routine bars, taverns, lounges, nightclubs, and concert halls that comprised a city's entertainment district. They became part of an area's local legitimate economy rather than illegal parties in the underground economy.

"Legitimate" locations did not become venues for more modern raves or EDM only. They continue to house many different types of music scenes or clubbing lifestyles. Thus, EDM, for the most part, has to compete for locations and is often played at venues where other genres and styles are also featured. This has resulted in some EDM parties taking on a more routine, club culture style. Still others fight to retain or reproduce a more authentic rave form. Thus, EDM events merged into a city's or town's commercial entertainment district in some ways and extended it in others.

These observations further substantiate the focus on scenes in this study. Entertainment and other venues are important to the culture and the people and groups or tribes who help shape it. For example, individuals often work with clubs and lounges to host their music-based group or tribe in a certain nightclub or part of town on a specific night. Locations often, consequently, become part of the tribe's collective identity. This is a good example of where the concepts of scenes and tribes work well together.

Two other points require brief mention before proceeding with discussion of types of events. First, the continuum reflects how a "scene" and the events that comprise it have changed, an important example to support the alteration thesis of this book. It does not explain how new genres or styles of music evolve or die. In other words, the following paragraphs report on the different types of events and the cultural elements they showcase, not on the emergence of EDM genres like minimal techno, soulful house, happy hardcore, electro, and so on.

Many EDM events today host one genre of music only, and certain genres of EDM (drum and bass, break beat, etc.) have their own subscenes with unique styles, culture, and, perhaps, tribes. However, some modern types of EDM events showcase several genres at the same party much like original raves. Thus, any discussion of cultural change must consider how the rave scene changed via both the social context of parties and the musical genres and sub-scenes they host.

Second, because my study was conducted in Philadelphia, I am first and foremost reporting on change at the local level. There may be some differences in the rave or EDM scenes in other locations. For example, Hunt and colleagues (Hunt and Evans 2004, 2008; Hunt, Evans, and Kares 2007) have noted there are numerous massives (large EDM events) in northern California. Most fit definitions of music festivals or corporate raves offered in this book. However, as I noted in Chapter 1 and will discuss more in Chapters 6 and 7, my observations suggest that the forms I describe can be found elsewhere in the United States as well as more globally in the United Kingdom and Europe.

The Cultural Components of Raves and EDM Events

Ethos

One of the first themes I heard in people's stories about raves were descriptions of beliefs and attitudes that many said gave raves their culture and identity. They were describing an ethos, a set of underlying beliefs and attitudes of ravers. Members or participants in any collective typically embrace an ethos. Raves had a distinctive ethos called PLUR, an acronym for peace, love, unity, and respect.[8] PLUR helped define ravers' identity and derived from the 1960s–1970s era of liberalism, freedom of expression, tolerance and acceptance, and connection and unity. Generation X ravers viewed this ethos as a closer approximation of a society in which they desired to live. It was their utopia. My sources spoke about it when describing what a rave was, the early raves they attended, or the larger rave scene in general. Jim, a white male, proclaimed:

> PLUR is what started this whole entire thing. That's why I said it's all about unity. It's on my truck. The [PLUR] sticker's on my truck.

PLUR is also a type of solidarity. Solidarity is about community, close ties, kinship, and traditions among people. Defined this way, it is easy to see that raves' PLUR ethos promoted solidarity. Evan, cofounder of an EDM dance group, described PLUR in this way during a group interview:

> There was a party on Sundays called Body and Soul, which was the epitome of what house [music] was about. Community, people, blacks, whites, Latinos, gay, straight, Jew, Gentile, everybody. I could be dancing

with her, turn around and there will be a guy behind me and I'm dancing with him. Then turn around and I will be dancing with a Latino,
then turn around and I will be dancing with another African American
girl. And the music was all over the place too. You could go from the
most soulful, house music, to hard core, acid house in a few tracks.
But, everybody was there for the same reason. That is the spirit of
EDM. That community bond.

Sociologist Émile Durkheim (1933) has claimed that solidarity is difficult
to achieve and maintain in modern and highly urbanized societies, including
cities like Philadelphia. It may not be surprising, therefore, that as raves merged
with the larger and much more conventional clubbing industry, the PLUR
ethos and intimate solidarity would be compromised. Absent these things, the
EDM scene would lose much of the glue defining its collective identity. More
generally, then, when a scene expands and merges into mainstream society, its
solidarity often changes, causing a dilution in its collective identity. During
expansion, Jeffrey Alexander (2004) noted that many cultural elements also
change with a collective's increased growth and complexity, often showing no
particular attachment to its original form.

While ravers in the past may have lauded the PLUR ethos as one of its
major attractions or something that made it unique, some of the other respondents and informants now perceived it as silly or something they had outgrown.
I asked Allen, a black male, if PLUR was something people grew out of when
they come to their senses. He replied:

Yes and no. Of course everybody wants peace. Everybody wants unity.
Everybody wants respect. But they aren't doing anything to obtain it.
They are not organized and doing anything to attain those goals that
they set for themselves. They think okay, cool, peace, and respect.
Let's take some E pills and have a cuddle puddle.[9] I just got over it.

Conrad agreed with both the centrality of PLUR to rave culture and people's
aging out of it. He added:

Back then they [ravers] were young. They have matured now. Back then,
if you used the word PLUR, you were a candy kid. I'm waiting for the
next fashion trend to come back to our scene. When I started it was
Adidas[10] clothes and shoes. That is what it [PLUR] was. It had a lot to
do with the whole fashion thing. I mean, all these things—fashion and
PLUR—helped the culture.

People also described PLUR's relative absence in the contemporary scene.
Younger EDM fans even lacked consciousness about it at all. Dennis, a gay
white male, has never been to a rave or to anything he defines as one. When I

described the PLUR ethos to him, he told me, "I've actually heard of that." Then, I asked him if anything like it existed in the club events he attended currently and he offered an account about intimate solidarity:

> I don't know. I guess I'm less worried about like, you know, flirting there. So I guess it does feel more communal, in that respect. Because I guess from the times where I have gone to straight clubs, I don't feel that as much. I feel the much more individual aspect that I was talking about. I don't feel as community-oriented but I do understand what you're saying about the rave and what I think of when I hear the word *rave. Community* is a word that kind of underlies it all.

The cynical accounts of PLUR in the past and its denial in the present likely earmark a fundamental change in rave consciousness and identity. Why do scene insiders define the ethos this way? Why did PLUR not resonate more broadly or work its way into popular culture? As I mentioned in Chapter 1, this ethos was one thing that attracted me to EDM early on. I was troubled, then, to hear that PLUR was silly and on its way out. PLUR was, after all, raves' socially conscious ethos and the heart of their collective identity.

Organization

As the chat room dialogue above revealed, people's definitions of raves also center on how events were organized, where they were located, and other aspects of their physical settings. For example, raves are described as being organized by insiders, not business people or industry heavyweights, using innovative or word-of-mouth recruitment strategies. Web site postings, mobile phone messaging, and secret flyers were distributed or sent at the last minute to protect the secrecy of the party from police interference. Both published and anecdotal accounts locate raves at unlicensed venues, like warehouses, fields, or abandoned buildings in rural or isolated settings.[11]

These more organizational features helped contribute to raves' reputation as being deviant, because they were held in violation of legitimate rules for public gathering (e.g., for licenses, insurance, noise, crowds). However, such locations could accommodate the massive crowds—another defining characteristic—and provide protection against law enforcement. In fact, most of the early efforts to prevent or control raves were about violations of venue licensing and noise ordinances.[12]

Rick, a white male DJ, used these organizational criteria when distinguishing raves from more commercial EDM events:

> Raves are dark and dingy and in warehouses, very underworld stuff. Bizarre stuff happens there. Tough kids put on the raves. The underclass was the promoters. When upper-class business men saw there

was money to be made, they stole the business away. Now the scene is all safe and packaged up into clubs.

Structurally, people described raves as something very different from live concerts or a night out at a local bar. Tony, a black male, compared a rave to a routine night out at a club:

> Raves are a very, very different feeling. When I am going to the club, we have a VIP room, the bottle service, etc. That is a club. If I'm going to a rave, I will dance all night. It's going to be ridiculous. I do not really care about anything else.

Raves were very long and took place during the nighttime when most people were sleeping (e.g., 10:00 P.M. until 5:00 A.M.). Rather than showcasing one musical style or genre and a leading or main act like a concert, raves featured many different musical styles with better- and lesser-known DJs rotating equally. Typically, there were tents or rooms specializing by genre (e.g., hard house, drum and bass, techno, etc.) with each having several DJs spinning thirty minutes to two hours each (Bennett 2000; Reynolds 1999).

This organizational style was consistent with raves' ethos and helped define both their identity and difference from more mainstream entertainment events. By housing together different genre-specific rooms or tents (and the fans and DJs who loved them) and by equalizing the artists' exposure and performances, raves fostered connection, celebration of diversity, respect for difference, and musical enlightenment. This structure allowed for the focus to be on the experience of musical diversity rather than the characteristics or talents of a particular artist or the style of a certain genre. These organizational characteristics, again, denote raves' solidarity.

Identity Markers

A group's identity is often understood via symbols, including such things as language, style, props, gestures or mannerisms, and even body shape and size. Virtually all music scenes over time have showcased their identities via such things. For example, hippies—who listened to folk music and rock—in the 1970s wore tie-dyed shirts and their hair long, while smoking marijuana publicly in an attempt to demonstrate a pro-freedom, antiwar group identity (Miller 1999). Modern-day commercial hip hop artists fashion a materialistically empowered identity via expensive jewelry and cars that signify the rags-to-riches stories of oppressed minority citizens of the inner city (Kitwana 2002).

Originally raves had no specific style. However, a rave image emerged over time, featuring baggy track or parachute pants, t-shirts with rave or antiestablishment messages, and comfortable shoes or trainers (sneakers). Bright and

Figure 2.1　Weaving glow sticks at a Philadelphia EDM party.

neon colors dominated. Over time, this style of dress lost popularity, even among scene insiders. For example, Allen told me, "I just got sick of looking at kids dressed in pants way too big with jelly bean bracelets. It just made me sick. I wanted to see cute girls in tight clothes." People like Allen became critical of rave attire worn by the young man wearing glow sticks in Figure 2.1. Rave props (e.g., neon bracelets, pacifiers, lollipops, and stuffed animals) not only completed the outfit but earmarked an image consistent with the PLUR ethos and the celebration of a childlike existence that embraced a utopian society.

Incidentally, many of these props had an entirely different meaning outside the scene and were not embraced by same-age peers, a point I elaborate on in Chapter 4.

While there was no definitive language or slang, there was a range of things ravers talked about. Elaborate details on the technological aspects of EDM's production, musical form and the mixshow journey, DJ talent and activities, dancing, drugs (euphoria and managing side effects), and socially charged subjects related to PLUR (e.g., tolerance of diversity in society and protection of the environment) encapsulated ravers' talk.

As mentioned in Chapter 1, the flyers used to promote raves showcased these and still other identity markers as well. For example, early rave flyers used

Figure 2.2 A Galactic Beat Troopers flyer.

bold and brilliant neon color, animated characters, antiestablishment messages, and childlike themes to promote upcoming raves (see Figure 2.2). Raves' identity markers displayed their collective identity, and they were very different not only from other music scenes but also from the rest of mainstream society in the latter twentieth century and early twenty-first. They never really resonated outside of raves. This has not been the case with other music scenes. Consider hip hop fashion today and its crossover appeal to other socioeconomic classes and racial or ethnic groups (Kitwana 2002).

Norms and Behaviors

Like other scenes, ravers engaged in certain behaviors. Most ravers I spoke with told me dancing to electronically produced music was the primary activity at a rave and that identity markers (clothes and props) centered on it. The dancing took on a unique form, which departs from styles seen elsewhere. For example, ravers danced individually but in unison with others around them. Their dancing simultaneously embodied the values of independence and connection, running consistent with raves' collective identity. Evan and James described dancing's purpose this way:

> JAMES: There is a transcendence that occurs when you are dancing that reconnects you with something that you have no contact with originally. I don't actually think we are alienated from our physical form. I think we are alienated from our meditative form. Dancing completely takes you to that place that we are all searching for.
> EVAN: Whether it be going to church, whatever.
> JAMES: Dancing just happens to be our vehicle of getting there and it is something that I think every person in this room wants to transfer to people who are kind of lost in their own drama, in their own life, and who are concerned with things that aren't real. Dancing is something that reconnects us with real life.

Related behaviors included hanging out and chatting with friends, often on the ground in small, intimate groups called cuddle puddles, as opposed to courtship activities common to other types of music scenes. Jim described the difference this way: "If you're *looking* for a typical good-looking girl, like all done up, like you're not at a rave. You know what I mean." That raves did not value sexual courting and conquest is logical with the PLUR ethos but is yet another factor that rendered them somewhat strange to mainstream "socializing" venues of both the past and present.[13]

Both the extensive dancing and absence of "hooking up" activities were facilitated by what many[14] believe to be rave's defining element: the use of illegal drugs such as ecstasy, acid, ketamine, and GHB (the so-called club drugs). Take, for example, Dennis (twenty-three years old), who has never been to a rave but who regularly attends EDM events:

> Rave and drugs kind of go hand in hand to me. And I know that's not necessarily the case anymore, but I'll always view them that way.

Critics have suggested raves' ethos and solidarity were simply by-products of such psychedelic-induced states. They have labeled the rave scene another drug subculture rather than a bona fide youth-oriented collective.[15]

As previously stated, illegal drug use has been documented extensively in both U.K. and U.S. scholarship on raves. Furthermore, many of the respondents and informants reconstructed their rave experiences as being saturated with illegal drug use. Trent, another white male, told me about his experiences with drugs and subsequent addiction while participating in rave culture:

> TRENT: I started pretty much spending all my time focusing on finding some way to spin [DJ-ing at raves]. And as I was doing that, I started progressing from ecstasy, you know what I mean, to other drugs.
> TAMMY: Like?
> TRENT: Like Special K, coke . . . those were, like, the kind of party drugs, and stuff like that. I could definitely tell it was starting to affect me. Like, out of all the drugs I had been on, you know, ecstasy affected my memory the worst. I could feel my brain like short-circuiting, you know what I mean?

It is easy to understand how raves' cultural meaning could be trivialized into a hedonistic phenomenon. For example, ecstasy's psychedelic qualities foster feelings of connection, utopia, love, and overall well-being, while its amphetamine-like composition permits exertion of high levels of energy for long periods of dancing. Edward, an Asian male, provides evidence that indeed one of the primary rave activities—dancing—was drug-related:

> When I first started going to clubs, I was taking so many drugs, not because I wanted to learn how to dance, just because I wanted to take so many drugs. But once I started to learn how to dance I pulled away from doing so many drugs because it was taking away from my dance.

These properties call into question the existence of PLUR, raves' asexual vibe, cuddle puddles, ability to dance all night, claims of spiritual enlightenment, social equality, and so forth. For example, the most popular rave drug is ecstasy, which is both a psychedelic and a stimulant. Thus, could the critics be correct about raves as another drug subculture if most of the cultural, lifestyle, organizational, and behavioral traits of them can be traced back to illicit drugs?

TABLE 2.1 BREAKDOWN OF DIRECT OBSERVATION AT EDM EVENTS IN PHILADELPHIA

Type of EDM Event	Number Attended	Average Hrs Observed
Underground Parties	2–4	3
Corporate Raves	5–8	5
Music Festivals	0	0
Monthlies	10–12	3
Weeklies	8–10	2.5
Superstar One-offs	8–12	4.5
Total	**33–46[a]**	**Average = 3.6 hrs[b]**

[a] I report a range in events here because I did not formally record field notes on all of the events I attended during the three years of my study. I have formal field notes on thirty-three events but gauge I attended up to forty-six based on casual referencing to them in my field notebook.
[b] I report averages here, but they do not fully reflect the number of hours I observed EDM events. Early in the project, I stayed much longer than the average shows. However, as I began reaching saturation—hearing and seeing many of the same things over and over again (Glaser and Strauss 1967)—I learned how to economize my observational time.

Contemporary Varieties of Raves: The Rave–Club Culture Continuum

During the period of my study, Philadelphia's EDM scene contained many parties that attracted artists and fans from across the country and around the world.[16] Are these events raves? The following vignettes illustrate the varieties of EDM events I found in Philadelphia. Table 2.1 shows the number and types of events I attended and where I made observations.[17] Along with the interview data, these vignettes serve as the basis for the continuum. I place the events on the rave–club culture continuum according to the cultural components (ethos, identity markers, organization, norms, and behaviors) they possess. The continuum is depicted in Figure 2.3, and a breakdown of the cultural components of modern EDM events by type of party is shown in Table 2.2. I begin my discussion of these events with the most rave-like event today—underground parties—and end with the most commercialized variety—superstar one-offs.

Authentic Raves ←————————————————→ **Commercial Club Events**

Underground Parties, Corporate Raves, Music Festivals, Monthlies, Weeklies, Superstar One-offs

Figure 2.3 The rave–club culture continuum.

TABLE 2.2   CULTURAL ELEMENTS OF RAVES BY TYPE OF CONTEMPORARY
EDM PARTY

Party Type	Ethos	Organization	Identity Markers	Behaviors
Underground Parties	Strong 1 and 2	3, 4, 5, 6, 10, sometimes 8, 9	Modernized 11, few 12, strong 13	Strong 14–15, moderate 16, 17, 18
Corporate Raves	Moderate 1 and 2	7, 8, 9, and 10	Classic and modernized 11, strong 12, moderate 13	Strong 14–18
Music Festivals	Modest 1 and 2	6, 7, 8, 9	Classic and modernized 11, strong 12, modest 13	Strong 14, 16, 18, moderate 15, 17
Monthlies	Moderate 1 and 2	Occasional 4 and 6	Modernized 11, few 12, strong 13	Strong 15 and 18 (minus cuddle puddles), moderate 14, 16, modest 17
Weeklies	Moderate to strong 1, modest 2	None	Modernized 11, strong 13	Strong 15 and 18 (minus cuddle puddles), modest 14, 16, 17
Superstar One-offs	1 and 2 highly variable	7, 10	Highly variable, but generally modest on 11–13	Strong 17, moderate 14, 15, 16, modest 18

Key to Cultural Elements of Raves

Ethos: (1) PLUR or intimate solidarity, (2) leftist or progressive (antigovernment and anticorporate) politics

Organization: (3) Grassroots, nonbusiness owners, (4) secretive, underground marketing, (5) unlicensed venues, (6) transport sound and light show equipment, (7) massive crowds, (8) musical diversity by area, (9) numerous rotating DJs (equity), (10) extended, after hours

Identity Markers: (11) Fashion (parachute pants, antiestablishment t-shirts, sneakers), (12) props (pacifiers, glow sticks, neon accessories, backpacks, stuffed animals), (13) language—range of discourse, music, E, leftist political issues

Norms and Behaviors: (14) Dancing, (15) music appreciation, (16) drug use, (17) DJ worshiping, (18) cuddle puddles

Underground Parties

Most of the underground parties I have attended or heard about over the years, both inside and outside of Philadelphia, mimic classic rave organization and replicate many of rave's cultural elements. For example, Table 2.2 shows underground parties have the strongest or closest fit to the classic rave's ethos, organization, identity markers, and behaviors than the other types of EDM events. I got a good sense about this back in the summer of 2005.

AN UNDERGROUND PARTY IN PHILADELPHIA

For half an hour now, I have been driving around northern Philadelphia trying to find an art gallery for an underground techno party. It is 11:15 P.M. and I am unfamiliar with this part of town. All I see are run-down homes and low-end bars and restaurants to my left and huge, desolate brick buildings in what appears to be an industrial wasteland on my right. This area seems unlikely for an art gallery. I think I am lost. I pull over and make a phone call.

How stupid! I was looking for a swanky gallery in a gentrified area. Chris just told me the gallery is in an old warehouse on the fourth floor. I make a right on the next street and head toward the water. A few blocks down, I feel my car vibrate under me to a hard, steady bassline and give a sigh of relief that I must be close. In between two massive factory-type buildings with broken-out windows, I see some cars lining the street. I roll up behind them and park my car.

I take another look at the flyer and then peer across the street to a tattooed, bald white guy blocking what appears to be an entrance to the building on my right. I step out of my car with digital camera and phone. Mr. Tattoo asks what I am looking for before I even cross the street. I shout, "The Rhythm City party."

As I walk closer, I see him check out my camera and phone. His look is disapproving. He asks, "Who do you know here?" I mention a few names and he gives me a "Hmmm." Just as my impatience builds, he admonishes, "You're gonna have to leave the camera and your phone if it's got a camera on it." Irritated, I walk back to my car and deposit my camera and phone only to return to find him ranting against the U.S. government. Turns out Mr. Tattoo talks like this all the time, as a few of my friends inside later told me.

Never before have I been to an underground party in such a location. The party promoters rent out this gallery from its owner, who happens to live and work in the building. From what I can see, it does not look as if anyone or any other business occupied it. It is dirty and in disrepair. Later, a few of the event promoters told me they preferred this location because it is out of earshot of the police.

In order to be somewhat in compliance with liquor laws in case of a raid, the venue did not sell alcoholic beverages. Instead, they were selling water, soda, smoothies, and vegetarian food, which I have never seen before at an EDM event. Alongside the falafel, hummus, and chips are flyers and pamphlets for different left-wing causes: the anti-fur campaign, environmental protection, just say no to child labor, and others. Adjacent to that is the "free" beer counter.

This event has a distinctive feel to it, which likely follows from its location and organization (secretive setting, well protected, in unlicensed venue), ethos (liberalism, earth and animal friendly), intimate solidarity, norms (music and dance), and participants (most were techno loyalists). Three techno DJs are going to perform. One assembles his music live, meaning he creates music on the spot by sampling sounds from different electronic machines and a laptop computer. I watch carefully along with others.

Back at the DJ booth, I notice several people walking back and forth to the bathroom. Some are rubbing their noses and sporting the sniffles; others are two steps ahead of a cloud of marijuana smoke. Like that at other parties I have been to, this drug use does not seem to be producing many complications.

Underground parties are organizationally the closest thing I found to original raves. While in London, I learned of a special type of underground party, called the squat party,[18] that was more like what people described as authentic raves. However, I did not hear about any squat parties in Philadelphia. Underground parties are held in both legal and illegal venues not licensed for the purpose for which they are used. Consequently, they adopt unique strategies to get around licensing regulations and the officials (police) who might enforce them. Furthermore, they are still largely promoted via word of mouth or by flyering at carefully selected venues and other events. This marketing style is an attempt to protect the event from official interference and prevent scene outsiders from attending. Clearly, Mr. Tattoo provided an example of this gate-keeping function.

Underground parties replicate many of the cultural elements of raves; however, like the other types of events, some of these have been modernized. For example, the vibe is typically one of solidarity. More than at the other types of events I have attended or heard about, there is usually some level of political progressiveness present, consistent with the PLUR ethos. This was evidenced by the vegetarian food for sale and the table of pamphlets and flyers on left-wing causes. Incidentally, I am on e-mail lists of several underground party groups in New York and London. I regularly receive e-mails about upcoming parties that showcase some level of social and political activism.

For these cultural and organizational reasons, in addition to their insistence on showcasing underground music, the people I talked with led me to classify underground parties as closest to the rave side of the continuum. There was a sense that they were strictly about musical exposure and consumption, without any of the profit motives of superstar club nights or corporate raves. In this way, then, underground parties were perceived by many as closer to authentic raves than any of the other events, even though they are seldom as massively attended as were raves in the past.

Corporate Raves

When Conrad told me that he sells a nine-hour vacation for $40, he was speaking about a corporate rave.[19] I call them corporate raves because they fuse more authentic rave culture from the past with a more modern-day, legitimate business style and purpose. In other words, they celebrate the nonmaterial aspects of rave culture, but their organization has been professionalized. This organizational shift has altered the DIY or grassroots character of raves. Corporate raves are at least one type of event that provides an example of the middle ground—between authenticity and full-blown commercialism—that scenes come to occupy over time. Their components are illustrated in Table 2.2 and were easy to see early in my project.

In the summer of 2005, my graduate assistant, Philip Kavanaugh, and I attended a corporate rave in Philadelphia to conduct direct observation. We arrived around midnight to find the event packed. Together, we estimated there were already 3,000 people there, ranging between eighteen and thirty years old. Whites predominated, with Asians the second most frequent minority group, followed by African Americans and Middle Easterners.[20]

The place was split up into five different genre-based rooms or tents, each with a list of about nine DJs scheduled to play one hour each between 9:00 p.m. and 6:00 a.m.[21] There was hard house in the main indoor room, deep and funky house downstairs in the Velvet room, hard techno in a side room on the main floor, drum and bass in an outdoor tent off the techno room, and a main house tent adjacent to that. The DJ talent was stellar by any EDM fan's standards. It was hard to believe that $40 gave you this much exposure. We suspected that some of the bigger names must have lowered their price for the event. Our suspicion was confirmed later in a conversation with the event's promoter.

We saw candy kids,[22] glow sticks, and break dancing all over the place. While the candy kids sported a more rave-like style, they were outnumbered by people in causal attire that I often see at weeklies and monthlies. In addition to the glow sticks, other rave props included bottles of water—by far the preferred drink here—and illicit drugs.

Because I was busy scouting the site with Philip and talking to staff, plus listening to some of my own favorite DJs, my first conversation with a raver did not happen until 2:30 a.m. Then I met a young white male in the Navy, Pat from Virginia, who had come with a group of friends. They were sitting in a cuddle puddle near the main tent area. Pat and I first talked about being in the Navy and attending raves but moved on quickly to how far he and his friends traveled to events like this. I learned distance was no real obstacle for them to hear good music and dance. Their raving was more limited by cash flow, that is, did they have enough for gas, shared lodging at a cheap hotel, entrance fees, and desired chemicals. They did not budget money for beverages. Like Aidan and Connor from Chapter 1, each had a water bottle they said they refilled in the bathroom.

Sitting close to them, in another cuddle puddle, was a group of young men and women (age eighteen to twenty-two) from the Pocono Mountains. They blatantly discussed using E and offered me some. I declined and warned them that a security officer just told me two guys got booted out of the party for selling E, after trying to pass a bag of 150 pills off as premenstrual drugs. We all laughed and they shrugged off my caution.

By 3:40 a.m., Philip and I noticed the crowd was beginning to thin out. The drum and bass tent stayed crowded, as did the main floor, but other areas of the club started to empty. The break dance groups were still going strong, taking turns in dance circles in the main room and the drum and bass tent. Still, most people looked to be tiring, including us.

So we headed for chill areas, which were now quite crowded. Philip took the outside one and I stayed in the main chill area inside. There, I saw some people sick on E, like one young white woman who spewed a milky-white substance from her mouth every fifteen seconds for about a minute. I could tell it was an E-sick due to the vomit's color and texture. My impression was confirmed when her friend sitting beside me outed himself as a dealer and her as a user, when bragging about his unusually strong batch of ecstasy. After her heaving, she returned to chatting with friends and then headed upstairs to dance.

By 5:00 A.M., the main room and drum and bass tents were still crowded, but the other areas and rooms had cleared out considerably. There must have been at least five hundred still at the party, maybe more. Those remaining were young—eighteen, mid-twenties, or so. I left the rave at closing—6:00 A.M.—and headed over to the "official" after-party at another big night-club in Philadelphia.

Corporate raves are one variation of today's new branded EDM parties and, on the face of it, they look to be a modern-day rave. They are massive in size, feature many different kinds of EDM music with numerous DJs in heavy rotation, showcase both traditional and modernized rave identity markers, re-create a PLUR-like ethos and strong sense of intimate solidarity, and house behaviors commonly associated with raves.

What distinguishes them from classic raves is their professionalized, organizational style. They are heavily promoted via mainstream marketing techniques (internet Web sites and chat rooms and city newspapers and fanzines of all kinds) in addition to being flyered publicly for months in advance. They are held in licensed venues, conform to alcohol and zoning regulations, and often hire additional security to maintain order and enforce policies. Thus unlike raves in the past, corporate raves today are in full cooperation, and many times collaboration, with legitimate business. In many ways, corporate raves—like this one and Explosion! (Chapter 1)—adopt commercial characteristics in order to secure wider profits and broaden the party's or brand's reputation. I discuss such cultural adaptation more so in Chapter 5.

Business people market their brands of corporate raves in the local entertainment industry. They do this in London and other U.S. cities as well.[23] Corporate raves often travel between cities and suburbs or change locations within them. However, cities the size of Philadelphia contain very few venues that could and would host such an event, thus making certain locations the chosen place for the same event over and over again.[24]

Over the course of my study, I have only heard the word *rave* used in the present to describe these kinds of events, even though underground parties are slightly more rave-like. Moreover, the EDM party card/flyer game I played with the guys at the record store—described in Chapter 1—produced consensus that these events were modern-day raves. It was during the playing of this game at the record store that the phrase *corporate rave* was coined.

Music Festivals

Another modern-day variation of raves is the EDM music festival. Many different genres of music and music scenes, not just EDM, host outdoor festivals in the United States and in different locations around the world. Rock, folk, women's music, and, more recently, hip hop and R & B festivals share some similarities with EDM festivals, including lots of diverse musical guests and talent, huge crowds, and outdoor locations during the warmer months. The Detroit Music festival, the Burningman festival in the Arizona desert, and the Ultra Music festival in Miami are three of the better-known EDM festivals in the United States; however, many others abound. In the United Kingdom and Europe, festivals for all types of music and scenes are plentiful. Some of the bigger EDM ones include Creamfields near Liverpool and Manchester, United Kingdom[25] (multiple genres of EDM); the Love Parade in Germany (techno oriented); and Sensation in the Netherlands (trance oriented).

EDM music festivals typically offer multiple genres of music, but they also might privilege certain genres or styles. They all feature long DJ lineups in diverse tents or areas of the field or campground. These organizational and structural traits liken the festival to the corporate rave. However, since they are not constrained by walls, music festivals tend to be quite large, allowing for the big crowds commonly attributed to raves.

The festival's organizational character tends to connote a slightly different vibe than a corporate rave and can attract a more diverse fan base. This can be explained by the sorts of people who attend corporate raves versus music festivals. For example, many people find it appealing to attend an outdoor music festival in the spring, summer, or early fall, no matter what music scene is hosting it. Thus, music festivals tend to draw a more diverse crowd that is not as loyal to EDM, compared to those attending a corporate rave or one of the other types of events. This diversity weakens the solidarity and vibe commonly associated with raves in the past.

Since most music festivals happen only once a year and since there are so few of them, attending one is considered a big deal. This cultural uniqueness leads to forms of behavior less commonly found at weeklies, monthlies, and underground parties. To begin, people stay at music festivals longer because they last all day. However, their hours deviate from the classic rave. Music festivals generally take place during the day and end earlier, in the United States, than raves in the past. Music festivals are also special because they are treated as a planned holiday or vacation. People gear up for them. Second, people do things at and for festivals they might not otherwise consider. This includes using vacation days, traveling out of town, paying sizable entrance fees,[26] and consuming illegal drugs.

To my knowledge, there are currently no EDM music festivals within the city limits of Philadelphia. However, there are a few close by that many city insiders classify as Philadelphia events, more or less. One such festival is Starscape in

Baltimore, Maryland. While I have never attended it myself, I have interviewed several people who have done so.[27] From this, I place EDM music festivals on the Philadelphia-based rave–club culture continuum because my respondents and informants told me about them and they are evidence that any local music scene transcends its own geographic borders. Subsequently, EDM music festivals are to the right of corporate raves and closer to the commercial side of the continuum (see Figure 2.3). Table 2.2 shows music festivals having a more moderate rave/EDM ethos and fewer organizational traits and rave-like behaviors than either the underground party or corporate rave. In addition, music festivals are attended by a lot of summer tourists, which also makes them deviate from early raves and less like underground parties or corporate raves. They are yet another variation of the middle ground between original raves and a more modernized or commercial party, indicating additional efforts toward cultural adaptation (Chapter 5).

Monthlies

It was the last Wednesday in September 2005 and I decided to attend one of my favorite monthlies: Paul Ferris's party at Liquid. I have been to this party numerous times since I began this project and have come to adore it. I find here many of the things I love about the EDM scene: excellent house music, brilliantly assembled by a wonderful DJ; an intimate dance floor; a peaceful, friendly vibe anchored in an intimate solidarity; and scene insiders whom I have befriended over time.

Outside, one of my key informants, Jamil, a mid-thirties black male who doubles as security staff and club manager, greeted me with a big hug and a kiss on my right cheek. He asked me how things were going (with the project), and when I told him very well, he replied, "Have a good time tonight." I paid the $7 cover charge and walked inside to find about 60 people in the 125-capacity club.

Standing in front of me were two other key informants, Bill and Rick, twenty-something white male DJs and producers, apparently back from Europe with their record label's owners. With excitement, they told me about their tour and that one of their tracks was recently played on Radio One (BBC) by Fergie, a superstar DJ in the United Kingdom. I was extremely happy for them but disappointed to learn that their newfound social and cultural success was not earning them any money.

Knowing that the EDM scene—like other music scenes—was dependent on new sounds to stay alive and that newly created genres could help spawn, revive, or transform a scene, I asked Rick and Bill what kind of music Ferris was playing. As usual, I really liked what he was spinning. Both knew Ferris better than I and had been up in the DJ booth earlier that night. They insisted he was playing German techno, even though it sounded progressive to me. Rick and Bill insisted that German techno was "all the rage in Europe" and proclaimed that progressive was "over." After some more debate about the music's structure and form, we compromised and agreed to shut up and listen to Ferris's magic.

Around us were white, black, and Asian males and females in their mid-twenties to early thirties, casually dressed with drinks in hand. Most were listening or dancing to the DJ. A few others hovered at the bar, chatting with friends or staff. It stayed like that for the rest of my time there. I did not see a lot of heavy drinking or drug use. Just a few guys appeared to be rolling,[28] which I surmised from their trance-like presence on the dance floor and sweat-saturated shirts and faces. I left at 2:00 A.M. and got home at 3:00 A.M., Thursday morning.

The monthly is another modern EDM event, both similar to and different from the weekly. Monthlies are also lodged between original raves and commercial club culture; however, their middle-ground position is unique compared to corporate raves or music festivals. This is because they are genre specific, representative of a subscene, and often hosted and populated by specific groups or tribes with distinctive identities and lifestyles.

Monthlies tend to have strong reputations and draw good-sized crowds. Typically, they connote status, especially for scene stakeholders, such as DJs and promoters. Venues offer them larger budgets than weeklies, on average, and in turn they are promoted more heavily. This includes flyering around town at retail locations and at other nighttime events, a more grassroots form of marketing consistent with the rave era. However, marketing for these events is also showcased in special announcements in local rags and Web sites.

Monthlies are a bigger deal to scene insiders than are weeklies. What I mean by this is that participants typically assign monthlies higher cultural value. Much of this has to do with their scarcity, in comparison to the weekly, which many take for granted. Specifically, there is a sense that missing a weekly is not as big a deal. There will be another in seven days. Mitchell provided a resident DJ's perspective on this:

> I don't like having a weekly residency in Philadelphia, just because they [people] are like, "Oh, well, you know, if we miss him this week, we can go next week." They think it's routine, instead of being something more special, like once a month.

In addition, monthlies often have wide reputations, transcending the local region. I have met many out-of-towners who have traveled to Philadelphia specifically for them. While they might also come to town for weeklies, I have not met anyone who has done so.

Missing a monthly is a bigger problem, not only because of the time lapse between them but also because they tend to have a more special flair than weeklies. Promoters are able to craft monthlies, due to their larger budgets and lesser frequency, uniquely and spend more time on their promotion. For example, the host DJ—like Ferris—might showcase a guest DJ who is traveling through the area. Guest DJs tend to have strong EDM reputations and slightly different style, thus enabling them to bring out more people. Monthlies are also more often CD release parties (for the resident DJ, someone on his label, or the guest DJ) and serve as fundraisers for social and political causes that fit with the scene's ethos and collective identity.

Monthlies might showcase more identity markers of traditional rave culture, but most of these are likely modernized EDM signifiers of tribal identities. For example, another popular monthly, Discobreakz, was held in a very large underground bar in Philadelphia's warehouse district where other famous rave venues were once located, including Conrad's flagship rave venue of the mid- to late 1990s. This location tended to earmark the party as being born out of the rave spirit while remaining true to the contemporary EDM underground. Discobreakz showcased break beat music and the local DJs who excelled in spinning it. It also was a party favored by local dance crews.[29]

Most differences between weeklies' and monthlies' norms and behaviors have to do with monthlies' more often being offered on weekends as opposed to weeknights. Since monthlies are more often held on weekend evenings and are considered more "special" events, some of the more traditional rave-like behaviors can be found at them. This includes greater frequency of rave styles of dance and consumption of illicit substances. Of course, as noted, monthlies can occur during the week and contain similar behaviors, albeit to a much lesser extent.

These norms and behaviors have been somewhat altered to the more genre-specific nature of the contemporary EDM scene. For example, the hard drum and bass scene and the monthlies that comprise it have been characterized as having a more aggressive vibe and being overpopulated by younger fans (especially males) who are more into drinking. People often told me that a popular drug on this scene was crystal methamphetamine. On the other hand, the monthly house (deep, soulful, and vocal) scene caters to an older crowd, can be status oriented, and features drugs like cocaine. Thus it must be clarified here that the classification of EDM events into weeklies, monthlies, and other types is further complicated by the presence of genre-specific subscenes and their respective parties.[30]

While monthlies are a lot like weeklies, they depart in important ways that make them more like raves. Much of this has to do with their relative uniqueness in comparison to the weekly. Other explanations center on their vibe and reputation. In short, monthlies tend to feature a closer organizational and cultural fit to classic raves, yet they are not perceived by anyone as authentic raves. As shown in Table 2.2, monthlies have a moderate rave-like ethos but very few organizational similarities to classic raves or even corporate raves, underground parties, or music festivals. They also are parties with fewer rave-like behaviors than the other varieties. For these reasons, I locate monthlies to the right of music festivals in Figure 2.3.

Weeklies

It was a Monday night in January of 2004 when I headed to Twilight around midnight for the Rich Love weekly. When I arrived, people were spilling outside of the club onto the sidewalk and the bouncer was having a good time chatting with them. I pushed my way into the tiny, smoked-filled room and said hello to the resident DJ. He came out from behind his decks[31] for a quick kiss and hug, just like he did with others over the course of the evening. Rich, the resident DJ, was spinning deep house at his infamous weekly. Deep house is richly textured, post-disco music with strong basslines, overlapping melodies, and soulful vocals. It is often simultaneously passionate and light or uplifting. Rich has a local reputation of being one of the best in town to mix this genre. And from the looks of it, that reputation was not in question tonight.

Despite the heavy crowd, I managed to grab a seat on a wall bench. Down here, the smoke-thick air seemed a bit clearer and I found I could breathe more easily. I noticed a discernable "alternative" style among the crowd, both in clothes and hair, including the white male with dreadlocks, Justin, who was sitting near to me at one of the few tables. I welcomed this aesthetic break from Abercrombie-mania on my college campus.

I struck up a conversation with Justin about the music, which led to a disclosure about my project on EDM culture. He took the occasion to dole out considerable cynicism about the scene. Justin ranted about the absence of "real" house music and even criticized the music the DJ was spinning a few feet away. Justin preferred rave-era house music, especially the pioneering stuff from Chicago and the United Kingdom.[32] When I asked him about the rave scene, he lost interest, grabbed my card, and walked away. I suspected I would never hear from him again and I did not.

Sitting on the other side of me was a young white female, Stephanie—who, as it turns out, was eavesdropping on my conversation with Justin. Her first words to me were to just disregard him because he was "jaded." She, on the other hand, would be happy to chat with me.

Stephanie was quick to establish her credentials as a loyalist.[33] She had attended the Winter Music Conference[34] four times, groupie-style: she makes last-minute decisions to go based on shared transport with friends and the ability to crash on people's hotel room floors.

Stephanie told me this weekly was among the best EDM events in the city. I asked what made it so good and she answered, "The music, DJ, and people." Then she asked a few questions about my project and I told her I was interested in how the scene had changed over time and what benefits and consequences people experienced from it. Stephanie homed right in on the *consequences* word and gave me a diatribe on scene drug use. She said house heads nowadays typically use marijuana and cocaine during the week and save ecstasy for the weekends or special occasions. She had much to say about ecstasy, something she had used frequently in the past. She was very cautious about the depression that followed its consumption, which now was an impediment to her work week.

Our discussion ended shortly after Stephanie and I got up and headed for the bar. I ordered a Coke—my usual—and turned around to watch the crowd. In no time, I was dancing with everyone else, but no one in particular. I spent the next hour and a half on my feet, dancing, chatting, and laughing with Philadelphia's house music loyalists.

The Rich Love weekly at Twilight is an example of, perhaps, the most common type of EDM event in Philadelphia. Weeklies are typically created and hosted by a resident DJ—like Rich—and specialize by musical genre (e.g., breaks, deep house, minimal techno) at commercially licensed venues—mostly bars, lounges, or small nightclubs, like Twilight. The DJ usually, but not always, spins himself or herself[35] the entire event rather than sharing the time slot with several others, as was customary in the raves of the late 1980s and 1990s.

For DJ stakeholders, getting a weekly is a major coup and establishes their reputation in the local EDM scene and the citywide entertainment industry. Their specialization by genre and hosting by a regular DJ are a departure from the original rave form, which can compromise its collective identity of diversity and tolerance (of music and its fans types) and equity (multiple DJs in a more status-neutral rotation). However, such specialization can also work to define smaller, more intimate subscenes with tribes, for example, house heads, who have unique identities or lifestyles.

Weeklies do not consciously perpetuate a PLUR ethos, yet they often convey a vibe anchored heavily in intimate solidarity. This is partially because attendees tend to know each other—and the often very friendly and interactive DJ—and share strong EDM ties. This is what I witnessed at Twilight. Weeklies are populated by mostly local residents with a strong commitment to the genre and scene, for example, loyalists (like Stephanie and Justin), although others attend for diverse reasons. Newcomers or less committed fans often learn about them via word-of-mouth from friends or those having more experience with and commitment to the scene. Still others hear about them via chat rooms.

Most in attendance are music focused or interested in hanging out with their friends. They are not primarily motivated by drinking, drugs, or courtship/sexuality, even though I have occasionally seen and heard about drug use at weeklies. They are generally not sexually charged environments, although courting and intimacy can and do take place at them. It is not, however, a primary objective of participants. People also tend to profess loyalty to weeklies, incorporating them as part of a normal week.

Weeklies are listed by area rags (e.g., O'Neal's "City Nights" column of the *Philadelphia City Paper*) and Web sites, but they are not rigorously promoted, that is, flyered, unless there is a special event on a given week. They rely, for the most part, on their strong geographical and cultural reputations. Weeklies do not showcase many identity markers from the early rave era. One main reason for this has to do with where they are located and the crowds they attract. Because entry to them is for twenty-one-and-over patrons, they attract an older crowd (older than ravers in the past) who do not dress in a rave style. In fact, the rave style of dress is "out" even among EDM fans who attend weeklies. The older style has given way to more casual, alternative styles, including cargo pants or jeans, t-shirts, and sneakers or Diesel flats or knock-offs for males and tighter jeans and more-revealing tops for females with higher-heeled shoes. Both Stephanie and Justin sported such fashions.

Furthermore, since these events happen on weeknights, they are much shorter in duration than an authentic rave. Most end at 2:00 A.M., which is dictated by alcohol regulations for nightlife venues in Philadelphia. This prevents attendees from staying out later and consuming too much alcohol or drugs. Many attendees have 9:00 A.M.–5:00 P.M. jobs and cannot stay out all night long anyway due to morning obligations. Also, since the clubs hosting weeklies are often small, certain rave styles of dance, for example, glow-stick maneuvering, are limited.

Taken together, weeklies are unlike original raves, but they are also not like a typical night at a commercial bar or club in Philadelphia. Based on the traits reviewed in this chapter, which are depicted in Table 2.2, I would situate them near the center of the rave–club culture continuum but to the right of monthlies and toward the more commercial side. Weeklies' nonmaterial culture is reflective of the authentic rave era, but their organization and behaviors are much more commercial and conventional.

Superstar One-offs

It is about 1:00 P.M. on Sunday, and I just finished my "morning" coffee after waking at noon. I was at the Deep Dish party last night until 5:00 A.M., so I am feeling sluggish after six hours of sleep.

Last night was a big superstar DJ event with a rave-era flair. Psychedelic videos with social and political references surrounded the DJs' progressive house style. Behind a modest setup on the main room's stage, the DJs stood casually dressed in t-shirts and jeans, chatting to other insiders between tracks. They were having a grand ole time and the crowd, myself included, loved watching them.

I remember thinking you could never tell from the DJs' dress, demeanor, and interaction they were "superstars." The Deep Dish duo has been repeatedly ranked among the best DJs in the world. They were paid a few thousand dollars to spin records last night and will travel to many other venues—earning the same amount or more—within the next few weeks on a U.S. tour. Instead of exploiting their status and credentials, as they could have, they were busy creating a typical EDM vibe, one centered on music and dance, not on hooking up or status.

The event drew a multiethnic crowd. As usual, white males were most prevalent, followed by Asian males and females and then people from the Middle East. I met people from the United Kingdom, Jordan, and Iran as well as from various U.S. states, including a group of five white males and females who drove in from Cleveland to see the show. They were rolling, and so were, it seemed to me, several others. I heard some people saying their friends were sick on ecstasy and saw some signs (seated, holding heads between hands and sweating profusely) of others close to it. Still, sickness was rare and I observed few other consequences. I left the party at 5:00 A.M., trying to imagine what the night's diehards might look like at 10:00 A.M. when the party ended.

Over the course of my study, I have been to many superstar one-offs (one-time parties showcasing a main act or "star"). It is very hard to pass them up if you are a fan of EDM music even though there are valid reasons for not going. For example, there is a sense, among scene insiders (which I eventually became), that such events are culturally problematic: they violate the "true" nature of the underground EDM spirit in a few important ways. The events are held at huge clubs that are very commercialized, and they attract all kinds of people for reasons other than those respected by insiders. While I have found this to be the case and have, myself, been annoyed by or discouraged from attending certain superstar one-offs, I often deviated from my fellow EDM insiders to attend them in clubs I did not care for with nuisance clubbers. I did so in order to hear a certain artist I adored or, more often, to cover an event for my research.

I have found that whether the superstar one-off fits with the EDM or rave spirit depends a lot on the reputation, status, and cost of the DJ.[36] To a large extent, it is the DJ's reputation and value in the global EDM scene that shape this event's fit with either rave or commercial club culture. The DJ's reputation and style help shape the event's organization, marketing, vibe, and identity.

Organizationally, superstar one-offs are very heavily promoted via both grassroots endeavors and more conventional marketing strategies. This makes them different from classic raves. Promotion must be rigorous and span out across many types of party people because the economic costs of the event require it. In short, superstar one-offs are among the most expensive events to pull off. As a result, you can often find out about them via flyers posted around town or distributed by stakeholders at other events, weeks in advance. In addition, leading area rags and citywide entertainment Web pages announce them and, at times, offer promotional incentives (e.g., reductions in entrance fees or drink specials) for prospective clubbers.

Unlike the weekly or monthly, there is often a partnering between event promoters and professional entertainment companies, with occasional sponsorship by commercial retailers.[37] The desire for such business collaborations is both culturally and economically based. On the one hand, the event promoter is typically interested in bringing a big-name DJ to the area because he or she wants to expose residents to the DJ's talent, keep the EDM scene alive, and elevate his or her own reputation, the DJ's, and the city's in the national or global EDM community. Conrad explained this to me:

> Paul Van Dyk, in my opinion, is a savior of the scene, because when he comes into a market, he exposes so many other people who would not normally listen to dance, to take a chance on dance. The event generates height on such a local level that people will say, "Okay I'll spend $15, we are going to go out anyway, let's try this Paul Van Dyk party

tonight." They come, he opens up the door and exposes new people to it. Why wouldn't you want that?

Other stakeholders, such as local club owners or entertainment promotional companies, have little cultural interest in the event. They do not care so much about what kind of music is playing or what scene is being served. They care about profits. Thus, there exists extreme pressure on promoters to pull off profitable one-offs since they require cooperation with these businesses and cost so much to put on.

The presence of rave identity markers at superstar one-offs varies by the DJ's reputation, the vibe he or she creates, and the types of fans who attend them. For example, since things like fashion, language, and props are showcased by individuals, an event's markers will vary by the types of people who attend them. Since superstar one-offs require massive audiences, they must attract people other than EDM insiders or former ravers. Consequently, more often than the other events, they are populated by the full range of fans described in the next chapter. Given the range in fans and motives for attendance, rave-like identity markers are fairly scarce at superstar one-offs.

In conclusion, superstar one-offs are among the most popular EDM events in town and do much to energize the scene. Still, they are less like authentic raves than any of the other parties because their organization is heavily professional and commercial, their cultural spirit is highly contingent on the DJ, and their fan base is too highly variable to experience any sense of solidarity or collective identity. Given this, I would classify superstar one-offs closer to the club culture side of the EDM continuum (see Figures 2.1 and 2.2 for more detail).

Conclusions

While the authenticity of raves has been and can still be debated, one conclusion from my work is that there are very few, if any, EDM parties in Philadelphia today that contain all of the cultural elements of the original raves in the 1980s and 1990s. I reviewed how my respondents and key informants characterized an "authentic" rave as having many cultural elements (see Table 2.2 for a list). Of course, debate might persist over how many or which of these elements constitutes an authentic rave. Still, the fact remains that there are very few unlicensed, illegal, massive indoor or outdoor all-night dance parties operating with a PLUR ethos and rave identity markers and behaviors today in Philadelphia or other U.S. cities. This is also the case in the United Kingdom and Europe. Thus, if we define raves by these cultural elements, then it is safe to say that we are in a post-rave era. Furthermore, most of the institutions, agencies, groups, and communication outlets that serviced rave culture have also disbanded or diminished in visibility.

Scene insiders I spoke with believe the rave era is over and in its place is a socially modernized and fragmented EDM scene that plays itself out in diverse types of events. These parties are lodged between "underground" authenticity and the "commercial" mainstream. They each possess different levels and versions of the cultural traits described in Table 2.2. None boast completely authentic or completely commercial ones. Instead, they possess gradations of rave authenticity and EDM or club culture commercialism. Consequently, understanding the cultural space between authenticity and commercialism hinges on the cultural traits that define scenes and how participants at the grassroots or local level or business owners or industry actors manufacture or manipulate them. Therefore, further understanding of top-down or bottom-up negotiations of a scene's cultural space is needed from future research.

There is more here to learn than this. First, this chapter has provided evidence of raves' significant alteration over time. While the rave–club culture continuum shows how raves have changed, it does not address why they have done so. While authenticity discussions point to commercial forces that may have altered raves, other factors likely played a role as well. Chapter 4 directly addresses why raves have undergone such alteration and decline. Second, while it is important to understand how people define reality or authenticity, I think it's more interesting to use their narratives and experience to learn about the production of culture, lifestyle, identity, and interaction in everyday life. Certainly, important lessons from this are relevant for other activities and social contexts.

In this vein, the next chapter considers the various types of EDM fans I found during my research. I review their backgrounds, behaviors, and personal identities that contributed to the lifestyle and culture of raves and the EDM scene. This typology also helps define events' place on the rave–club culture continuum. In other words, an event's fit with rave or commercial club culture is also partially dependent on the fans who attend them. In addition, the next chapter explores why people gravitate to the EDM scene, stay attached to it, or grow out of it over time. Thus, clubbers' profiles and identity narratives play a fundamental role in raves' alteration and decline.

3

Loyalists, Spillovers, and Other Party People

Personal and Collective Identities in the Post-rave Era

How can I change the world if I can't even change myself?
—"Salva Mea" (Save Me), Faithless

Early in my enthusiasm for dance music, my friend Adrienne introduced me to Faithless, a U.K.-based electronic dance group composed of Rollo, Sister Bliss, and Maxi Jazz. With many guest collaborators—including Dido as a vocalist in the "Salva Mea" track—Faithless has produced many classic dance anthems that helped define the 1990s global rave scene.

Dido's opening vocals in "Salva Mea" are about personal identity and collective action. They are about the connection between ourselves and to something larger than us, for example, groups around us, our society or culture, or even the world. The link between personal and collective identities in the contemporary EDM scene is the subject matter of this chapter. It addresses such questions as, Who participates in the EDM scene? What motivates their participation? How have they shaped the rave culture? Each of these questions taps into matters of personal and collective identity. Therefore, it is my hope that by explicating the forms these identities take, as well as the substance and motives behind them, further understanding of raves' alteration and decline will be gained.

This objective follows from my witnessing and hearing numerous incidents and stories about personal and collective identity, human connection, and social change in the dance music scene in Philadelphia and elsewhere. I have always found these encounters comforting, especially after September 11, 2001, when the United States and the world at large seemed to be growing more disconnected and chaotic.

One such experience occurred in the summer of 2004, while I was visiting Ibiza, Spain, with three undergraduate students on a university-funded research expedition. There, I learned how powerful dance music could be in fostering connection to a common objective among dissimilar people, despite personal discomfort. Let me explain.

It was about 2:30 A.M. and I was on the dance floor at Pacha, a very large[1] and posh nightclub in Ibiza, Spain. Beautiful people, about one thousand of them, from all over the world surrounded me. Dancing close to me were two women from Hungary, Gitta and Hanja, and a young man from Germany, Gebhard. We yelled our names to each other over the music and became fast clubbing friends.

The hard, driving bassline of the progressive house music synchronized our movement and made us smile and gasp for air. After about thirty minutes or so, Gebhard turned to me and said something. I had no idea what he was talking about but guessed it had something to do with his arms, since he was pointing to them. I shrugged my shoulders and yelled back, "I can't understand you." He repeated himself and again I drew a blank. He could not understand me either.

Gebhard seemed distressed about something, which did not make sense to me. We were having a great time dancing and the DJ was killing it.[2] Worried, I asked him, "Do your arms hurt?" He gave me a quizzical look and I repeated, "Your arms, is there something wrong with them?" Our verbal disconnect remained, but we continued to move in sync with the music. I moved closer to Gitta and Hanja to see if, somehow, they could help me talk to Gebhard. They just smiled and uttered something that neither Gebhard nor I could decipher.

At this moment, I remembered that I was an English-speaking American among a multiethnic, multilingual crowd in a European nation. Over the course of the night, I met people from England, France, Scotland, Australia, Denmark, Amsterdam, Brazil, and, of course, Spain—both the mainland and the Balaeric islands. I also saw Asians and people of Middle Eastern descent on the dance floor. We were in Ibiza, Spain, capital of the global EDM scene. English was one of four languages printed on café menus here. People like Gebhard, Gitta, Hanja, and I visited Ibiza for the same reason: a love of EDM. This singular purpose bonded us and overpowered our cultural difference.

I turned back to see Gebhard put his nose under his arm and make a sour face. Then he yelled "Sorry" over the music. I finally figured out he was concerned about his body odor and worried about offending me. Then he said "You help me?" I felt lost and stupid. Gebhard obviously knew more English than I did German. I tried to tell him that I did not have anything for him, that I could not smell him and that even if I could, it would not matter. But I realized again that words were almost useless.

Suddenly, the music's bass and drumline stopped, leaving only an ethereal melody. People were stilled, including Gebhard, Gitta, Hanja, and I. This brought me relief, yet consternation. I was grateful for the break in the dancing—I was getting tired—but worried that the near silence might amplify my language barrier with my new friends. Gebhard, Gitta, and Hanja seemed to share my fear as we gave each other a quick, somewhat awkward smile and then looked toward the DJ booth for help.

Soon, the DJ rescued us. He cued in a faint bassline and I saw Gebhard start tapping his foot. As the melody and bassline swelled, each of us began patting our hands against our legs, counting together the four-four pattern.[3] We smiled when we heard the snare kick in and could now feel the bass vibrate the floor beneath us. With excitement, we looked at each other anticipating the crescendo. As it peaked, we threw our hands up in the air, let out a scream, and found ourselves reunited in movement. Gone were concerns about language barriers and personal hygiene.

Collective and Personal Identities in the EDM Scene

Collective

For me, being at Pacha that night felt like the ethos of peace, love, unity, and respect was still possible, not only in the post-rave era but also a wartorn world. While it might seem insignificant to some, Gebhard, Gitta, Hanja, and I—complete strangers from different parts of the world—found a way to overcome an embarrassing situation, communicate, and bond with each other to EDM's persistent and fundamental objective: dancing. The music which brought us to Ibiza also helped us resolve our problems by allowing us to establish shared identity and the mutual compassion that often follows from it.

My experience at Pacha that night illustrated the persistence of some elements of rave culture in a highly commercialized venue hosting a superstar one-off. Some might claim this disrupts the rave–club culture continuum. Yet this kind of experience, I have found, is much more likely to occur in Europe or the United Kingdom, where EDM still has a very strong following. It was far less likely in the United States. Chapter 6 discusses these differences and others between the United States, London, and Ibiza, Spain. They likely indicate that the rave–club culture continuum, described in Chapter 2, does not perfectly capture all events and their cultural components.[4]

Sociologists have a long history of studying collective and group identities in such social situations as the Civil Rights movement, union activities, war, and rebellion as well as the identity issues of race, ethnicity, religion, sexual orientation, and disability (Cerulo 1997; Goldberg 2003; Snow 2001; Snow and McAdam 2001). Over time, sociologists have also discussed the role of music in establishing collective or shared identity and in influencing social movements. Work by Denison and Peterson,[5] Frith,[6] and Eyerman[7] are standouts among them. Much of this literature describes collective identities as having boundaries for membership and clear and actively pursued political goals,[8] which were often articulated in lyrical content. Lyrics helped articulate the concerns of groups and their causes, especially during the Civil Rights era or the period closely surrounding it.

Certainly, music's language helps define collective identities and outline agendas of collective action. Political goals and standards for membership do so as well. Artists from many genres—rock, folk, jazz, hip hop—have also sung about changing the world or some small part of it. What happens, however, when music does not have much language or express a direct political message? Absent these things, how does music help define collective identities, culture, and lifestyles change? On what other aspects of the music scene does this broader objective fall?

I remember thinking that night at Pacha, and at other EDM events in the United States and abroad, how glad I was that dance music had so little language. Some might think this a shortcoming, since language allows people to communicate and transmit culture.[9] Without it, they might wonder how effective the EDM scene is in conveying ideology, beliefs, routines, norms, or values. However, Chapter 2 described that such cultural elements were present in the past rave scene and have persisted—albeit to a lesser degree—in the current EDM scene.[10]

At another level, however, the answer to such questions likely requires recognizing that the EDM scene possesses a unique culture, one not specific to a single national culture. Such cultures allow people from diverse countries or localities to connect with something more neutral, universal, and inclusive. This is what Gebhard, Gitta, Hanja, and I experienced that night at Pacha. While lyrics might transmit culture more directly and efficiently, the stories told in songs might resonate with or be understood by some and not others. More recent work[11] on music scenes highlights the role of ritual activity (e.g., dancing and other forms of gathering), rather than language, in facilitating collective identity. This is one reason I have been grateful for the relative absence of lyrics in the music at EDM parties. No particular story or set of ideas was being told in any one language.[12] As a result, the connection between Gebhard, Hanja, Gitta, and I was equalized.

More than this, though, lyrics focus one's attention, while music without many words is more interpretational and can allow freedom of thought and spontaneous bonding with others via ritual activity. In a recent study about white power music, Robert Futrell and colleagues (2006) noted that "actors identify with and commit to one another as they collectively participate in music performances, such as singing and dancing."[13] This acts to heighten emotional energy and feelings of solidarity, a point also made by Kai Finkentscher (2000) with raves' predecessor, disco. When techno DJ Chris Leibing told me and some guys at the record store before his 2003 show at Liquid, "I find that lyrics just get in the way. They are an unwanted interference," he was referring to language's directive and potentially divisive nature. Given these things, it may be that the solidarity conveyed in dance music's collective identity is quite strong, as it is based on a more socially spontaneous consensus rather than identification with a specific set of ideas conveyed by a certain language.[14]

Raves were, and some current EDM events are, environments where participants created an alternative existence or lifestyle with antimainstream values, anticommercial styles, and anticorporate standards. This scene is where the cultural components discussed in Chapter 2 rule the day. Activities, ethos, and organization are leisure oriented and represent a utopian existence reminiscent of the past, rather than being expressly political and directed toward social action. The rave collective identity was both oppositional and "other" because it staked a claim against the government agencies and policies in addition to the corporate-controlled record and clubbing industries. Furthermore, it embraced the values of community, connection, and PLUR, which at the time raves came into existence (the 1980s) was resistant to larger cultures of the time in both the United States and United Kingdom.[15] This substantiates raves as more of a scene with a unique culture rather than a traditional social movement or subculture with politically or socially defined goals. Given this, any kind of social change likely to emanate from raves or the more modern EDM scene is likely to be less political and not geared toward changing mainstream society.

In addition to this alternative content, the rave collective identity was "other" in another respect: members' and participants' social status. In the early days, raves were populated by society's outcasts, teenagers and young adults who were not part of popular school-based groups and who would not typically associate with each other outside of the rave.[16] Thus raves became places where "outcasts" or those defined as "different" from some mainstream standard could congregate, connect with others, and find belonging.

One of the most dramatic aspects of alteration, which contributed to raves' decline, was in the content and solidarity of this rave-era collective identity. Today, older Gen Xers and their younger Generation Y counterparts confront an EDM scene spread onto a rave–club culture continuum that contains no singular or unified collective "other" identity.[17] On the contrary, the highly fragmented EDM scene presently has variations of "otherness." The contemporary EDM identity is a much more diffuse entity.[18] As indicated in Chapter 2, it has a compromised ethos (PLUR has lost its stronghold), more specialized and commercial organization, and both alternative and mainstream identity markers and cultural components. Thus, the people involved in the scene today are likely to have different motives and needs for participation and exude new, more outrageous, or more mainstream styles and behaviors. Eventually, my discussions with the respondents and informants and my observations at EDM events produced a typology—a set of ideal types—of modern-day party people with varied interests, stakes, involvement in the scene, and attachment to raves' collective identity.

Personal

An additionally important yet neglected matter is how individuals link up with a music scene's more collective purpose and lifestyle. This refers to the personal change side in the line from the "Salva Mea" track. For example, few have explored the relationship between individuals' personal identities and the larger group or collective identities, purposes, and styles of particular music scenes.[19] Also, there is little understanding of how the individual and group identity relationship forms and changes over time and varies among those involved in the scene.

This gap also characterizes literature about the past rave culture or the more current EDM scene. For example, U.S. scholars have studied potentially destructive consequences of raving and club drug use among individuals.[20] Typically, they have downplayed connections between raving, identity, culture, and consequence. Such an approach might, however, improve the understanding of the various public health and social consequences in question.[21] On the other hand, U.K. scholars' work focuses heavily on the collective identity and EDM lifestyle without equal attention to matters of personal identity.[22]

In this chapter, I also report on personal identities in the EDM scene and how they were inspired by many things, including personal discord, simple leisure pursuits, artistic appreciation, and social and political consciousness. I accomplish this task by describing how the respondents'[23] and key informants'[24] personal identities are connected, to varying degrees, to the contemporary EDM scene in Philadelphia. My interviews with some respondents and key informants, those especially active in the early rave scene, revealed that "other" or marginal identities were formed early in life, especially within their own families, but also their neighborhoods, schools, or religious groups. For some, this outsider status, during what many consider the most alienating period of human existence, adolescence (Epstein 1998), is what motivated their participation in the rave scene. For such people, the EDM experience was about linking themselves to something greater or, at least, to something that "mattered," as indicated in the "Salva Mea" track. For others, it was leisure activity that yielded pleasurable experiences and, at times, destructive consequences. For still others, it was all of these things and more. These identity stories begin deep within the subjects' backgrounds. Biographical markers shaped personal identities and inspired gravitation to raves or the modern EDM scene. Thus, it is by understanding the myriad backgrounds and current interactional styles of scene participants that we can make sense of the links between personal and collective identity in the post-rave era. Furthermore, this articulation should prove useful in further informing raves' alteration and decline as well as identity and change matters in other youth scenes.

Backgrounds of Respondents
and Key Informants

The people[25] I interviewed were young adults, ranging between twenty-two and forty years of age. Ravers in the late 1980s and early to mid-1990s were, generally, much younger than this.[26] This upward age-shift is largely a result of the organizational change in raves discussed in Chapter 2, which will be further explained in the next chapter. As raves and EDM parties moved into licensed bars, lounges, and nightclubs,[27] they had to abide by the twenty-one-year-old minimum age requirement stipulated by liquor laws. Corporate raves are capable of admitting those eighteen and over because they are often held at nightclubs large enough to secure different zoning and alcohol policies. Music festivals can also do the same because they are held outside under different alcohol regulations.

Prior work on the rave scene has documented considerable race, ethnicity, and socioeconomic diversity among ravers.[28] In fact, the acceptance and celebration of all kinds of diversity were considered a core rave value in the past, and my respondents and informants continued to endorse it in the present. Yet, during the time I spent studying the Philadelphia scene, I found EDM events far less diverse than participants indicated. Instead, heterosexual white males from modest to privileged backgrounds predominated, with white females comprising the second most prevalent group. Asians (especially Koreans and Chinese) and African Americans from comparable socioeconomic backgrounds were the most prevalent minority groups. Again, males were a majority among them.

Table 3.1 shows 69 percent are male (twenty white, nine black, five Asian) and 31 percent are female (thirteen white, two black). Other studies[29] have also found raves and the EDM scene disproportionately male, especially scene stakeholders like event promoters and DJs. My interview pool reflects this as well. Specifically, sixteen of the forty-nine were DJs. Among them were six white males, four black males, three Asian males, two white females, and one black female. There were seven producers[30] and seven promoters among them. Producers were white males for the most part, with the exception of one black male. Promoters were about equally male and female and mostly white, with the exception of one black male.[31]

TABLE 3.1   BREAKDOWN OF DEMOGRAPHIC CHARACTERISTICS

Race/Sex	Fan	DJ	Producer	Promoter	Total
White Male	5	6	6	3	20
White Female	8	2	0	3	13
Black Male	3	4	1	1	9
Black Female	1	1	0	0	2
Asian Male	2	3	0	0	5
Total	**19**	**16**	**7**	**7**	**49**

The people I interviewed were mostly from middle-class and working-class families. All but one had a high school diploma and a slight majority some college education, mostly at schools in the Philadelphia and New Jersey area including Temple, Drexel, University of Pennsylvania, University of the Arts, Rutgers (Camden, Newark, and New Brunswick campuses), and various community and technical colleges.

Their levels of employment ranged from blue collar (e.g., electricians or auto repair) and service positions (e.g., waitress, bartender, retail clerk) to technical and artistic-oriented white-collar jobs in computer programming, systems administration, interior design, and marketing research. The respondents' incomes ranged from modest (about $15,000 a year) to "comfortable" (a high of $60,000 a year). A few of the key informants had incomes much higher than this, since they were internationally known DJs and producers. While they did not give me an actual figure, others in my study who knew them well told me they earned a million dollars or more per year working full-time in the dance music industry. However, most people in my study had yearly earnings in the $20,000–$30,000 range. Thus, very few were wealthy by any standard.

Most respondents were single, with the exception of a handful. Even fewer were parents. In general, about half of the pool had significant others, but very few lived with them. Most were heterosexual. Some identified as bisexual and five were openly gay. One pattern I noticed throughout my study, across locations in the United States and Europe, was how difficult it was for people to maintain interpersonal relationships while professionally involved in the scene. Heavy workloads, traveling, and time spent in clubs and bars, and the temptations and complications that accompanied them, were cited as reasons for this.

EDM Participant Typology

Long ago, sociologist Max Weber (1994) noted that "ideal types" are constructed by people (e.g., clubbers) to help them make sense of their worlds and those with whom they interact. To varying degrees, many people rely on typologies or classification schemes to organize information, manage impressions, perform "appropriate" behaviors, and understand their environments. Daily, we also classify to earmark membership, search for authenticity, and negotiate identity. Whether such representations are theoretical or empirical, based on ideas or experience, does not seem to matter much. In fact, Weber reminded us that "ideal types" are not found in reality.

Still, investigators use claims about ideal types to ascertain similarities and differences in concrete cases and to inform broader issues—such as the link between personal and collective identities. During my fieldwork, six ideal types of party people emerged: loyalists, stakeholders, clubbers, hustlers, pretenders, and spillovers. Grounded in the respondents' and informants' narratives, as well as my direct observation of club events, these ideal types not only inform the link between personal and collective identities, they also helped further define the rave–club culture continuum described in Chapter 2. For example, one of my key informants, Tony, a techno DJ and employee at the record store, offered up a classification the first time I talked with him. He defined insiders as those

> loyal to electronic music and true believers in the rave concept. "Outsiders" are routine party people who chose events for convenience and like dance events because they run way past normal bar hours.

It is important to remember here that my entry to the EDM scene (see Chapter 1) was via a bunch of insiders—DJs, producers, music store employees, long-term fans, and EDM Web site regulars. Many had strong opinions about who was an insider and who was an outsider. It is important to remember that these types do not objectively exist but are formed by scene participants in efforts to note authenticity and to symbolically demarcate membership and belonging. Yet, the EDM scene is a very loose or informal one, as membership is open to anyone.

Over time, however, my fieldwork yielded a more elaborate typology of EDM scene participants, who could be sorted into insiders versus outsiders and further subdivided from there. Specifically, I found three types of insiders (loyalists, stakeholders, and hustlers) and three types of outsiders (clubbers, pretenders, and spillovers), each with different motives for interaction in and connection to the EDM scene and the events that comprised it. Interestingly, their personal and collective identity needs also varied.

Insiders: Loyalists, Stakeholders, and Hustlers

Insiders were described as those who view EDM events as part of a scene with a unique culture and collective identity they endorse. They are deeply committed to finding the latest underground music. Insiders draw social boundaries in two respects. The first is between their scene and the larger commercial clubbing district in Philadelphia. This was described in Chapter 2 and is elaborated on in this chapter. A second distinction is between the EDM scene and the larger society. Loyalists remain opposed to the pop culture mainstream, but they now, as working adults, have a more relaxed attitude about corporate America than did ravers from the past. Still, they are the most likely to believe that raves were, or the contemporary EDM scene is, a place in which they can carve out an alternative way of life and achieve personal transformation. *Their ability to shape this scene by activity, communication, or both gives them a belief that they are changing a social world that matters to them.* And because the EDM scene is linked to other national, virtual, and global (Bennett 2000) EDM scenes, insiders are further empowered in their beliefs, solidarity, and collective identity. In the following text I describe three types of insiders I found during my research. They include loyalists, stakeholders, and hustlers.

They can be differentially situated on the rave–club culture continuum, because even though they are scene insiders, they vary in allegiance to the EDM identity, cultural components, and ideology.

Loyalists

As you can see in Table 3.2, loyalists were the most common type of insider I interviewed. They are deeply committed to underground, as opposed to more commercialized, dance music and they demonstrated the strongest and most consistent ties to the EDM scene. Loyalists spend a lot of money on hard-to-find and cutting-edge dance music and incorporate it into most aspects of their daily lives. Once I asked DJ Modest, a white male, how he could afford his weekly trips to the record store, and he answered, "Vinyl before food!"

Loyalists consistently told me they chose events by the music or the DJ who was playing or that they attend weeklies and monthlies[32] put on by their scene friends. At times, they admitted being music snobs, candidly critiquing events and those who attended them. They were the ones most likely to participate in EDM chat rooms or message boards, which provided them a venue for their

TABLE 3.2   RESPONDENTS AND KEY INFORMANTS[a]
             BY FAN TYPES

Fan Types	Number
Insiders	
Loyalist	18
Stakeholder[b]	21
Hustler[c]	2
Outsiders	
Clubber[d]	5
Pretender	3
Spillover[e]	0
Total	**49**

[a]The table reiterates the heavy influence of insiders in my interview data. While my direct observations of club events, and my casual conversations with people while there, corroborated findings about outsiders, it is important to remember that the fan typology is heavily influenced by scene insiders' perspectives.
[b]All but one of these stakeholders can also be classified as loyalists.
[c]One hustler was also a stakeholder, but his illegal moneymaking in the scene dominated his legal, professional stakes, thus earning him the hustler designation.
[d]Two of these four clubbers were on their way to becoming loyalists at the time of my interview.
[e]I did not interview any people who could be considered spillovers. This ideal type was constructed by claims made by other respondents and informants and from what I witnessed at EDM events, that is, people who crashed after-hour EDM parties when the bar they were attending closed. Because of this, I do not offer a specific profile of a spillover.

scene commentary.[33] The conversation I had with Parker, a black male and self-proclaimed techno head and EDM loyalist, illustrates these insider traits:

TAMMY: How do you choose an event?

PARKER: One, do I know anyone who's playing? Do I know the DJs, or know of the DJs? I don't have to know them personally, but I have to know their work, their music. So, that's first and foremost.

TAMMY: Are there any venues you won't go to?

PARKER: Anything on Riverfront Drive without a really, really, really good reason. Meaning my friends have to be working there or playing there, or personally inviting me to go there and I really had no other choice but to say yes.

TAMMY: Now does Riverfront Drive include Summerfield Blvd?

PARKER: No, because Big City Lounge is there.

TAMMY: Yeah, there is a big house night there Friday night. Oh, but you're a techno guy.

PARKER: I do house occasionally, but I'm not really a house head.

The loyalists I met and talked to are different from yesterday's raver or candy kid. First, they are typically older and more mature. They dress casually and comfortably, like the guy in Figure 3.1, while out at events and do not sport the candy-kid style from the past or modern club-culture chic. Many did a lot of drugs as ravers but have dramatically scaled back since then. Most use some type of illegal drug—mostly marijuana—and consume alcohol, but their levels of consumption are dramatically less than what they used to be. Also, yesterday's raver and today's corporate rave attendee is more into a diversity of music, while the loyalist is more genre-committed, as illustrated in the conversation with Parker.

In numerous places, I indicated that males dominated the EDM scene. It's worth specifying here that males seemed even more likely to be scene insiders, including loyalists, but especially stakeholders and hustlers.[34] Therefore, I decided to profile a female loyalist in the following paragraphs to give some representation to women where they were most plentiful.

Profile: Michelle is a twenty-seven-year-old female of Irish and Cherokee descent. During our interview, she described herself as friendly, bitchy, artistic, a flip-flopper, and unsure of what she wants to do with her life. On the other hand, she told me her top values were honesty, love, independence, and ambition. She works full-time for Federal Express and is currently "on pause" from college at a local university.

Michelle grew up mostly in New Jersey and was raised by her mother and other female relatives. She claims to have had a normal childhood, even while moving around a lot—twenty-three times exactly. Thus, she attended many schools, including three different high schools. This made it very difficult to participate in school activities or make many friends. When I asked her if she

Figure 3.1   Loyalists at Liquid, 2004.

had a favorite school, she told me, "I didn't really like high school at all. So, I got my G.E.D. when I was sixteen." She described her family's financial status as "probably lower class, but not where we were like ghetto poor, you know what I mean? Every time we would move into an apartment and then they would raise the rent, we would have to move because we couldn't afford it."

Like many other loyalists, Michelle recalls her life as fundamentally linked to music. Her childhood hobbies were playing clarinet in a band and listening and dancing to disco with her mother. Michelle cited this as an early indication of her eventual EDM loyalty. Today, she prefers progressive house and break beat music and is quite active in the message boards that serve those subscenes in Philadelphia.

In 1999, after just turning twenty-one, she began attending Epic, the leading indoor rave club at the time in Philadelphia. Quickly, she became a raver and subscribed to the identity and lifestyle. This included considerable drug use, which was ecstasy nearly every time—about once a week—she went to Epic or another rave-era event. It cost her a best friend and left her with some memory problems.

Today, Michelle remains active in the local EDM scene, attending EDM events—mostly weeklies and monthlies—about three times a month. Like most other loyalists, she chooses an event based on who is playing or what music will be offered. She looks for reputable DJs who play the latest underground stuff.

A second criterion Michelle uses for choosing events is its vibe and the kind of scene to which it is allied. She prefers events with a modern-day rave-cultural feel. These feature an intimacy between participants, a mutual love of underground music, and disregard for various status symbols—dress, accouterment, and certain drugs—that accompany many commercialized events in the city's clubbing district. In fact, Michelle does not do many drugs today. She told me she had not rolled in several years.

Loyalists like Michelle regularly classify and criticize outsiders, who they believe are contaminating the scene. She told me:

> It's not like how things used to be where everybody kind of knew each other, wanted to know each other. It's not like that anymore. There's some people who are really there because they're feeling the music. They are really going there for, for the same reasons I feel I go—to listen to good music and be put into that, that Zen, you know what I mean? And then there's some people who you can tell, it's like they don't really care who the DJ is. For them, it's kind of like a status symbol, or they're like a socialite-type deal. You know, it's always like, "Oh, I have to arrive fashionably late," and, "Oh, what's this person wearing, what's that person wearing?" Me, I could really care less.

Like most other loyalists, Michelle's love for dance music has not dwindled over time. When I asked her what she loved so much about it, she mentioned things consistent with my own sentiments and those of others described above:

> MICHELLE: I can close my eyes and I can, you know, listen to a DJ play a set, or listen to a CD that I have, or whatever, and it kind of like almost puts me into another place. You know what I mean?
> TAMMY: Can you describe that place for me?
> MICHELLE: It's kind of like floating around. I'm floating around and everything's real calm, real peaceful, you know; I'm not all stressed out.

Thus, she told me she listens to dance music all the time: at work, while driving, or just tooling around her apartment.

As indicated in Table 3.3, the loyalists I talked to most often attended weeklies and monthlies and showed up at superstar one-offs if the feature DJ specialized in their preferred genre or had a stellar EDM reputation. In addition to this, they also told me they had attended one or more of the leading EDM festivals at some point in time. Their underground elitism, however, keeps them away from the larger and more commercialized events on the rave–club culture continuum depicted in Chapter 2. Given all of this, I situate loyalists on the rave or far left side of the rave–club culture continuum, based on their identity connection, cultural allegiance, and event attendance.

TABLE 3.3   ESTIMATES OF EDM EVENT ATTENDANCE BY PARTICIPANT TYPES

	Insiders			Outsiders		
	Loyalists	Stakeholders	Hustlers	Clubbers	Pretenders	Spillovers
Underground Parties	Dominant	Dominant	Regular	Occasional	Rare	Rare
Corporate Raves	Occasional	Regular	Dominant	Regular	Regular	Occasional
Music Festivals	Occasional	Occasional	Dominant	Regular	Regular	Rare
Monthlies	Dominant	Dominant	Occasional	Occasional	Occasional	Occasional
Weeklies	Dominant	Dominant	Rare	Rare	Occasional	Rare
Superstar One-offs	Occasional	Regular	Regular	Dominant	Dominant	Regular

Stakeholders

A second type of scene insider I interviewed is the stakeholder. Stakeholders are the scene's professionals, seeking to make a living from or earning income in it. They are DJs, producers, event promoters, and other marketing specialists, and visual, sound, or media technicians or aides. Most are also loyalists, but their professional stakes in the scene have the potential to either shore up or undermine their commitment to the EDM culture and collective identity.

Stakeholders are the movers and shakers in the scene. They make things happen on a weekly basis. Thus, they have played an important role in shaping rave culture and will continue to influence the EDM scene in the future. Their activities require straddling the EDM scene and mainstream institutions. Stakeholders must negotiate with conventional and legitimate businesses of many kinds[35] in order to play, create, and distribute dance music and to organize dance events. Take, for example, Leo, a white male, who is a popular DJ locally with a monthly at Liquid, one of the most popular underground spots for EDM music. During our interview, he told me about the financial complications in bringing outside talent to a small venue even though it had a solid scene reputation:

LEO: I wanna bring in DJs who haven't been here before so people can experience something new.

TAMMY: Do you have resources to bring them in? I mean, can you pay them?

LEO: Well, the owner will put up the money, and the promoter—me— will get a fee for putting it together. I mean if I put up my own money, I'd be planning on making it back at the door, but especially with a DJ from out of town, I'd rather have to not take that chance on myself, you know? And if it's someone like Tiesto, I couldn't come up with like $20,000.

TAMMY: But you might be able to pay somebody $1,000 for a set?

LEO: Yeah, but usually the most important thing at Liquid . . . DJs play there for nowhere near what they normally get because they hear about how good the party is. So everyone is lucky because great talent comes in to play for a lot less than what they normally would get paid somewhere else.

Most of the stakeholders I spoke with, like Eve Falcon, a Los Angeles DJ shown in Figure 3.2, began as dance music enthusiasts who developed business interests during their participation in the scene. Conrad, from Chapter 2, is another case in point. Because of this, they possess a bifurcated tie to the scene, one anchored in leisure activity versus professional endeavors, or artistic appreciation versus cash and economics. At times, this dual role often placed them in a unique and precarious position regarding EDM culture and collective identity. Most are extremely devoted to the music, culture, and scene but find they must adjust to external and often commercialized demands of the ever-changing clubbing industry. Consider the following profile of a typical stakeholder in my study:

Profile: Kurt is a twenty-three-year-old Chinese American male whose parents emigrated to the United States when he was nine years old. He is currently a U.S. citizen. He has no brothers or sisters, claiming, "Nope, I'm a single child,

Figure 3.2 A DJ stakeholder spinning at a local nightclub, 2004.

just like that policy says."[36] Thus, he grew up solo in suburban New Jersey in the 1980s in a nonreligious household with solidly middle-class parents. He attended a school with few other Asians and opted out of most conventional peer activities for music-related interests. He told me that even his musical tastes were different from those of others at the time, as he was into alternative and punk rock and then post-1970s disco, followed by dance music (e.g., break beat and trance). He had loads of CDs as a teen and took pride in collecting them.

Later in high school, Kurt discovered www.clubradio.net and became a bedroom DJ,[37] posting shows on the Internet. Soon afterward, he started playing out locally and became a fan of local DJs. He decided a move to Philadelphia was in order so he could be closer to the scene. He enrolled in the Philadelphia Art Institute to study graphic design. He has not finished his degree yet but claimed he intended to soon.

Kurt attended his first rave as a teenager in the late 1990s. Back then, he identified as a raver and bought into raves' collective identity and many of the cultural elements described in Chapter 2. This included considerable drug use. "When I first started going to the parties," he told me, "I used a lot of E. Then, for a couple of months' stretch, I did lots of acid and maybe like one or two pills a week, but then I cut it out."

His drug use escalated during his weekly attendance at Philadelphia's two popular rave clubs, Epic and The Lighthouse, in the late 1990s. But shortly after he started attending those more legal raves, his drug use fell off because he started working for Epic. Over time, he continued to work in Philadelphia's EDM scene, and his drug use decreased even more. He explains this fall-off in drug use as a result of his rising stake in the scene. Today, he told me he likes to drink beer and smoke marijuana. However, drugs like cocaine, ecstasy, and acid are largely a thing of the past.

Today, Kurt is busy working as a promoter in Philadelphia's EDM scene. He holds no full-time, day job. All of his money comes sporadically from marketing and promoting EDM events. Currently, he believes much of rave culture is and was silly, especially the rave style of dress and the PLUR ethos. He used to believe in the PLUR concept. He even told me his top five current values were love, stability, community, staying busy, and having fun. Still, he thinks PLUR is silly. While his denigration of rave culture and its collective identity is anchored mostly in his growing out of raver style and behaviors, it can also be explained by his becoming a businessman operating in today's clubbing industry.

This business objective and identity have even replaced music appreciation as his top priority for scene involvement. For example, Kurt seldom goes to an EDM event that he is not either working or promoting. If he does, it is usually to a familiar stakeholder's event to network or accrue the clubbing clout he needs to succeed in his own efforts.[38]

And while he has been and remains an EDM loyalist, Kurt's professional and economic interests might lead him elsewhere. He spent the final fifteen minutes of our interview educating me about the mash-up and hipster scene,[39] which as a businessman in the leisure industry he thought would be wise to invest in. Kurt explained:

> I don't know how much longer clubs are going to afford to continue having dance music parties. There simply isn't enough demand.

The conflict between cultural integrity and business motivation has been discussed previously in studies about music scenes. Howard Becker's classic 1963 *Outsiders*, a study of jazz musicians, is certainly a standout, as is David Grazian's (2003) more recent study of the blues in Chicago. This conflict is also what distinguishes Kurt from Michelle as two different types of scene insiders. Michelle can remain primarily focused on the cultural aspects of the scene, while Kurt must worry more about economics, even if that means compromising his cultural interests and social ties. This is a fundamental claim Theodor Adorno (1991) made when discussing how art forms, and their appreciation, get corrupted when commercial interests enter the picture. For all of these reasons, stakeholders can be located left on the rave end of the rave–club culture continuum; however, their business interests imbue them with more mobility to shift toward the commercial end.

It is important to reiterate here that because insiders, such as stakeholders, have such tenuous connections to the underground EDM scene and powerful demands and incentives to accommodate the commercial clubbing industry, they have been critical actors in shaping the rave's alteration and, ironically, its decline. This is a point I explore more fully in Chapters 4 and 5.

Hustlers

While most of the insiders I interviewed could be classified as loyalists and stakeholders, I also ran into a third type that did not necessarily fit the other two categories. As you can see in Table 3.2, I interviewed only two such people. However, I commonly saw them at events and had casual conversations with them about their work.

Hustlers provide support services (e.g., they set up and maintain Web sites and message boards) and sell miscellaneous legal and illegal goods (e.g., t-shirts, glow sticks and lollipops, and drugs) in the EDM scene. Like those of stakeholders, their objectives are economic and they may not have been ravers or currently subscribe to EDM cultural ideals and activities. Unlike that of stakeholders, however, their work is more like a cottage industry that exists under radar of law enforcement and quite often even the club and bar owners who house them.[40]

Their presence in the scene is welcomed by some and not by others. For example, drug-dealing hustlers can be old-time ravers and current stakeholders who sell drugs to a small circle of their EDM friends in a very close network.[41] This includes some local DJs who are trying to make a living on the scene.[42] Most of these sales are done in private residences and before EDM events. On the other hand, drug hustlers can also be independents and music outsiders who crash the larger, more commercial events like corporate raves, music festivals, and superstar one-offs to sell drugs widely to anyone.

Other types of "legitimate" hustlers sell legal goods like rave-like accouterments—glow sticks, lollipops, temporary tattoos—at corporate raves with full cooperation of party promoters and venue managers or owners. T-shirts and CDs are typically sold by a representative of a DJ or group from a subscene, also with full cooperation of party promoters and club staff. Like both loyalists and stakeholders, hustlers also sport a casual, comfy style at events that departs from both past rave and current club culture fashion.

During my interviewing and interaction, I witnessed and heard about a lot of illegal hustler activity taking place at EDM events. On several occasions[43] people pointed out drug dealers to me during events or the dealers identified themselves to me by offering me ecstasy, GHB, ketamine, cocaine, and crystal methamphetamine. Some of these people agreed to do interviews and gave me their phone numbers, but my calls went unreturned. This was usually the case with those hustlers who were strangers to me. The insider hustlers I interviewed or spoke with had phased out of their illegal hustler activities in the EDM scene and were now loyalists and stakeholders. Therefore, my profile is of this latter type and should be understood accordingly.

Profile: Allen is a thirty-year-old black male who describes himself as an artist, musician, farmer, and teacher who values honesty, loyalty, justice, integrity, and spirituality. He is from a lower-middle-class background, raised in a Philadelphia suburb by his mother, an elementary school teacher, and his father, a commercial portrait photographer. He has one older sister whom he has never really been close to, largely because she is much older.

Allen described his childhood as interesting yet stressful. He had a strong relationship with his mother but a problematic one with his father. They had communication problems and different ideas about Allen's life. For example, Allen was a musically oriented child. He played the recorder and the violin and generally loved music. However, his father wanted him to play the trumpet. Allen's entry into dance music began just after high school when he went on a road trip to follow the Grateful Dead. He recounted:

> I was at a Grateful Dead show in Oregon and we were walking in the parking lot and I heard this music playing in the distance. I was like, "What the hell is that?" and we kept looking for it. Then, we pulled up to a U-Haul truck with a pair of turntables in the back, and kids were spinning like West Coast trance music.

Back in Philadelphia a few years later, Allen started attending illegal raves and eventually got involved in putting them together. In a very short time, he was promoting large raves and was selling keg beer and nitrous gas at them. The money from these events rolled in, but so did trouble with the cops:

ALLEN: We started getting really big, to the point where clubs would open up and no one [clubbers] would show up. And because of that, we got raided by the cops. The first time I got raided, they thought they had me. They [police] spent $180,000. They came in a mobile unit, an RV, 4 vans, and like all these cops. They found one dime bag of weed on the floor and that was it. They spent $180,000 of taxpayers' money to get one dime bag of weed.

TAMMY: Shouldn't there have been plenty of E and other drugs around?

ALLEN: Well maybe, but tough luck [with a very large grin on his face].

Like many others, Allen told me he consumed a lot of acid and ecstasy in his raving days but grew out of it by the time he was in his mid-twenties. On the decline in his drug use, he claimed, "One night I couldn't afford a pill, and I walked around the club and I was sober. And I was like, 'I look like that when I'm fucked on E? I'm not doing that shit again.'"

Today, Allen owns an art gallery and still has a hand in legal party promotion. While his illegal hustler activities at EDM events have stopped and his own drug use has shifted to occasional marijuana use, he provided lurid detail about other hustlers he currently knew operating in the scene. He described this in a story about a recent drug bust at a club:

The other night, we were in this bar and this one black kid was selling pot. I guess he asked the wrong person if they wanted to buy a bag and they gripped him off and they took him outside. They [club managers] were going to call the cops to get him arrested. We were just sitting there and we looked at the managers and thought there are ten white coke dealers sitting inside this place, but they're gonna fuck with this one kid because he is selling pot?

There are many kinds of hustlers in the EDM scene and they cannot easily be subsumed into one classification. At the very minimum, there is a noticeable difference between those who provide legal support services and those who solely sell illegal drugs at events. Keep in mind, however, that some do both. Hustlers who provide legal support services or retail-types of goods are a welcomed part of the scene, and they typically are also loyalists or very close friends of loyalists. This type of hustler embraces much of EDM culture and could be situated near the center of the rave–club culture continuum. It is only their economic objectives that place them to the right of loyalists.

Drug-dealing hustlers, who show up at corporate raves, music festivals, and superstar one-offs with large bags of pills or packages of crystal methamphetamine or cocaine, are largely unwelcome members to the scene. Insiders believe they threaten the vitality and culture of the EDM scene. Still, loyalists seldom run into them because such drug-dealing hustlers typically attend different events. Thus, this type of hustler is positioned further toward the clubbing side of the continuum.

Outsiders—Clubbers, Pretenders, and Spillovers

Outsiders are believed to less often view EDM events as part of a particular scene or cultural entity. Moreover, they are described as not embracing its collective identity, displaying many identity markers, or experiencing such cultural components as PLUR or another type of solidarity that demarcate the current EDM scene. For example, outsiders are more likely to adopt commercial club culture styles of dress as personified in popular culture. These styles are gendered, sexualized, and more carefully assembled.

Outsiders are not especially committed to dance music, and they might not understand the difference between underground and more commercial tracks or mixshows. Their musical tastes are more closely wedded to popular radio and other media such as MTV, VH1, and BET. At EDM events, they seem to be more focused on common barroom and clubbing activities, such as drinking or courting the opposite sex, rather than adhering to any cultural lifestyle of the EDM scene. I found three types of outsiders during my fieldwork. They are clubbers, pretenders, and spillovers. They too are ideal types that can be situated on the rave–club culture continuum, and because of this, they have played a role in raves' alteration and decline.

Clubbers

Scene insiders are not the only ones to identify a category of party people called clubbers. It is a classification used by many before and can act as a generic term for all people who frequent bars, lounges, nightclubs, and other venues. Many stellar books have been written about clubbers in many different scenes over time, for example, Thornton's (1996) book *Club Cultures: Music, Media, and Subcultural Capital*, Malbon's (1999) book *Clubbing: Dancing, Ecstasy, and Vitality*, and Bennett's (2001) *Cultures of Popular Music*, an excellent collection about clubbers in many scenes. On the EDM scene, scene insiders designated clubbers in a similar way, yet their definitions and my research expanded on this category.

Clubbers are committed to going out late at night to socialize, drink, and dance. Thus, they spend considerable time in the nighttime leisure economy.

They are often loyal to a venue or to promotional gimmicks, such as drink specials, guest sponsorship, contests, or special events (e.g., a fashion show at a club or an eighties night).

At times, clubbers also congregate at events that specialize by musical genre, but do it at a more general level than insiders. For example, during my three years of observation, I ran into lots of people who liked dance music parties but did not necessarily care who the DJ was or what subgenre was being featured. Because some clubbers are regulars at certain venues, they deal with the music played there. Thus, they like dance music (or are tolerant of it), but they have little cultural identification with the scene. Like the others, clubbers also like EDM events due to their organizational characteristic of running long and extending alcohol consumption. Thus, they consume considerable alcohol, but also illegal drugs on occasion.

Culturally, clubbers seem to embrace a more pop culture style rather than an EDM one. And unlike pretenders, they are not perceived by insiders in a hostile way as exploiters of the scene. On the contrary, many loyalists and stakeholders view them as potential or future fans of the EDM scene. Next, I profile T.J., who seemed to epitomize the clubbers I met and heard about during my fieldwork.

Profile: T.J. is a thirty-four-year-old Asian male who was born in the Philippines. He came to the United States when he was nine years old with his father. His mother stayed behind. He works full-time as a mechanic for a paper industry and makes a good wage. He is one of the few married respondents with children I interviewed.

T.J.'s wife also works full-time, as an assistant at a law firm, so together they live a comfortable life. And while T.J. and his wife might be equal financially, he runs a patriarchal household. He does not allow his wife to go out clubbing with him. She must stay home to watch the children.

T.J. is from a large family. His father was married twice and has numerous children from each marriage. T.J. was raised to value family, which remains a current priority and an important value. He also has other conventional values, including work and friends. He described himself as follows:

> I'm a simple person and so friendly. I trust people, very quickly. I don't want to do anything bad to someone else. I just want to make myself and others happy. And I help people a lot. If they ask me to help them, I can't say no.

Dancing is T.J.'s favorite hobby, and he has excelled in it since he was a child. In his adolescence, he danced to pop artists like Michael Jackson but later got into techno, which is a word he used to describe all EDM, something an insider would probably not do. He has no rave experience and no special story about entry to the EDM scene. He likes many forms of music, including pop, hip hop, rock, and techno. Like other clubbers and outsiders, he does not know much about dance music. Consider the following exchange:

TAMMY: If I looked in your CD case, what would I find?
T.J.: Techno, Alternative Rock . . .
TAMMY: Can you give me some examples of bands or artists?
T.J.: Aerosmith and Axl Rose, Guns N' Roses.
TAMMY: What about techno artists?
T.J.: I really don't know about the music, I just have this CD called "Three Minutes" or something.

Every weekend, for the past year or so, T.J. has gone clubbing at the same two venues with the same two guys. He goes to dance and to be seen, because to him, clubbing is about style and status. He conforms to commercial fashion and makes dancing a competition. He explained this when talking with me:

If you go to the club, you have to wear nice clothes. Me, I always wear nice clothes. That's why every time I go, people look at me. Sometimes the girls, they do like this, "Oh you got cowboy boots." And I say "Yeah, I want to wear it, I want to look good at the club." When I dance, you know, everyone is looking at me. That's what I go out for.

T.J. told me he tends to drink a lot when he goes clubbing. He spends an average of $100 a night on shots of alcohol and Heineken and, of course, the cover charge, typically $15–$20. Occasionally, he does ecstasy and other club drugs. However, alcohol is what gets him into trouble. His wife complains about the money he spends on booze, and he has been in numerous altercations because of it. This is one reason he does not permit his wife to go out with him. He explained:

I had been drinking about three or four bottles and somebody tried to touch my sister in a dirty dancing kind of way. I saw the guy and I got mad. I don't want some guy doing like that on my sister and so I protected her. I talked to the guy and you know he doesn't listen to me so I swung my elbow in his jaw.

While T.J.'s ideals and behaviors run contrary to the EDM culture, clubbers like him are necessary to keep the EDM scene alive. Repeatedly, I heard from scene insiders that bringing outside talent to the area was one of the few ways to keep the scene alive and help it grow. To do this requires investment by club owners and promoters. They are willing to take this risk on EDM, in a city that is dominated by hip hop, if they are confident in getting their money back. Thus, superstar one-offs, corporate raves, and music festivals must appeal to a group other than insiders. Clubbers would be among the most welcome, due to

Figure 3.3   A pretender at a superstar one-off, 2004.

their affection for dancing, musical preferences, and generally benign behaviors at EDM events. Given this, I would situate clubbers on the right side of center on the rave–club culture continuum.

Pretenders

According to insiders, the primary defining element of a pretender is a temporary attachment and counterfeit loyalty to the EDM scene in order to build some sort of clout or status among their peers. The young man in Figure 3.3 represents one such pretender. Other derogatory names used were "posers" and "frat boys." Pretenders were also perceived, by insiders, as exploiters of certain aspects of EDM culture, for example, drugs and events' long hours.

The pretenders I learned about usually frequented the most commercial or sensational EDM events. As Table 3.3 shows, they are especially fond of superstar one-offs, but they also attend corporate raves and music festivals. They attend these events to boast about hearing a certain celebrity DJ—thus increasing their clubbing capital[44]—or to indulge in certain types of drug use, which they tend to overdo, so that they experience negative consequences. They may or may not have ever raved and what they know about raves was their deviance, which is part of what attracts pretenders to the scene.

As you can see in Table 3.2, I interviewed only two people who could be considered pretenders. However, my direct observation at EDM events and casual conversations with people attending them corroborated this ideal type. The profile I offer comes from field notes I took at a corporate rave in 2004. Because I got the information live at an event and its duration was much shorter, it does not have the same level of detail as the other profiles.

Profile: Last night around 3:00 A.M. I met a twenty-two-year-old white male who boasted about doing ten E tablets since the party started around 10:00 P.M. His clothes were completely soaked with sweat, including his pants and shirt. Sweat kept beading up on his forehead while talking to me, requiring him to wipe it with his shirt tail every fifteen seconds or so. I said something about this to him and he attributed it to the dancing and pills. He also noted he had lost twenty-five pounds in the past two months. I noticed his clothes were rather loose.

He told me he had been up for two days straight and would return to the closing party[45] on Sunday evening before finally sleeping on Monday. Then, in an attempt to impress me, he invited me to a private after-party in south Philadelphia. I asked him how he would stay up that long (three days straight) and he made a comical gesture of pill-popping.

I tried to engage him in a conversation about DJs, music, and other events he had been to. He told me he liked dance music but only rattled off big names like Paul Oakenfold or Louie DeVito when I asked him who he listened to. Paul Oakenfold is, perhaps, the best-known EDM DJ and commands the highest salary in the world (see the *Guinness Book of World Records*), while Louie Devito has made millions selling highly commercialized vocal house music on CD. Then I told him I hoped to see him at an upcoming weekly or monthly because I was going to have to pass on his after-party invitation. He replied he really only comes out for the big events, saying, "I'm really not that into it."

As our conversation about the music wound down, he told me he was unemployed and would start looking for another job on Tuesday. He had recently lost a construction job and he blew through any money he had in the bank. He wanted to talk more and was interested in my project, but he had to get back on the dance floor with his friends. He tried to give me his cell number but could not remember it. So, he gave me another one. It was disconnected when I called it two days later.

The pretenders I encountered during my fieldwork ranged considerably. Some were much older than this particular young man, and many had more resources. Based on my work, pretenders seemed to vary across gender, social class, and race and ethnic background. In demographic terms, then, pretenders did not seem to differ significantly from the insiders. However, there were some significant cultural differences.

One disparity between the pretenders and loyalists, stakeholders, and hustlers is that pretenders tended to view the EDM scene as a deviant subculture, a place to break free of conventional rules to engage in highly hedonistic behaviors. A second is pretenders' treatment of the event and DJ as a status symbols to shore up their clubbing capital (Thornton 1996).

Since they do not identify with the rave culture of the past or the current version in today's EDM scene, they also do not share any collective identity. Furthermore, since their attendance is at the most commercial events and is motivated by more hedonistic interests, I situate them on the clubbing or right side of the rave–club culture continuum. Ironically, the EDM scene also needs pretenders in order to thrive. I discuss this point more in the following text and in the next chapter.

Spillovers

Perhaps the most culturally foreign outsider to the EDM scene is the spillover. Spillovers were described as those who "crashed" EDM events simply to prolong their partying into the early morning hours, after the bar or club they were attending closed for the night or issued "last call." "Spilling over" is typically a weekend phenomenon, since extended-hour parties seldom take place during the week.

Spillovers are believed to be interested in commercial nightlife activities, such as drinking alcohol and courting or hooking up with the opposite sex. Because of these motivations, they could be among the most intoxicated and disruptive people at EDM events.

As previously noted in Chapter 2, most Philadelphia bars and clubs close at 2:00 A.M., giving last call around 1:45 A.M. or so. EDM events typically secure extended drinking permits in order to stay open until 3:30 A.M. or later. At some of the larger and more commercial venues, I regularly noticed a wave of differently dressed men and women enter the club between 1:30 and 2:30 A.M. Some came as heterosexual couples, while others came in small groups of same-sex friends, most often males. Many were visibly intoxicated and hung out near the bar, watching the dance floor. They were often rowdy and got into altercations with others, including security personnel who were charged with enforcing safety rules.

Unlike clubbers and pretenders, who have some interest in EDM music or culture and activities, spillovers seem to have very little. Their respect for the culture of events also seemed paltry. For example, I often saw drunken male spillovers ask women to dance or begin dancing with women in a form deviant to the EDM style (see Figure 3.4). This included grinding as a dyad or moving together in a synchronized fashion. While these activities and styles are standard to the commercial clubbing scene, they are alien to the EDM one (see Chapter 2) and often drew protest and scorn from insiders. In fact, insiders were quick to discuss how spillovers ruined things. During our interview, Carla, a white female loyalist, told me:

Figure 3.4   A spillover "crashing" the trance room at a local nightclub.

In beginning of the night [EDM party] I love the people, it's a great time. I'm having a good time, and 1:30 A.M. rolls around and the "bar" crowd starts coming in just because the party is open until 3:30 A.M. and drinks are served until 3:00 A.M. Everything changes. It becomes more crowded, number one, so you get pushed a lot. And people become ruder. We [loyalists] get pushed out of the way. We get hit on. It just gets more annoying, and I usually like to get out of there when those people start coming.

Personal Identities and the Link to Raves and the EDM Scene

I wanna take a look at the world behind these eyes,
Every nook, every cranny re-organize,
Realize my face don't fit the way I feel.
What's real?

—"Salva Mea" (Save Me), Faithless

Toward the end of the "Salva Mea" track, Maxi Jazz, the lead vocalist for Faithless, raps about linking individual sense of self to something larger and more external. Thus far, I have focused more on the collective identities of the rave and modern EDM scenes and ideal types of party people currently active therein. In a few places, however, I noted there were some important personal identity matters that connected people—differentially—to the EDM scene. For example, you might have noticed that in each of the insider profiles—Michelle, Kurt, and Allen—there were themes of childhood and adolescent trauma or alienation that inspired linkages to alternative groups, including the rave scene. These experiences were most common among the scene insiders and former ravers with whom I met and talked. On the other hand, they were not as common among insiders who had not raved in the 1990s or among outsiders.

In this last section, then, I want to discuss the personal identity motivations and links to the contemporary EDM scene. I discovered three general patterns of personal connection to the EDM scene: alienation and rave culture appeal, avoidance of sexuality and gender norms and ideals, and merging technological fascinations with artistic outlets. I cannot proclaim complete confidence in these patterns for all party people, insiders or outsiders, since the representation of them in my study is uneven. Moreover, there are likely many individual pathways to scenes and leisure pursuits. It is my wish, however, to simply open dialogue about personal identity stories by reporting on some preliminary patterns.

Alienation and Rave/EDM Scene Appeal

The personal identity discussion begins with two types of alienation,[46] commonly discussed by sociologists, which were widespread among scene insiders and former ravers. Each alienation type worked to define personal identities and motivate links to the larger EDM collective identity.

The first type of alienation refers to a perceived sense of comparative social and economic handicap between the individual and some larger entity: a group, clique, neighborhood, or society around him or her.[47] Instances of this social marginalization might include growing up in poverty or in financially stressed households, as was the case with Michelle, where stress might range from being unable to provide or secure basic sustenance needs to living beyond one's means or "keeping up with the Joneses," as was the case with Kurt.

The second type of alienation is more about feelings and beliefs that are anchored in detachment. Many have written about this type, including me. For example, I previously[48] described personal marginalization as early experiences in life that distance people from local norms, statuses, and experiences considered "normal." Examples include, but certainly are not limited to, death or divorce of parents or caretakers, child abuse and other personal injury traumas, constant geographic moves of the family, and childhood assumption of adult responsibilities.

Both social and personal marginalization or alienation can lead to a strong sense of difference and need to belong. Belonging is relevant here since it can motivate an individual's connection to something external—a group (e.g., tribe) or scene and the collective identities groups or scenes celebrate. The quest to belong to something greater than oneself, where one fits in, is also a very strong motivator of behavior. Thus, degrees of belonging to a scene might produce diverse behavioral responses. Compare Michelle or Kurt to T.J. or the corporate rave pretender.

Finally, when a child or adolescent is defined by others or defines himself or herself as "other" or different, he or she will likely seek out a location in which to belong, one in which to obtain an insider status. Since the individuals in search of such locations are recognized as different and "other," it is likely they will join sites that are also alternative. This personal identity pathway was common among the respondents and key informants, especially insiders who were once ravers. Themes related to this trajectory helped define their personal identities and motivated them toward the rave and EDM scene where they found a way to "fit their face and feelings to a new social world," just as Maxi Jazz raps in the "Salva Mea" track.

One of the first patterns to emerge was a perceived outsider status within one's own family or at school as a child or teenager. This outsider status emanated from either personal or social marginalization. For example, Pat, a black male, conveyed a social marginalization experience:

> In the high school I was wearing clothes that didn't have a label on them. I was antilabel at that point. When I was like maybe in seventh or eighth grade, it was all about having what these kids had. Later in high school, everyone wanted the clothes with label on it, but I didn't care. And the fact that I was pretty much slack, my room was full of records, and they [siblings] would occasionally say, "What is going on? You are so weird, you're so strange." Nobody else was like that at the time.

On the other hand, Glen, a white male, described the connection between personal marginalization—due to parental discord—and the rave and EDM scenes during our interview:

> GLEN: I was on Ritalin as a child, which kept me awake all night, which was when I would play around with music. And then my parents divorced and things got really emotional. The music, I suppose, was triggered in me from growing up in a not-so-perfect environment, getting picked on, not being good at sports like any other strange kid.
>
> TAMMY: So you're saying that music was a way to kind of adapt to these things?
>
> GLEN: Something to attach myself to and you know kind of avoid people.

TAMMY: What do you have in common with these people besides the music?

GLEN: A lot of political philosophies. We all hate George W. Bush. A lot of my friends are vegetarians. A lot of them were a little on the weird side as a child.

Insiders who reported having such outsider statuses within their own families or at school got involved in "alternative" groups, usually of lower social status among their peers, in order to rectify their identity problems. This was an important second pattern in the personal identity stories. Trent, a white male, told me:

Events that led up to me dropping out of school and stuff like that . . . I guess I was kinda looking for a place. I didn't realize it, but now I look back at it, it was like an immediate way to fit in and get attention, to gain some kind of control back in my life. At parties, I was over bothering the DJ. I started asking him how he got into it, what was involved, the price of equipment, and this and that. And he explained to me the value of Technics 1200s, which I wanted. So, within the next coming weeks, I gathered what money I had and bought two brand new Techniques, cartridges and needles, and I had this shitty little mixer that he gave me—I traded him a record for it. He was my direct communication to subculture. I didn't know where to buy records at, or how to get involved, but it was my goal. Like, everything else I did in my life, as far as like girlfriend, or job, or whatever, everything came second to this. And so I started kind of surrounding myself with that whole scene.

While many young people, as others have noted,[49] may have similar experiences and needs that might so compel them, perhaps one reason raves were chosen by the people I talked with had to do with a third similarity: a musical upbringing. Many of the insiders I interviewed and met with told me about having musically oriented parents or being trained musically as children and teenagers. If you will recall, this was the case with Michelle, Kurt, and Allen. Thus, involvement in the past rave or current EDM scene was like a tailored way to fit into something larger than them, just as the "Salva Mea" track indicates.

Avoidance of Gender and Sexuality-Based Ideals

Certainly, social and personal alienation were important motivators of collective identification with the past rave and current EDM scenes for some. However, there were other avenues as well, featuring milder forms of "otherness" or resistance of conventional or pop culture ideals, which made the EDM scene appealing.

One of these had to do with a desire to avoid gendered norms and styles in commercial club culture. LeBlanc's (1999) study of girls' gender resistance in the punk subculture documents similar phenomena. A second was a rejection of club culture's sexually charged ethos. Recall from Chapter 2 sentiment from respondents and key informants that the more commercial scene was about image and hooking up, among other things. Several people I interviewed or chatted with informally at events told me they did not like these aspects of commercial club hip hop and house parties. Rich, a black male DJ, explained this to me:

> I've seen ten guys all around a girl, one or two girls, and maybe the girls are getting off on it because it's like all these guys. But to look at the guys. . . . I don't understand it. I don't understand how it happened, you know? I don't understand how the guys have gotten so out of control and how they let this happen.

People like Rich appreciated EDM's more androgynous or asexual cultural qualities. Both women and men told me they liked attending trance, techno, or house parties because they tired of the more predatory nature of commercialized events. They attended EDM parties because they appreciated the relative absence of a sexualized environment and preferred dancing in an individual and nonsexualized style. Dennis explained:

> I mean, because I can go with my friends too and we're sharing the experience together. And we can dance together and kinda harmonize our bodies, I guess. I kinda like being part of something but you're still individual, because even when I go and dance with my friends, I don't interconnect dance with them. I feel I can dance better when I'm dancing in my own individual space as opposed interacting with someone else's space.

To them, socializing at night was about more than just "hooking up" or "getting laid." They wanted to hang out with friends, dance, and have fun without being pressured to look or act in a conventional and highly sexualized fashion. Insiders, as well as clubbers, most often reported such personal motives. Michelle explained the differences between the scenes and why she prefers EDM events:

> MICHELLE: Okay, the guys at the house event would probably stare or look, but not say anything. But at hip hop events, guys would probably be like, "Yo, yo, what's up baby?" Like all up on you, like try to get up on you and grind on you when you dance. And at Paradise Joe's [large Top 40 venue] they would suddenly have the balls to go up and talk to you because they drank about ten beers.
>
> TAMMY: What type of interaction with guys would you prefer?

MICHELLE: Just regular house guys.

TAMMY: Why?

MICHELLE: If you can't come up to me and just be yourself, like if you have to drink ten beers, or you have to pretend that you're like, this big time player or whatever, this big tough guy, then I don't want to be bothered at all.

Technological Fascination

A third pathway to the EDM scene was particularly common among males and had to do with EDM's origins in state-of-the-art electronic technologies. Many males I interviewed or chatted with informally were into electronic gadgets and games as children and teenagers. Tony, a black male, described this child-hood pattern:

I have been messing around computers and microphones, musical wires, cables, and keyboards as long as I could remember. . . . We used to ma-nipulate, take over the computers and mix the records. We would take any extra money we had to buy equipment, gear, microphones, cheap keyboards, mixers, et cetera. We'd hook that up through the whole stu-dio. So, I was always the tech guy, the resident tech you know.

They were currently pursuing degrees or occupying jobs with considerable ana-lytic, technical, or computer-based skills and requirements.

Males' more analytical traits and interests welcomed a creative, artistic merger with computerized EDM. Recall that EDM is produced by machines, computers, and other unconventional instruments (e.g., the Roland 303 syn-thesizer) via the piecing together of samples. One does not necessarily need musical training in order to play or produce dance music. Take, for example, Thad, an upper-class white male who is currently an Internet designer. He sees EDM as providing an ideal balance between the right and left sides of his brain, claiming, "Playing and producing the music is an activity where I can use my computer skills to fulfill my artistic ideas. It's a perfect intellectual mix." Many of the male DJs I spoke with went on at length discussing the mathematical and technical sides of electronica. Over wonton soup at an Asian restaurant, Thad even discussed sound waves and how they were recorded.

Left-leaning sociologists have discussed technology as having a singular and negative impact on human relations. However, these male EDM fans re-ported the opposite: technology permitted them to fuse their analytic skills and interests with more creative and artistic ones. Whatever the case, elec-tronically produced music—whether it is trance, techno, house, hip hop, or electro—will likely be produced by all kinds of people for a long time. At the ROAR protest in 2003 (see Chapter 1 for reference), I heard a music industry representative proclaim:

They [the federal government] can't abolish dance music because we live in a techno culture. The music is driven by computers and technology. It cannot be stopped!

Conclusions

This chapter has shown that raves' alteration and decline have taken place not only because the culture and organization of EDM events have changed (into six new types of parties) but also because the collective identity of rave culture has been diluted over time. To review, the collective identity of raves has changed from one anchored more in a close-knit and all-inclusive solidarity to a diffuse and specialized one (see also Kavanaugh and Anderson 2008). This kind of alteration in collective identity happens often to things that expand, become more complex, and encounter financial opportunity (Alexander 2004). This was the case with raves' predecessor: the hippie counterculture of the 1960s. Consequently, the EDM scene is less grand and all-inclusive today. What exists, instead, are smaller, more specialized subscenes, based mostly around genres of music, six types of events that vary in allegiance to authentic rave culture.

Even though authentic raves have declined—EDM lives on in popular culture because it has expanded its social boundaries and has adapted, to some degree, to commercial culture. In the course of doing this, EDM has attracted different people with diverse stakes and interests in the music and the events that showcase it. This has been a necessary requirement for EDM to expand, yet it has compromised and altered its singular and unique culture and identity.

Chapter 3 has, therefore, assisted our understanding of raves' alteration and decline by explaining changes in collective identities of the scene and by identifying the ideal types of people currently participating in it. This chapter indicates that how people identify themselves personally and more collectively helps to define and change cultural entities. Establishing shared identity with others is a powerful exercise, for it allows mutual compassion to flourish, while differential identification often leads to conflict and complications.

Yet another important finding has to do with outsiders and social change. People who are outcasts or perceived as different have numerous possibilities to remedy their identity situations. Two include changing themselves to fit mainstream or conventional ideals, or searching for an alternative place—like the EDM scene with its unique culture—that betters fits, supports, and celebrates who they are or want to be. In these alternative places, so-called outsiders become insiders who need not change anything about themselves to be accepted and flourish individually. *Still, they can live a different or alternative lifestyle and even change the social world most important to them through their activities in this cultural collective and space while coexisting in mainstream society. And there exists a distinct possibility that they could have some impact on the larger, conventional society in which their mini-world is located. These are the kinds of social change EDM insiders and other outcasts in conventional society are likely to accomplish.*

Today, the EDM scene is not, however, just populated by society's outcasts. It houses varieties of both alternatives and conventionals. Moreover, even scene-insiders or those that society would consider more alternative have gone more "mainstream" as they have grown older, reconciled personal demons, ceased many deviant behaviors, and accepted raves' fusion with commercial culture. This raises an interesting question about social change: does a scene's ability to continue an alternative lifestyle or impact the mainstream falter or gain momentum as it expands? I offer some insights about this in Chapters 6 and 7, but before I do so, we need to understand *why* raves transformed culturally now that we understand *how* they have done so. Thus, Chapters 4 and 5 describe the reasons for raves' alteration and decline and the types of cultural work currently at play.

4

From 1990s Massives to Raves' Death?

Forces of Cultural Change

Each generation has their time and place to dance.
Raves were ours.
—Curtis, an EDM loyalist

What produced the alteration and decline of raves, a music scene that was once a significant youth phenomenon and site of mainstream opposition? To what extent did rave culture change or falter because it could not accommodate the transience, tastes, or aging of its fans? How did commercial interests affect its trajectory? To what extent was it torpedoed or catapulted by its own form and expression? What role did the state play in altering rave culture and the EDM scene's existence over time? Finally, how are the forces of alteration and decline related to each other, and what can we learn by articulating their interconnections?

Evidence of raves' decline was provided in Chapter 1, both at the local and national levels in the United States. And even though scholars, government officials, scene insiders, outsiders, or the general public might be in disagreement about whether raves exist today,[1] Chapters 2 and 3 show that rave culture, its social organization and cultural form, has transformed dramatically in fewer than ten years since its heyday in the mid- to late 1990s, accounting for a clear case of scene alteration.

The purpose of this chapter is to consider the reasons for the coming and going of music scenes; to move toward an explanation of scene alteration and decline. It is primarily concerned with raves as a music scene with a unique culture rather than with the proliferation or popularity of dance music as a genre or set of genres, although the relationship between them must be addressed.[2]

Elaborating these forces of cultural change will help elucidate raves' alteration and decline by tracing a relatively under-studied part of raves' trajectory:

from their peak in the late 1990s to their diminished and fragmented state in the early twenty-first century. Recall from previous chapters that much research documented the ascent of raves, but few analysts have systematically investigated their transformation since that time. This chapter attempts to fill that gap.

Although there have been many studies of music scenes, youth subcultures, and other peripheral cultural entities that have taught us about resistance, collective identity, social change, youth style, deviance, and otherness, those works have elaborated on the emergence, existence, and substance of those entities or scenes more often than they have explained their transformation over time.[3] The result is that models or explanations of cultural change that could help us predict and understand the trajectories of other scenes ahead of time are scarce.

Perhaps even more important, then, is this chapter's broader goal of uncovering an explanation of cultural change that may be useful for analyzing other music or "alternative" scenes and lifestyles. For example, the discussion of raves' alteration and decline draws heavily from the sociological study of economics and music, collective and group identity, and deviance and social control. Thus, explicating the forces of cultural change will inform numerous sociological literatures and improve our understanding of the fate of social worlds over time.

Situating the Forces of Change

To date, the sociology of culture and music, including that on raves (Bennett 2000, 2001; Malbon 1999; McRobbie 1994; Reynolds 1999; Thornton 1996), tells a unilateral story of how grassroots cultural production gives way to commercial takeover, following Negus's (1999) culture-as-industry perspective. This account raises at least three questions worthy of systematic investigation. First, are economics or culture industry forces the only ones capable of altering scenes, or may social, cultural, and political factors do so as well? Second, and closely related, may a scene transform because of changes in its cultural traits? These cultural elements may be vulnerable to influence, manipulation, and control not just by economic forces but also by such things as social control policies, identity demands, consequences from deviance, and evolving tastes in music. Third, does actual or attempted commercialization guarantee scene expansion or even continued existence of a scene, or can it work to produce the opposite: scene decline? This too might have something to do with the vulnerability of a scene's cultural elements.

Understanding scene alteration and decline requires focusing on all cultural elements of a music scene, not just a particular cultural product (e.g., music). Therefore, we must go beyond the culture and economics narrative to consider how things such as group identity, style markers, behaviors and activities, and norms and values might have also played a role in raves' alteration and decline. In other words, while commercialization and the culture industry may play an important role in transforming a scene's music, they are not sufficient to explain an entire scene's alteration or decline.

In this chapter, I discuss five forces behind a scene's trajectory, one of which includes commercialization. Two additional forces, generational schism and cultural hedonism or "otherness," have not received much attention in music scene research. Insights about them can be gleaned from the collective and group identity and deviance literatures. The other two, formal social control and genre fragmentation, have been discussed in other academic studies of music scenes, including, but not limited to, work on the rave scene. However, my fieldwork revealed some nuances in how these forces worked.

The following paragraphs discuss these five forces of raves' cultural transformation. I present these five forces in order of their prominence in my fieldwork and their conceptual connection to each other. After describing each, I illustrate their interconnections. In doing so, I am attempting to build an explanatory model of cultural change. Briefly, the five forces include generational schism, commercialization, cultural otherness and self-destruction, social control, and genre-based subscene fragmentation.

Generational Schism

During my research, I noted a generational schism that reduced enthusiasm for and participation in the EDM scene and rave culture. Specifically, Generation Xers, who originated and participated in early raves, had dramatically scaled back their attendance at raves and their connections to the EDM scene, while potential new and younger recruits—Generation Y—did not gravitate to them in sufficient numbers. Since any scene or cultural entity requires a mass of people in order to thrive and transmit culture, this generational disinvestment helped facilitate raves' demise. What explains this generational break?

To begin, it is essential to understand that *generation*, as I use it here, is simultaneously a cultural as well as a demographic entity (Ulrich and Harris 2003). Thus, *Generation X* refers to the unique subcultural identity created and embraced by the cohort born in 1965–1980. Generation Xers are between the ages of twenty-nine and forty-four. On the other hand, *Generation Y* refers to the cohort born between 1977 and 2003. Today, they are between the ages of six and thirty-two, overlapping, to some extent, with Generation X. While older members of Generation Y would be able to attend most rave-like events today, many of them—adolescents—would be shut out due to the twenty-one-year-old requirement of most events, bars, and nightclubs. Thus, Generation Y is cut off from the EDM scene today in ways that Generation X was not blocked from attending raves at more informal venues. This would ultimately lead to raves' decline.[4]

Detachment of Generation X

All demographic cohorts have certain ideologies, styles, and interests that develop over time from their experiences in society and the mainstream culture it endorses.[5] Recall from Chapter 1 that the Baby Boom's liberalism of the 1960s and 1970s gave way to a more conservative consumer culture in the 1980s. Generation X—children of Baby Boomers—would grow up during a new pro-corporate, pro-commodity era. It would define them as material beings situated on "career arcs," which ultimately produced feelings of alienation and marginality because of the economy's troubled state in the 1980s.[6] Given this, is it any wonder that the rave and EDM scenes (with the PLUR ethos and celebration of anticorporate values and underground music) would be so appealing, especially among those who were not attracted by the conformity mainstream activities required?[7]

If alienation and discontent from the mainstream fuel attachment to and participation in peripheral cultural entities,[8] it stands to reason that the reverse would also be true: increased attachment to conventional interests and activities likely produces detachment from those that are marginal. Therefore, one aspect of the generational schism—which helped alter rave culture—was Generation X's shift in attachment from the alternative, underground rave lifestyle to conventional institutions and routines.

Many of the study participants mentioned how the increase in conventional ties over time made it difficult to stay closely connected to the past rave and modern EDM scenes, something Bennett (2006) and Davis (2006) also addressed in their studies of aging punk fans. As the Generation Xers finished school, took up full-time jobs in the workforce or started careers, and got more serious about relationships and family, their alienation from mainstream life began to diminish. They no longer had the same incentive to resist the conservative consumer culture they once rejected as teenagers or college-aged ravers. Subsequently, their identification with an "alternative" collective identity and lifestyle began to fade. Allen told me:

> Everybody grew up. It is weird. I will go out now and I will see kids from way back in the day and be like, "Wow, you have changed."

Mary and I discussed how family ties changed her participation in rave culture:

TAMMY: Why did you stop going?

MARY: The children. I went up until I was like four months pregnant with my first.

TAMMY: What kind of connection do you now feel to the dance music scene?

MARY: A very weak connection. I've lost touch. Like I've said, I can't just go out anymore. I mean, I have some control over that, but I don't want to just leave my kids every weekend. I feel more obligated, sort of like a mother guilt issue.

Many EDM loyalists and former ravers told me about the difficulty in attending events, especially those held on weeknights. This is no surprise, since raves were a nocturnal culture that required daytime recuperation. Thad, a former raver and EDM stakeholder, told me how he must balance a 9:00 A.M. to 5:00 P.M. conventional job with his nighttime DJ-ing and clubbing activities. This forced him to forgo many events or to carefully select them. He bemoaned:

> It's not like in the old days when I was working at my record store and could go out all of the time. Now, I have to be at the office at 9 A.M., sometimes sooner, Monday through Friday. It makes Monday night at Twilight—one of my favorite weeklies—very difficult.

There also was a second, albeit more subtle, aspect of Generation X's investment in a more conventional lifestyle that led to a detachment from rave culture. It had to do with a rejection of raves' grassroots organizational style and a growing preference for club culture's more "civilized" and professional setup. In short, as the Generation X respondents aged into corporate society, they developed tastes for its commercialized operational style and comforts and a disliking for raves. Mary explained this to me:

MARY: I was so disgusted because of the conditions they had at the place [outdoor rave].
TAMMY: Explain that to me.
MARY: It was like a ski lodge or something up near the Poconos [Mountains] and there was no air and it was so hot in there. People were passing out, and they weren't letting anyone near the door to get air. They were making everybody stay inside, with the doors closed. They wouldn't let anybody leave. If you left, you had to leave for good, you couldn't come back in. I think there were four stalls in the girls' bathroom. I had to use the bathroom, and when I went into the stall, the toilet paper was stuck to the side of the toilet seat. I literally had to stand on the seat to go to the bathroom. It was the most disgusting thing I've ever had to do.

DJ stakeholders expressed the same preference for commercial club culture venues. They took comfort in the club's DJ equipment, sound systems, and light shows. These nightclub resources alleviated the grassroots burden of securing, transporting, and setting up such apparatus in the middle of a field, at a warehouse, or at any other facility that was not already equipped and designed accordingly. Nearly every rave-era DJ I spoke with confirmed this preference. Rich told me:

> You know, raves were edgy and at that time, I liked that. But the DJ setups were not good. Clubs are just more secure and they have better equipment. But raves were more fun. What ya gonna do?

A third aspect of Generation X's detachment from rave culture and the EDM scene has to do with aging, rave's cultural components, and simple burn-out. Specifically, as Gen X ravers aged, dancing all night (often under the influence of drugs or alcohol) on multiple nights a week or on weekends became too difficult, tiring, and eventually boring. Sylvan (2005) noted that raves required tremendous amounts of physical and emotional energy. For many of the respondents, dancing or staying out until 4:00 or 5:00 A.M. became increasingly difficult and undesirable. In short, raves' organizational style (long hours) and cultural activities (dancing and drug taking) are hard on people. Carla lamented:

> It just seems like I am getting old and burned out. I don't like to do the same thing every weekend. I am getting at the point where I [would] rather do things during the day and go out one night, not both nights. Or even just going out to a couple in one month. It is expensive, number one, and I don't like spending my entire weekend either drunk or trying recover from being drunk.

Incidentally, other Generation X music scenes, for example, alternative or grunge rock, did not have similar organizational and cultural "hurdles" since they were organized more conventionally.[9] Again, raves' cultural elements and social organization are what helped make them unique and, perhaps, ultimately so problematic. Therefore, in order to persist over time, scenes must adopt cultural and organization styles that permit the continued involvement of their fan base. They must secure these ideologically, logistically, and practically. The structure, culture, and concept of raves did not allow this. Leonard, a thirty-something newcomer, told me:

> Someday, I'm going to get married. I can see that once I get married, it's [clubbing] gone. Like, I see this [going to house music events] as a distraction 'til something else. It's something to do. It's part of a social scene. I'll have my CDs, but I wouldn't say I'd be significantly connected after a certain time.

Failure to Recruit Generation Y

If the detachment of aging Gen Xers from rave culture and the EDM scene was inevitable, then successful recruitment of younger newcomers would have been essential in keeping the scene viable. In other words, if you cannot pre-vent people from leaving a scene, perhaps you can recruit new ones to replace them.

The recruitment of new members to music scenes relies heavily on adoles-cents and young adults (see also DiMaggio and Mukhtar 2004). Thus, to fill the gap left by aging Gen Xers, Generation Y had to be recruited to breathe life back into rave culture. To reiterate, Generation Y generally refers to those born between 1977 and 2003. It is the last generation of people born in the twenti-eth century. To provide a reference point, the twenty-one-year-old who at-tended a superstar one-off in 2005 was born in 1984 and is solidly part of Generation Y. As I indicated in Chapter 3, my respondents and key informants ranged between twenty and forty years of age when I talked with them in 2003–2004. Thus, they span Generations X and Y.

Generation Y has come of age in a society fully entrenched in a materialis-tic ethos and lifestyle where hip hop's stories of oppression by and resistance against the white power structure and celebration of materialism and bling (expensive and ornate jewelry and other accessories) predominate. This is the case in Philadelphia and elsewhere.[10]

I witnessed commercial hip hop's dominance among young clubbers in Philadelphia on most nights I conducted direct observation. For example, there are four main clubbing or nightlife areas in the city of Philadelphia. The small-est is housed in the city's gay-friendly district, and the clubs and bars there play mostly dance music, although hip hop is becoming more popular. Two of the other clubbing areas are more heterosexual oriented and cater to young profes-sionals. Both areas have numerous bars and clubs that predominately play commercial hip hop, although old school hip hop, Top 40, salsa, and mash-up can also be found there. In the city's "superclub district," hip hop dominates. While conducting direct observation on Friday or Saturday nights, I noticed huge lines of young clubbers outside of clubs and bars playing hip hop. Often, the dance music party I was attending had a much smaller crowd. Given the dominance of hip hop in these nightlife areas and the numbers of young club-bers attending them, I took this as further evidence of Generation Y's prefer-ence for commercial hip hop in Philadelphia.

My observations were confirmed by the respondents and key informants I interviewed. When I asked about the recruitment of new and younger people to the EDM scene, former ravers and current EDM insiders (especially stake-holders) were in unison about the younger generation being a difficult sell for dance music due to hip hop's dominance. Trent complained:

> I was starting to spin out, I guess, at like different places, mainly in the Northeast, like, bars and stuff like that. But, I got a few spots up there and nobody wanted to hear that [dance] kind of music. They couldn't identify with it.

TAMMY: What did they want to hear?

TRENT: They wanted to hear hip hop and mainstream music, you know what I mean? If they didn't know it or if it didn't have words, they couldn't understand it, I guess.

When I asked Allen about younger people's presence at EDM parties, he drew a blank and replied:

That is something we are all trying to figure out, because everybody went to commercial hip hop, everybody disappeared.

When I mentioned to Rich, the DJ from Twilight in Chapter 2, that it seemed like today's youth preferred hip hop, he ranted:

When I played for the University of Minnesota, I would bring a radio so I could tape the Chicago mixed shows in '90 and '91. And I would get Bad Boy Bill, Julian Jumping Perez, and Frankie "Hollywood" Rodri-guez, and they'd be playing all kinds of house and rave. But you can't find that, you know, and the kids in Chicago aren't getting into that, kids in Detroit, kids in Philadelphia, you know. I mean Robbie Tronco [famous EDM DJ] used to be on the radio. I mean, if they're not getting that now, like younger kids, who are at home and are able to listen to the radio . . . you know, they want to hear Snoop Dogg and stuff like that.

Another reason for the failure of the EDM scene to recruit younger people from Generation Y could be raves' association with drugs, a connection routinely reinforced by the media[11] in the 1990s, which alienated many young people. The rave loyalists and scene insiders I talked with were convinced of this point, and they often cited compelling evidence to support their viewpoint. Take, for ex-ample, my conversation with James and Evan of a local EDM dance group:

JAMES: You see, people think raves are dirty. No one wants their kids to go to raves.
TAMMY: Are you saying EDM is just not regenerating its base?
JAMES: Yes, it's not. You want to know why? Because the media brought it to the point like, if you are a raver, you are a crackhead. Did you see that report by Barbara Walters?
TAMMY: Barbara Walters? When did she do an interview or exposé?
EVAN: Oh my God. They did songs with her documentary or whatever it was. It was so bad. They demonized EDM so bad that people dis-associated with it. Kids today don't want to grow up and listen to dance music.

By the 1990s, most school-aged children were exposed to national drug prevention programs, like D.A.R.E., and other War on Drugs campaigns, which also demonized the rave scene. Recall Dennis's statement from Chapter 2 about the inherent connection between raves and drugs. Dennis is part of Generation Y, and even though he attends EDM events and loves dance music, he has never raved and he refuses to be part of any scene with heavy drug use. He told me:

> I'm remembering an episode of *90210*[12] or something like that, where they had to go to this one grocery store and ask for the map and the map would lead them to this place in the desert and then all these people would be in this like warehouse in the desert. Lots of bright lights and fog there. Lots of drugs!

By the time of my study, the EDM scene had been fully stigmatized as a drug subculture and official data seemed to suggest it impacted Generation Y's drug use. For example, the leading youth drug use survey, the Monitoring the Future Study,[13] shows MDMA or ecstasy use steadily increasing between 1998 and 2001 (the height of the U.S. rave scene) among school kids but decreasing between 2002 and 2005. Thus, the generational effect overlaps with two other forces of cultural transformation: self-destruction or hedonism, and formal social control. Both helped stigmatize rave culture and the EDM scene, acting to reduce their allure to Generation Y.

To sum up, one major force of raves' decline had to do with population loss stemming from detachment by aged-out Gen Xers and disinterest by Generation Y. My work shows the rave scene simply lost its hold on its founders and failed to significantly attract the next generation. This generational schism primarily produced scene decline. Therefore, in order to persist over time, a music scene—and likely other cultural entities—must sufficiently possess a critical mass of members[14] by either retaining those who founded it or recruiting new members.

The key to understanding this generational schism centers on how tastes and preferences are established historically and change over time. People and groups (e.g., Generation X) create culture and cultural entities—like music scenes—at specific points in time and in response to what is going on around them. The connections they establish to these cultural creations change over time and may not resonate with other groups (Generation Y). Because birth cohorts are not simply demographic groups, but rather sociocultural entities that both shape and are defined by history, they must be considered an important force of cultural change.

The Commercialization of Raves and Rave Culture

A second force of change pertains to the commercialization of raves, EDM music, and the motives and activities of people—particularly stakeholders—

involved with them. The basic claim is that commercial interests infiltrated rave culture and helped professionalize it for profit. In an attempt to expand and professionalize the rave scene, I maintain, the forces of commercialization primarily altered it and, subsequently, helped produce its decline.

As indicated, this force has dominated studies on changing music scenes. Many studies argue that recording companies, mainstream media, and retail businesses corrupt underground or grassroots music scenes where "authentic" music begins.[15] Typically, music is considered authentic when it is underground, produced in a DIY fashion outside the mainstream music industry, written or produced with high artistic integrity rather than simplified to fit pop culture, and unknown to the masses and kept close to scene insiders.

Commercialism is believed to corrupt all of this.[16] It brings music out of its small underground scene and into the larger conventional society. Commercialism forces musicians—or DJs, in the case of EDM—to trade creativity and complexity for formulas (i.e., verse-chorus-verse) that people can recognize. And in the process of doing this, commercialism fundamentally, and often permanently, alters cultures, scenes, and insiders. Some find the cultural change repugnant, while others applaud it.

Whatever one's viewpoint, the cultural fallout from commercialization is an under-studied aspect of a music scene's trajectory. Therefore, by elaborating on the commercialization of the rave scene, I hope not only to articulate how and why it happened but also to illustrate the consequences for the EDM scene and lifestyle.

Raves' Partnership with Legitimate Clubs

Accounts of raves' origins by people such as Matthew Collin (1997), Andrew Hill (2002), Steve Redhead (1993, 1997), and Simon Reynolds (1999) concur that raves' roots officially began in the immediate aftermath of disco's death in the late 1970s and early 1980s. Soon thereafter, acid house came onto the scene at underground clubs in Manchester and London. The parties became very big and were frequently raided by the cops, causing promoters to move them outside the city to obscure locations that could accommodate the massive crowd size and evade law enforcement. Thus, it is both ironic and cyclical that raves should later be lured back into nightclubs. This time, however, things would be different.

Club owners in the 1990s saw the popularity of raves as a way to make money. They began approaching rave promoters and DJs to bring the parties inside for a sort of joint partnership. Conrad, a former rave-era promoter and rave nightclub owner, described this:

> What they were doing at that time, is that they [rave promoters] were all throwing illegal, warehouse parties, so the clubs in New York had the bright idea, we will shut them down. We have room for three thousand

people. We will bring all the parties and the DJs and this whole culture to our club. We will partner with the promoters. We will make the money and then that's it. We will have parties, but they will be in clubs. What ended up happening? It is the birth of the Lime Light, the Tunnel, and clubs like that all owned by the same group of individuals. I believe that every party that was underground at that time, well, there was no other place for these parties to go. There was such a demand for them.

While Conrad's story[17] refers to New York City, the same thing happened in Philadelphia. In fact, some former rave promoters I spoke with bought large nightclubs—Epic and The Lighthouse—that later housed Philadelphia's rave scene at its peak.

For stakeholders, this was considered a very smart business move with many benefits. However, it had created consequences for rave culture: it positioned the EDM scene's ethos closer to "corporate" or big business principles that Gen X ravers once rejected. And profiteering and PLUR are very strange bedfellows.

Many DJs welcomed the partnership with legitimate nightclubs because, as Rick indicated, grassroots organizational strategies were problematic and labor intensive. Moreover, letting the club take care of equipment and logistics freed DJs to focus on their music and promoters on better marketing strategies for their parties. Plus, bringing the event inside to a legal environment secured it from police interference, again freeing up the DJ and promoter to specialize in their tasks and professionalize them.

A major consequence of raves' partnership with legitimate nightclubs was the loss of the youngest ravers at events. Nightclubs must adhere to a city's zoning and alcohol laws, which often disallow entrance to people under twenty-one years of age. At times, clubs can get special permits to admit people aged eighteen years and over, but few can permit anyone under eighteen. The result is that younger people—a target recruitment pool—found it harder to attend raves, to locate dance music, and to experience the scene and culture. Thus, this aspect of commercialization added to the generational schism between Generations X and Y. Over time, teens would gravitate to the music they had access to: the hip hop and rock played on MTV and mainstream radio. Thus, rave culture's partnership with legitimate nightclubs professionalized and commercialized raves, and in so doing, it altered raves' ethos, changed their grassroots organization, and cut out a large portion of their potential fan base—younger ravers who could not meet the twenty-one-year-old age requirement of legal clubbing venues. This illustrates the connections between general schism and commercialization as forces of alteration and decline. It also shows how the expansion goal of commercialization backfired by cutting out younger (Generation Y) participants.

The Professionalization of the EDM DJ

Recall from Chapter 2 that, in early rave culture, DJ-ing was egalitarian: DJs traded off with each other, played for similar amounts of time, and were paid modestly (Melechi 1993). They were largely a faceless group with collective goals such as musical enlightenment and taking fans on journeys and keeping them dancing all night.

As raves and dance music grew in popularity, DJ-ing became considered an art form (Fikentscher 2000; Herman 2006), especially with constant technological advances in equipment to produce and mix music.[18] Nightclubs facilitated the professionalization of DJ-ing since they had the resources to invest in sound and lighting equipment. Rich, who began DJ-ing at raves, told me:

> Well, at that time, you really had to be into it and into the music. Because it wasn't about money. There weren't superstar DJs at that time. And it's not really about that anymore in a lot of circles, because, you know, whenever there's success or the chance of success where people can make money, and travel, and do things that they really wouldn't be able to do any other way, I don't know. You get a lot of people now who, they have an agenda. Back then, people didn't have agendas, it was just, "Hey, we're having this party." Play some records.

Superstar DJs had emerged by the time raves peaked, permanently changing the egalitarian principles that governed raves in many respects (that is, DJs received equal compensation and time slots in joint or shared rotation).[19] "Main acts" became marketing tools to attract people to events. DJs themselves realized there was now a "profession" they could pursue that had a discernible career arc. There was also lots of money to be made.

Yet another important step in the professionalization of the rave-era DJ was the eventual valuation of original music production over the live spinning of records. Many DJs I spoke with told me that to get gigs today they had to produce their own music and that it had to achieve some popularity within the local or more national, and perhaps international, scenes. Promoters told me that selling their events to the public required DJs at the cutting edge of musical production. In fact, during my study, scene stakeholders distinguished between DJs and producers or artists. DJs were those who played other people's music, while producers were artists who generated their own. Glen, a younger, Generation Y DJ, told me:

> It's not the rave scene like a couple years ago when you have some tickets and some promoters and get booked out in the Northeast. Like now you have to have a good record out. If you can get the record out, then people are like "Oh, maybe we should bring this guy into town."

In order to navigate the EDM DJ career path, one has to produce new music, becoming more of an artist rather than a mere DJ. This is yet another instance of raves' commercialization into the mainstream music industry: the trademark musical product of raves (a DJ-ed mixshow) loses its cultural value to the more mainstream commodity of an original track or CD.

Over the course of my study, I have talked with many DJs about their dreams of self-supported playing and making music rather than having to split their time and energy between conventional 9-to-5 jobs and nighttime gigs.[20] The professionalization of DJ-ing and the national and international success of some rave-era DJs made this dream seem possible. Anyone who excelled at mixing and produced a hit track might actually become a pop star, or better yet an "artist," and enjoy the perks that accompanied it. After all, Michael Cohen, VP of commercial marketing at Warner Music Group, in a 2000 *Billboard* interview with Paoletta, proclaimed, "The DJ is now the pop artist."[21]

The competitive business of DJ-ing and the EDM DJ's quest to earn respect in the legitimate music industry are yet another aspect of commercialization that inadvertently compromised rave culture. To begin, aspiring EDM DJs often disassociated themselves from the word *rave* because it was perceived to diminish the respectability of the DJ's work. DJs who emerged from raves as "professionals" were aware of being closely associated with rave culture could give them a courtesy stigma,[22] which might undermine their careers. Thus, the shamans or leaders of the rave culture grew to prefer being called "main acts," "artists," or "producers," all names with more currency in the mainstream pop music industry. Many DJs I spoke with would like to be taken seriously as artists, giving them another reason to avoid the highly stigmatized word *rave* and its childlike culture.

The professionalization of DJ-ing weakened the ethos and organization of raves, and the rise of superstar DJs tested a local scene's ability to support them. When superstar DJs request large sums of money to spin for a few hours, clubs in cities like Philadelphia have a difficult time paying them, and young people—like Aidan and Connor from Chapter 1—have a difficult time going to hear them. Cities like Los Angeles or New York, where dance music has a stronger hold and that are larger and have bigger leisure industries, can regularly afford to bring in such talent. Many of the superstar one-offs I attended in Philadelphia had crowds too small to cover event expenses, resulting in losses for promoters and club owners. Thus, while many believe superstar DJs are necessary to energize[23] a local scene, their exorbitant fees impede that goal. The ability of organizers and promoters to keep the scene fresh with guest DJs becomes problematic when DJs charge fees the events or participants cannot afford. High DJ prices can lead to scene stagnation because they prohibit events and clubs from bringing in different or well-known talent. Fans begin to underappreciate the hardworking and talented local DJs,[24] even though they are the ones who originate, preserve, and shape local scenes. Moreover, hearing a superstar DJ play is now a primary motivation for attending an event, often overshadowing other interests more closely connected with rave culture.[25] Jim told me:

The commercialization of the scene kind of takes away from why people are really there. You can flip it around and say it's really helping the scene by introducing it to a lot more people via big DJs, but basically there's no intimacy.

The DJ's transition from a faceless, collective-oriented rave shaman to a superstar artist is a significant development, one resulting from the commercialization of rave culture and the professionalization of the DJ as a pop artist. While this transition has benefited a small proportion of DJs, it has damaged the collective identity and cultural cohesion of rave culture and current EDM scenes. Furthermore, it has impacted the frequency of events and attendance at them due to the rising financial costs of superstar DJs.

The leaders of rave culture, EDM DJs, shifted their allegiance from the cultural collective that helped establish them in the first place in favor of participation and recognition in the mainstream music industry. In doing so, rave culture lost many strong leaders and found the very norms that characterized that leadership (equity in time spinning between DJs, modest pay, and their humble self-images) altered. EDM DJs abandoned these things because of commercialism's temptations and, perhaps, the very strong U.S. ideal of individualism that encourages all of us to prioritize our personal needs and interests above the collective. Any social movement or cultural entity—like a music scene—needs leaders in place to help navigate members toward goals (or to fashion a lifestyle) and to preserve its culture and identity. It is essential for those leaders to stay connected to these collective interests.

Branding EDM Parties

In Chapter 2, I described a rave–club culture continuum with six types of EDM parties. At least two on that continuum, music festivals and corporate raves, are versions of "branded" parties, entertainment events with a unique style, format, and content marketed widely as products or brands. In short, EDM events are brands to be marketed and sold just like other events in entertainment industries today.

Branded parties are the business of professional entrepreneurs or entertainment groups.[26] Examples include the Buzzlife and Explosion! corporate raves in Philadelphia and the Ultra Music festival in Miami. To some extent, weeklies and monthlies, especially those hosted by well-known national or international DJs (e.g., Deep Dish's Yoshitoshi party at Pacha or Balearic People at Penelope nightclub, both in Ibiza, or the Hed Kandi nights in London), are also branded weeklies, but they typically are located in cities with larger, more lucrative EDM markets.

Branding EDM parties—formerly raves—replaces grassroots with professional organization and collective, empathy-based ideologies and cultural forms with an emphasis on pizzazz and profit. Branded parties are very expensive productions requiring tremendous attendance in order to turn a profit. Thus, promoters often must compromise some aspect of rave culture or depart from it in order to successfully market their brand. Some of these strategies include corporate sponsorship (another indication that Generation X was getting over its anticorporate ideology), recruitment of consumers outside the EDM enthusiast pool, and a sacrifice in rave style and activities for something closer to that of club culture or MTV chic. For example, branded EDM parties today place a higher value on sexuality and hooking up.

In addition, the organizational style of branded parties also departs from that of early raves. Marketing strategies are now out in the open and used well in advance of an event in order to draw large enough crowds to offset operating costs.

Taken together, industry insiders, especially local, national, and international stakeholders, see commercialization not as negative but as a positive step in EDM's evolution. To them, the commercialization of raves allowed EDM to gain cultural legitimacy—where people can make a livelihood out of working in the industry. So, the move toward commercialization of the EDM scene is viewed as an advance: from the underground rave culture to a bona fide place in the mainstream music industry, or from marginality to cultural legitimacy. Cristina Fisher wrote in *BPM* magazine:

> As the music became more widespread and gained a wider audience, venues grew to accommodate. Clubland took notice, and the movement became an opportunity for the music to gain cultural legitimacy and begin to reap financial rewards.[27] (p. 89)

Typically, the people who espouse this position are industry heavyweights who have achieved some modicum of success. They desire music's emancipation and for DJ-producers to be viewed as artists and players in the pop music industry. But not everyone holds these sentiments, and plenty of other scene insiders—DJs and fans alike—debate keeping things underground and authentic versus selling out to the mainstream.

In conclusion, commercialization primarily altered the rave scene and its culture. Specifically, commercial expansion corrupted the cultural elements and social organization of raves, replacing them with styles more similar to mainstream popular culture, in three ways. First, it lured raves indoors to legitimate nightclubs where the profit motives of club owners trumped the PLUR ethos and professionalized setups replaced grassroots organization. Second, commercialization altered raves' leaders, EDM DJs, into pop stars or artists capable of successful independent careers in the music industry. Third, raves (especially music festivals and corporate raves) also professionalized by becoming brands marketed for sale in the leisure industry. These transitions were aided by the profit motives of conventional businesses, including large entertainment groups, super nightclubs, clothing and other retailers, and record companies. They are a clear case of Negus's (1999) culture-as-industry mode of commercialization. As a result, raves' cultural form and social organization were permanently altered. Moreover, raves' partnership with the legitimate clubbing industry stymied recruitment of new members—Generation Y—thus exacerbating the generational schism and scene decline. Some individual stakeholders endorsed the shift, but other insiders like Hamilton, a long time EDM fan, lamented it:

> I think that the scene just allowed itself to be packaged and sold by MTV and Gap, and all those institutions. I don't want to buy my clothes at Gap. I don't want to look at MTV and see an EDM video. I like going to grimy warehouses with a shitty sound system and just being free. Now, there are people filming movies about it [EDM and raves]. It's lost something.

Cultural "Otherness," Hedonism, and Self-Destruction

Involvement in a scene that is peripheral to the mainstream or different from conventional styles, behaviors, and selves can be a stressful and undesirable experience for some but a comfortable, cool, and unifying experience for others (Irwin 1977). At times, it can even be both things simultaneously. In the earlier chapters of this book, I noted that rave culture and the EDM scene were an alternative entity whose unique culture showcased many identity markers, styles, and behaviors that were often unique and deviant yet widely embraced by those participating in the scene.[28]

It seems almost paradoxical, therefore, to write a few years after raves' peak that aspects of raves' cultural "otherness" would ultimately cause them to self-destruct. Raves' alternative ways would wind up not only turning off new recruits from Generation Y but also alienating some of the Generation Xers who helped launch the original culture and style in the first place. Thus, the premise behind this third force of change is that raves' cultural form and lifestyle were simply too alternative or deviant for their own good, eventually helping to bring about their own demise. Much of raves' aesthetic and lifestyle were rejected by scene insiders and outsiders. In addition, ravers ran into complications from their own debauchery and began criticizing the scene in a similar fashion as the wider public. Taken together, these forces provide evidence of scene decline.

Rejection of Style or Aesthetic

During my research, I found several different aspects of increased rejection of raves' style or cultural aesthetic. One pertained to rave style or fashion and other identity markers. For example, the childlike candy kid, wearing parachute pants, sucking on a pacifier, and weaving glow sticks (shown in Figure 2.1), simply became too weird, silly, and different.[29] It was not an image or fashion many insiders wanted to continue or outsiders cared to copy. Benjamin told me:

> You used to see all these people in baggy pants with glow sticks. To me it was very circus, very clown-like compared to, at the time, to the house music I was listening to. We got dressed up to go out. On a Saturday night at Club X, you were dressed in black pants, black shirt, you know, dressed normally. So to look at the two [raves versus commercial house scene] can't be any more extreme. So I appreciate both extremes, but I would rather be in a black shirt, black pants.

Moreover, the androgynous style and asexual vibe at raves alienated many clubbers, especially after raves came inside to legitimate clubs in entertainment districts. In most locations, clubbing (which is largely what raving became)[30] is about courtship and sexual intimacy, yet raves were notoriously asexual.

The rejection of rave culture's image and style was, in many ways, about rejecting the return to or pursuit of childhood innocence. Parker, a DJ and fan, retrospectively put down the rave image:

> Maybe it was the drugs they were on, and I was on, but people were hugging each other, and they were dancing all night, and they were jumping and screaming with glow sticks, and acting childish, and just being children doing drugs at a party.

More recently, scene heavyweights, at national and international levels, have called for a "makeover" of the EDM scene's style and image, one that more closely emulates the mainstream. For example, at the 2004 Winter Music Conference's panel on club culture, I listened to scene loyalists debate with major club owners about cleaning up the EDM scene's image to make it more successful in commercial club culture. For club owners, this included wearing better clothes and buying more alcohol than bottled water (a rave drink associated with drug use).

Finally, over time, flyers for upcoming events displayed identity markers that increasingly digressed from rave culture and aligned themselves more closely with commercial club culture. For example, flyer art shifted to darker, deeper colors (as opposed to raves' neon ones) with sexually charged language and images to advertise events. Especially common, on even the most rave-like event flyers, was the Barbie doll–proportioned, scantily clad female—a dramatic departure from raves' youthful "girl" wearing baggy pants and holding a stuffed animal.

Raves' Drug Use as a Turn-off

While the rejection of raves' stylistic "otherness" alienated people from the scene, a more urgent and devastating repudiation followed from stigmatizing drug use and its consequences. As indicated earlier, rave culture's association with drugs has been a major focal point for academic, media, and public policy attention. During my research, I uncovered two major ways that drugs worsened raves' image and contributed to their self-destruction: raves' drug use turned people off to the scene, and individuals suffered consequences from their own drug use at raves and EDM parties.

Many people I spoke with told me that raves' close connection with drug use was something they did not endorse or could no longer tolerate.[31] Often, these antidrug positions were held by stakeholders with professional interests in the scene. Suzanne, a DJ, blamed raves' troubles on club managers and rave promoters. She told me:

> The thing with the rave scene is that it is very close knit, and the club managers and the owners started messing up real bad, just messing with the kids. They had people coming in and selling drugs in there. Kids were getting robbed for drugs.[32]

Allen, a rave-era promoter, countered this by blaming individual drug use when I asked him about the cause of raves' demise:

> I say it was a dumb-ass drug addict that couldn't control their drug habits. And they were like, "Hey, let's do some drugs and die in a parking lot of a party before the party even starts!" It's stuff like that. As I've said, there are people that throw parties and are out there for the music, and then there are people out there for the drugs.

Certainly, Allen's perspective can be understood given the professional stakes he had in rave culture and those he enjoys in the contemporary EDM scene. Other such stakeholders shared his sentiment. For example, Tony, a former DJ and current light show and graphics expert, also dismissed ravers as "living in a candy-coated fantasy world," while Jesse Saunders, at the 2003 ROAR protest I attended, recounted stories of people laid out on the dance floor from drugs. In his words, "they are not hearing the music."

Other insiders shared these antidrug sentiments. For people like Leonard, drug use was stupid and a turn-off:

> I see pills, you know, I see people sniffing stuff. That's just crazy. And what blows my mind is that you have someone walking around the club with little vials of stuff, giving it to people and they drink it. How do you

drink something and you don't know what's in it? That blows my mind. They'll smoke weed too. Say I'm with a group of friends, and one of their friends comes in the group and he's smoking marijuana. I'm out. I just don't want to be associated with that stuff. You know what it is, I feel like it is a knucklehead element that associates with it [drugs].

The antidrug sentiment was also driven by personal concerns. Carla, a twenty-eight-year-old fan, discussed cocaine use among some of her clubgoing friends at an after-party:

It kind of scares me how it's [drug use] so accepted. Two weeks ago I was at my friend's house at an after-hours gathering and they had a dinner plate full of cocaine. I was like "I need to go." It was bad.

Drugs and Personal Consequences

Most of the people I interviewed told me they had used illegal drugs at some point in their lives and at raves or other EDM events. Marijuana and ecstasy were the most common drugs used; however, others discussed using LSD, ketamine, crystal methamphetamine, and cocaine. Their levels and frequency of illegal drug use varied considerably. For example, a slight majority were active drug users, smoking marijuana more than once a week, snorting cocaine on a monthly basis, and taking ecstasy more sporadically and often for special events. About a third of the respondents told me they quit using all drugs recently and only consume alcohol. Men reported considerably more drug use than females, a well-established pattern in the substance abuse literature.[33]

Drug use was initially very pleasurable for the people I spoke with, and it came without consequences. Glen described this during our interview:

My sister and her friends were ravers and would tell me crazy stories of going to parties, dressing real wild, taking all these drugs. I didn't go to a rave until like four years later. Seeing LSD in front of me for the first time was just like WOW! It was exciting. Whenever I went to a party, I was like "This is really cool, this is what I want to do. This is really wild, subversive. I want to be a part of this."

Drugs were viewed as simply part of rave culture and the EDM scene. Parker explained:

People were generally friendly, and maybe it was the drugs they were on, and I was on, but it was just a very sociable, very fraternal environment. People were hugging each other, and they were dancing all night.

Research[34] suggests that the psychedelic effects of ecstasy likely contributed to such feelings and sentiments since the drug has empathy-inducing qualities. However, ecstasy was also a good fit to rave culture in another respect: its stimulant properties facilitated dancing for long periods of time. A conversation with Glen confirmed ecstasy's dual attraction:

TAMMY: So you take ecstasy more for the hallucinogen effects or more speed?
GLEN: Well, I'll take either but I hope for something that's speedy.
TAMMY: Can you elaborate on why that is?
GLEN: Because if it's speedy I can party longer and just dance all night, you know?

For many, these initial, pleasurable experiences with drug use and raves took a negative turn. People ran into problems due to drugs—they lost friends, missed work, dropped out of school, or suffered mental or physical illness. These personal consequences facilitated their detachment from the scene. Recall from Chapter 3 Michelle's loss of a best friend and diminished memory due to weekly ecstasy use at raves and the twenty-three-year-old pretender I profiled who told me about taking ten ecstasy pills, losing massive weight, and being unemployed and broke.[35] Many reported personal consequences from drug use at raves that forced them to alter their clubbing activities and scale back their involvement in the scene. In addition, I know of several scene insiders who ran into drug-related problems over the course of my study. I lost contact with one key informant due to excessive ecstasy and ketamine use and with a second due to crystal methamphetamine abuse.

Theoretical Connection

Cultural theorist Theodor Adorno (1991) claimed that "culture industries" (i.e., businesses that produce and market cultural products like music and art) ensure continued obedience of people to market interests by homogenizing their cultural palates. In this way, the culture industry defines deviance or "otherness" or creates intolerance for it by producing a preference or bias for sameness and conformity.

This could be one operating premise behind the cultural hedonism and otherness force of cultural transformation. As raves were lured into partnership with legitimate nightclubs, outsiders to the scene were recruited by professionals to expand profits. These newcomers requested mainstream cultural products from the rave scene, including sexually oriented vibes and more mainstream styles. Raves' cultural elements—their asexual vibe and childlike fashion—were subsequently altered.[36] Generation X rave enthusiasts also rejected raves' cultural otherness as they aged into working professionals. They too came to believe some parts of rave culture were simply too outlandish. Thus, rave enthusiasts and outsiders began to converge in their tastes for commercialized products and forms, indicating, as Adorno warned, the power of culture industries to move people toward homogeneity and standardization as they age.

Still, there is another factor that torpedoed raves, and it has little to do with the cultural sameness or culture industries. Cultural hedonism, especially illicit drug consumption and other forms of deviance, by rave insiders or enthusiasts led to the scene's self-destruction and decline as people developed addictions to chemicals or suffered personal consequences from raves' lifestyle. Simply put, rave culture yielded too many bad consequences for those involved. The scene's allegiance to these forms and acts ultimately contributed to its internal corruption and decline.

Cultural hedonism has something in common with generational schism. Both refer to population loss of insiders or early participants and a failure to recruit new ones. The two differ, however, in reasons for that loss. For example, population loss due to cultural hedonism and too much otherness cuts at the essence of raves' cultural form and uniqueness. In other words, rave culture's grave was being dug when people, especially ravers and scene insiders, began defining raves' characteristics as too "other," weird, or excessive. When still others suffered too much consequence from the rave lifestyle, rave culture was covered in dirt and laid to rest. This force of change calls into question the ability of deviant or resistant cultures to persist over time.

Herein lies an interesting question: are there limits to how deviant or resistant a culture can become before it self-destructs and loses its members? Some of the best-known sociologists, such as Howard Becker and Kai Erickson, defined deviance in society but wrote little about its range or severity. Few have considered just how deviant or "other" something can become before it loses population, becomes disrespected, and eventually self-destructs. This force of change opens up that dialogue. Since marginal cultures—like the rave scene, the White Power movement, skater culture,[37] and various drug subcultures—exist in relation to core or mainstream cultures, it makes sense that they might retain more members and longevity if they do not stray too far from them.

On the other hand, deviance and otherness cannot not be viewed as something negative only or as indebted to societal conventions. Deviance and otherness can also be positive acts of resistance, innovation, challenge, diversity, and change.[38] In short, deviance often envisions a better world. The people profiled in this book needed such deviance and otherness to make sense of their lives (see Chapter 3). But they likely are not the only ones. Society itself requires some deviance and otherness in order to advance. And most so-called normal people—whoever they are—likely need deviants to reaffirm their humanity, not just their sense of what is right, wrong, or acceptable. Over time, scenes or social worlds must learn how to balance social convention with deviance or conformity with resistance in order to remain viable.

Fear, Panic, and Politics: The Formal Control of Rave Culture

On a fall night in 2004, I attended a techno party at a superclub in Philadelphia. I arrived around midnight, and after a quick pass through the club's hip hop and trance rooms, I made my way to the back room where the main techno event was located.

After an hour or so, I saw a young Asian couple having some difficulty near the dance floor. The young woman was completely out of it. She could not sit up on her own or keep her eyes open. Her boyfriend kept trying to help her, but he made little progress.

By 2:00 A.M., their situation worsened. The boyfriend tried to get his sick girlfriend to drink some water, but she threw it up immediately. A white frothy liquid spilled out of her mouth onto her jeans and the floor below. I walked over and asked him if she was okay and he said, "No." He was beginning to panic, saying over and over again that she was really sick and he did not know what to do. I asked him what she was sick on and he told me alcohol. I doubted him because her symptoms looked more like she had taken too much ecstasy. He insisted it was just alcohol.[39]

Like him, I began to worry about her. Clearly, she needed some kind of help, probably medical attention. Having just returned from a two-month trip to London for this project, I got it into my head that club staff could help us if we told them what was going on. I remembered that in London, some big nightclubs had medics on the premises to help reduce health consequences from things like cut feet, fights, or overconsumption of drugs and alcohol. So, I got a security guard, thinking he would assist the couple.

A tall, burly white man with a shaved head and a club staff t-shirt followed me to the couple while I explained the situation. As we approached, the security guard paused to look at the sick woman. Without hesitation, he picked her up and walked, or rather dragged her upright, toward the club's back exit. Her boyfriend and I followed, asking what the security guard was going to do.

Just outside, the security guard let go of the female and she fell to the ground. Her boyfriend rushed to her side and admonished, "What are you doing? She's sick." The security guard barked, "Sick people aren't allowed to stay. You gotta leave."

I stood outside thinking about how ridiculous and cruel this was. The boyfriend was completely focused on his girlfriend, so I walked back to the security guard and asked if he could call 911 for a medic. He just gave me a blank stare and then asked, "Are you coming back inside? You have five seconds to decide." I repeated my request for a medical call and he gave me a short diatribe about club liability. Basically, the club did not want responsibility for her situation, no matter what it was or what caused it.

At this venue, the policy in such situations is to call the police and then let them decide how to proceed. Such calls are problematic in Philadelphia and at a rave-like event anywhere. It might show a club's collusion in drug use and consequently a Rave Act violation. Thus, clubs do not make such calls and they do not provide medical help like some clubs in London. And no such call was made for this Asian couple.[40]

I brought this up in an interview with Benjamin, a long-time promoter on the rave and dance scenes. He explained:

> The Rave Act has taught us that we [promoters and club owners] have to say that there is a zero-tolerance policy and that there are no drugs going on inside the club. This is, of course, turning a blind eye to what is actually happening, but we can't admit that it's even going on, let alone saying, "We want to have a medic here just in case what isn't going on is happening."

In this section, I elaborate on a force of change that many believe explains the shift to raves' decline. The operating premise is that local, state, and federal policymaking and law enforcement attempted to eliminate raves and damage the EDM scene through legislation and its enforcement. This formal control agenda was a response to perceptions about how the rave scene became corrupted due to drug use and other types of debauchery or hedonism. The formal control of the rave scene altered raves' cultural form and social organization and eventually "chilled" their presence in society, leading to their decline.

A Brief History

The social control of rave culture began long before any specific rave law was passed. From raves' inception, an anti-rave movement started at the community level in both the United States and England. Cities passed ordinances designed to regulate rave activity. In the United States, the first efforts were to enforce juvenile curfews, fire codes, health and safety ordinances, liquor licenses, and codes for large public gatherings, in a sort of "broken windows" approach to crime control.[41] Eventually, these acts of regulation nudged raves toward commercialization via forced partnership with legitimate clubs.[42]

Later, the United States created drug laws to specifically target raves, especially the business people who stage them.[43] For example, federal rave-related drug laws were passed in the United States around the time of raves' peak. The Ecstasy Anti-Proliferation Act of 2000 scheduled club drugs with the Drug Enforcement Agency's Controlled Substances Act, increasing penalties for sale and use of drugs like ecstasy, GHB, and ketamine. The Vulnerability to Ecstasy Act of 2002—revised into the Illicit Drug Anti-Proliferation Act of 2003 (i.e., the Rave Act)—later made it a felony to provide a space for the purpose of illegal drug use. It was intended to hold rave promoters accountable for ravers' drug use. These new laws worked to reinvigorate a stale war on drugs, one in need of a new enemy after inner-city crack use began to decline in the late 1990s.[44]

There were various public health, political, social, and cultural factors that contributed to federal laws addressing raves and illegal drug use. To begin, in an era of punitive antidrug policy, an impending public health threat was perceived on the horizon when club drug use (ecstasy, ketamine, GHB, and Rohypnol) and health-related consequences increased significantly among young ravers in the 1990s.[45] For example, illegal ecstasy markets grew in urban and suburban areas.[46] Deaths due to drug-related overdose and dehydration at raves were widely publicized and scientific research quickly, yet erroneously, concluded that ecstasy produced long-term brain damage after only modest use.[47] These public health indicators frightened parents and policymakers into action in order to protect the mostly white, middle-class ravers and club-drug consumers. Rave promoters and ecstasy sellers were constructed as a dangerous new criminal class that needed to be controlled.

The Rave Act's author and leading proponent was U.S. Senator Joseph Biden. I learned about this from my Washington, D.C., interview with Bill Piper at the Drug Policy Alliance (DPA) in December of 2003. Piper was DPA's leading expert on the Rave Act, and at that time, DPA was busy lobbying Capitol Hill to protect the EDM scene from harsh drug law enforcement. Piper told me that Biden suggested to policymakers using his earlier Crack House law[48] to disrupt the rave scene and hold its promoters accountable. Piper's claim was substantiated, since the legislation was, in fact, fashioned after the early Crack House law.

Local law enforcement in places like New Orleans soon began a major assault on the culture. For example, Operation Rave Review, a special rave-related law enforcement initiative, was launched in 2000 after many drug overdoses at places like the New Orleans Palace Theatre,[49] which held hundreds of raves per year. Other notable club closings happened in Michigan, Wisconsin, Washington, D.C., and New York.

Social Control in Philadelphia

The evidence I gathered in Philadelphia was consistent with these national developments. The people I interviewed talked about social control of raves via nondrug policies and later by drug-related ones. Allen, a rave-era promoter, told me:

> Philadelphia was so much better back then [mid-1990s], because everything stayed open until like 6:00 in the morning. Everything stayed open late. And then all of a sudden the Republicans wanted to crack down on everything and started closing clubs down, and

saying you can't go past this time, if you do go to 6:00 a.m., you have
to buy a permit off of us. They tried to take control of everything.

TAMMY: Why do you say it was the Republicans that cracked down on
everything? This city has been controlled by a Democrat [Mayor
John Street] for years.

ALLEN: Yes, but it was a Republican governor that wanted to shut everything down. Tom Ridge, as soon as he came in, he started shutting
everything down.

Eventually, drug-related rave laws impacted the Philadelphia scene. While
they have not yet produced many individual arrests, several influential clubs
have been closed by them. Both Epic and The Lighthouse were closed in 1999
and 2000 under a cloud of drug-related suspicion. Conrad, the promoter from
Chapter 2, recounted firsthand experience with this force of change during our
interview:

My interpretation of a rave party is an unlicensed activity happening in
an unlicensed warehouse. I never considered myself a big rave promoter.
I made the mistake one time of calling one of my events a "rave." The
party got shut down because I printed the word, "rave," on the flyer.
"Rave" is a word the media latched onto that created this whole big
drug phenomenon. You know what? I've never been more frustrated in
my life until the day I went to Ozzfest. And keep in mind this is a Clear
Channel concert. America's favorite fucking family, the Osbournes,
excuse my language, but the guy's blatantly screaming, "Smoke some
pot! I just did a bump." I'm like, "Holy shit!" These guys fly under the
radar. It's unfair. We [people involved with raves] get killed because our
music is not accessible on the radio, our culture doesn't respond to traditional marketing, you can't see us on TV commercials.

Discussion about substance abuse in the United States often focuses on
two central themes. The first is that drugs are held primarily responsible for
many problems in a society (i.e., crime, violence, and youth rebellion). A second is that society's survival requires prohibition of the drugs in question
(Whyte 1979). These well-established ideals drive the constant criminalization
of substance abuse in the United States and set it off from more public health–
oriented approaches in other nations. The American public has been repeatedly told that illegal drug use of any kind—including club drug use at raves or
rave-like events—will immobilize youth (the future of our society), stymie industry and free-market capitalism, and devastate important social institutions
(e.g., religion and the family) that comprise the very fabric of society. These
themes shaped the local and federal control of rave culture, constituting a
fourth force of cultural change.

Social Control Recap

The key conclusions of this section, therefore, are that the social control of rave culture began in Philadelphia, like other national and international locations, with non–drug-related ordinances that helped force raves indoors to legitimate clubs, thus intersecting with the commercialization force. Furthermore, concerns about illegal drug use and other debauchery inspired federal U.S. drug-related legislation after raves peaked. This force levied a final blow to rave culture not solely from club closings but more powerfully via a "chill effect" that discouraged club owners and promoters from organizing such parties.

Frustrated by the enforcement of local ordinances and threatened by federal antidrug laws, many club owners and promoters have opted out of EDM events, even though most are not involved in illegal activity and do not even know who might be engaging in it at their clubs or parties. Instead, they increasingly choose to host other kinds of events —hip hop, mash-up, live performances, and others—not similarly controlled and which yield more money. Thus, while the chilling effect from rave laws may make it seem that general deterrence has been secured, my research has revealed that the leisure industry's relative abandonment of rave culture and the EDM scene has had more to do with securing greater profits from competing scenes, not solely from the fear or reality of social control. Thus, the social control of rave culture was inspired by concerns over cultural hedonism and deviance and ended up fueling scene commercialization and generational schism—two other forces of alteration and decline.

Genre Fragmentation and Subscenes

In the spring of 2001, M. Tye Comer[50] wrote that there were 100 recognized subgenres of EDM nationally and internationally. Since then, others have documented even more.[51] Musical expansion within the rave scene has produced genre-based fragmentation—a pronounced form of alteration—into various EDM subscenes today. Presently, genres host their own nights, at mostly weekly and monthly parties, and have developed their own cultural styles, cliques, and perhaps tribes. The musical expansion of rave culture has featured genre-based fragmentation, but how has this development impacted rave culture and the existence of raves?

This phenomenon accounts for a fifth force of transformation, one that directly altered raves' social organization but also produced a decline in the presence of large raves in a given locality. This genre-based subscene fragmentation had little to do with culture industries. Instead, it coalesced around participants' musical preferences and tastes and their desire for unique scenes and a more intimate solidarity than rave culture could deliver.

Sociologist Chad Allen Goldberg[52] has claimed that the bigger something gets, the more likely it is to fragment into something smaller and more familiar.

This is because larger collectives encounter difficulties in retaining cultural cohesion and group solidarity. Factions develop between members and over such things as objectives and collective identity. In-group purification efforts (e.g., ridding raves of less-favored genres and the people who support them or simply spinning off a smaller weekly party that specializes in the preferred music of choice) can restore cohesion. Solidarity among participants or their sense of intimacy with and ties to others becomes very difficult with expansion, resulting in reestablishing intimacy in smaller groups and settings.[53]

As you will recall from previous chapters, raves were often quite massive, eliciting crowds in the thousands. Some of today's rave-like music festivals and branded parties still report such attendance. Thus, while the growth in the size and frequency of raves may have bolstered their importance, the size—coupled with their popularity—also alienated people. Since raves' structure always featured many DJs playing diverse types of music, it was predictable that such a large entity with a broad collective identity would fragment into something smaller and more specialized.

Another related point about genre fragmentation follows from the work of Pierre Bourdieu.[54] Aesthetic genres, or tastes for different styles of music, correspond to social boundaries between groups or homophily, that is, birds of a feather flock together (McPherson, Smith-Lovin, and Cook 2001). In other words, groups claim certain EDM genres (e.g., breakbeat, drum and bass, techno) as their own and develop mini-scenes around them. Recall from Chapter 2 that many of the weeklies and monthlies featured one genre of music. These events typically do not house together several genres of music as did authentic raves. Such events and activities related to (chat room dialogue) are hosted by subscenes. Cameron, a record store owner, DJ, and producer, told me:

> In the rave days, all different kinds of music were played in one location. Today there is specialization, i.e., different venues and events boast different kinds of music.

This differentiation and fragmentation cut at the very core of what generated the PLUR ethos of rave culture: musical diversity and its mutual appreciation. Today, events, and sometimes clubs themselves, specialize by types of music, helping to spawn subscenes. Cliques, which voluntarily associate with one style of EDM, now predominate and host their own dance parties and message boards. Renee described this in our interview:

> If you're going to generalize, drum and bass is kind of on their own and they don't listen to anything else, so that's that kind of thing. And then there are the house heads, but there's all sorts of different kinds of house, but for the most part, if someone's into funky house, they're not going to listen to deep house. There's like a little house scene, too. And then we have our little breaks scene. It's all by genre, it really is. But

people float around. Like, you know I'm into everything, and so are a lot of people, but I'd still say there are subgenres.

Genre specialization has also created fan factions and disdain for others' tastes.[55] In some cases, subscene participants believed their taste in music was superior and condescended toward those with dissimilar tastes. Steven admonished:

The younger generation that wants to hear like DJ Silver [a local DJ] and shit like that, you know what I mean? There's nothing spiritual about that crap as far as I'm concerned. I won't go and listen to that.

Michelle further described the elements of fragmentation that characterize the contemporary EDM scene:

There are some people that don't really support this scene, like they will only go see drum and bass. They will not go to see other events. They say that they love the music, but they only love what they do. I know some DJs, they'll spin their own brand and then they'll leave.

In addition, fragmentation of the scene by genre also manifested itself as competition among those professionally associated with different genres (DJs, promoters), again undercutting raves' egalitarianism and PLUR ethos. Hamilton noted:

There are certain crews that overshadow a certain kind of music just because they don't like it and they want to promote a different style. That's where the separation is.

Finally, certain identity markers and practices of the original rave scene had even changed with the fragmentation into subscenes. For example, the subscenes boasted their own drugs of choice. We routinely heard about cocaine's dominance on the house scene, crystal methamphetamine on the drum and bass and jungle scenes, ecstasy and hallucinogens on the trance scene, and crystal methamphetamine and cocaine on the break beat scene. The biochemical and psychological effects of these extremely diverse drugs differentially work to connect people to or detach them from the PLUR ethos.[56]

However, in all the genre-specific subscenes, alcohol use has increased dramatically from modest levels during the rave era. Rave culture never really valued alcohol consumption. Alcohol further dehydrated the ecstasy user and often "interfered" with one's high. But with the commercialization of the culture and state-level control of it, legal substance consumption—alcohol as well as prescription painkillers and over-the-counter (OTC) medications—have become more common at EDM events of all kinds.

Conrad summed up the scene fragmentation force for me:

Today, it's like if you didn't like deep house, you're walking out the door. It wasn't always like that. Now, you have snobs. We hurt each other because we created these drum and base snobs, these house purists, people who only listen to drum and base and they won't venture out to the rest of the party [corporate rave], they will stay in one room the entire night. Then when you have your new kids coming in, they are totally confused about where to go in a mass setup like that. You can always spot who the new kid is. He is trying to learn. It is all foreign to him and he's probably more taken aback by the whole idea that there are all these different types of music going on at the same time, than thinking about the entire experience.

To sum up, a fifth force of alteration and decline pertains to cultural fragmentation based in genre specialization. The tremendous attendance at raves and the continued artistic development of the music produced this outcome. Simply put, raves grew too large and consumers began demanding specialization by genre as their musical tastes evolved. Consequently, the quest to hear only drum and bass or techno, house or break beat violated the musical diversity principle of raves. People no longer had to put up with other music and its enthusiasts if they did not want to. The demand for all-inclusive raves diminished.

Basic Tenets for an Explanation of Cultural Change

Social theories or explanations require more than the articulation of the forces, concepts, or variables at play. They also require an understanding of how the forces are linked to each other and to the outcomes (e.g., scene alteration and decline) in question. Table 4.1 and Figure 4.1 help clarify these points. Table 4.1 shows the relationships or connections among the five forces of change. Figure 4.1, on the other hand, shows the types of change—alteration or decline—that each force produced.

According to Table 4.1, there are several links among the five forces of change. Some worked to produce others. For example, commercialization, cultural "otherness," hedonism or self-destruction, and formal social control lead to generational schism, while the enforcement of local noise and public gathering ordinances also led to commercialization, that is, specifically to partnership with the legitimate clubbing industry.

Table 4.1 clearly shows that commercialization had the most connections to the other forces. In addition to influencing generational schism, it also led to cultural hedonism or "otherness" (i.e., the rejection of rave style and image) and to genre fragmentation (i.e., because of the professionalization of DJs and the

TABLE 4.1   INTERCONNECTIONS AMONG THE FIVE FORCES OF CHANGE EFFECT

Cause	Generational Schism	Commercialization	Formal Social Control	Cultural Otherness, Hedonism, Self-Destruction	Genre Fragmentation and Development of Subscenes
Commercialization	Partnership with legitimate clubs, professionalization of the EDM DJ, and branding of raves/EDM parties leads to the failure to recruit Generation Y			Partnership with legitimate clubs, the professionalization of EDM DJs, and branding EDM parties leads to a rejection of raves' image and style	Professionalization of EDM DJ and the branding of raves or EDM parties lead to specialized tastes and new social groups
Formal Social Control	Partnership with legitimate clubs cuts out Generation Y through age-related admission policies	Enforcement of local noise and gathering ordinances leads to raves' partnership with legitimate clubs		Reinforces stigma associated with raves as harmful venues for drug use	
Cultural Otherness, Hedonism, Self-Destruction	Drug use stigma, consequences from drugs, and a rejection of rave image and style lead to detachment of Gen X and failure to recruit Gen Y		Drug use stigma and consequences from drugs lead to federal antirave drug laws		

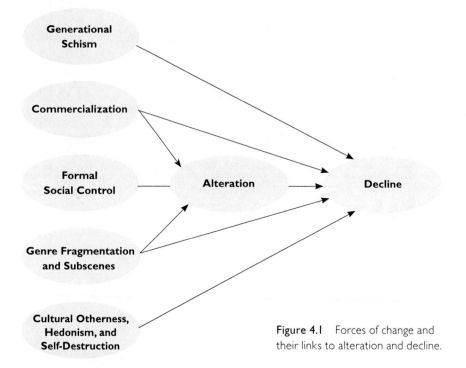

Figure 4.1   Forces of change and their links to alteration and decline.

branding of EDM parties). *These interconnections are, perhaps, another important contribution of this study, for even though previous studies may have discussed how some of these forces (e.g., commercialization or formal social control) helped produce scene change, none have articulated the interconnections between them or others.*

Still, more work is needed. As a general principle, explanations and theory are considered more reliable and useful if all of the interconnections or paths between forces, concepts, or variables can be accounted for. If not, they should be discarded or revised. As Table 4.1 shows, not all of the forces were linked together. During my fieldwork, for example, I did not find any connection between genre fragmentation or the development of subscenes and the other four forces. This does not necessarily mean there is not a connection. It simply means I did not find one. Future research is, therefore, needed to shore up the theoretical utility of this explanation of scene change.

Figure 4.1 illustrates the findings to the study's main research question: why did the rave scene experience cultural transformation? It shows which kind of cultural change—alteration, decline, or both—each of the five forces produced. Commercialization, formal social control, and genre fragmentation or subscene development led to both the alteration and decline of rave culture, thereby occupying what may seem to be a more prominent role in the explanation. Generational schism and cultural "otherness," hedonism or self-destruction, on the other hand, produced scene decline only. These findings and Figure 4.1 also demonstrate the significance of this study and the need for future research. Three of the five forces produced scene alteration and decline while the other two only scene decline. This provides further evidence that the pathways between the concepts and two types of change require enhancement before a formal theoretical model can be stated.

Despite the seeming dominance of commercialization and formal social control in Table 4.1 and Figure 4.1, however, it seems to me that generational schism is most central to raves' decline. I make this claim for numerous reasons. First, generational schism produced population loss for raves and EDM events; that is, people aged out of them and new ones were not sufficiently recruited. As a result, attendance at events dried up, leading to a reduction in the overall number of all-inclusive corporate raves and even the more genre-specific weeklies, monthlies, and superstar one-offs. Second, commercialization and formal social control helped produce scene decline primarily because they exacerbated generational schism; for example, the partnership with legitimate clubs disallowed younger people to hook into raves or modern EDM events. Third, cultural "otherness," hedonism, or self-destruction also intensified generational schism. Generation X ravers suffered drug-related consequences or burned out from drug use, while raves' drug-related stigma turned off younger Generation Y members, who have been bombarded with strong antidrug and anti-rave messages throughout their formative years and into adulthood. Finally, many sociologists have warned that the failure to retain a critical mass of people in any type of social world will ultimately lead to its decline. This is exactly what happened with generational schism. *What is new is that it is the detachment of one generation and the failure to recruit its successor that failed to yield the critical mass required.*

At a broader level, these conclusions indicate that explaining cultural change requires understanding culture's complexity and its close connection to other equally powerful domains of life. With respect to peripheral cultural collectives like music scenes, cultural change is—at the very least—linked to demographic composition, economics, socially based oppositions, politics and the state, shifting tastes and artistic development. More specifically, the finding of *generational schism* as a force of change signifies the intersection of demography and birth cohorts with culture. Cultural tastes are situated to birth cohorts and change over time. *Commercialization* reveals an eventual link between culture and economics, that is, if some aspect of a culture is potentially profitable, economic forces—especially in capitalist societies—will exploit and likely change it. *Alternative social entities* will always emerge to resist the mainstream, yet such resistance will struggle over time if its cultural form is too "other" and yields too many consequences for those involved. The very cultural composition of alternative social entities will inevitably confront *control by the state*, due to the fears, panics, and politics associated with it. In this capacity, the state acts as a *culturally "corrective" force*, one that forces conformity to social conventions. Finally, since art forms are a defining and driving force of culture, the development or expansion of art—like music—will also shape cultural entities and their trajectories.

There is evidence that the model of change articulated here may prove applicable to other music scenes and subcultures. Consider two cultural collectives: the B-Boys from the 1980s hip hop scene and hardcore punk. The documentary entitled *The Freshest Kids: A History of the B-Boys* (Image Entertainment 2001) indicates that commercialization altered the group via the professionalization of dancing (similar to the professionalization of DJ-ing). In the process, many B-Boys shifted to an "exchange" value orientation because the mainstream music industry created opportunities for them to pursue break-dancing careers. Numerous cultural traits of the collective were subsequently altered, including the dance form itself. With their success, some B-Boys also became increasingly involved in drugs and crime, while others suffered injuries from break dancing.[57] This deviance attracted negative attention from the media in much the same fashion as drug use and all-night dancing did at raves. This deviant behavior and unconventional organization led to more stigma and social control. Like raves, commercialization, deviance, and social control helped produce generational schism among the B-Boys and with break dancing. While break dancing was birthed in the 1970s, it lost its way to more conventional dance styles; that is, couples engaged in courtship activities. B-Boys aged out of break dancing and the generation that followed did not keep it going.

Many of these same forces can also be used to explain the demise of the hardcore punk subculture of the 1980s (see Reynolds 2006). This collective is also documented effectively in *American Hardcore* (Sony Pictures 2007). Hardcore punk was a grassroots collective at its origins, but musicians were soon lured into the mainstream music industry with promises of big paychecks and exciting careers. Like raves, punk music was accompanied by an alternative lifestyle and lots of deviance, for example, promiscuity, drug and alcohol abuse, violence, and other crime. Many of the people who started the scene left it; others suffered consequences from their involvement. Younger recruits were hard to come by. Such problems led to the subculture's self-destruction and fragmentation by the mid-1980s.

These examples underscore the utility of the described model in explaining music scene or subculture alteration and decline. Simply put, a culture's fate lies in attracting birth cohorts and demographic groups, the destruction in or diffusion of its elements and form, its exploitation via industry, and its suppression by the state. Thus, any study of cultural change, be it of music scenes or other youth-based entities, would benefit from understanding the connections between culture and the forces articulated here. They must, however, be treated as agents that intersect with one another, not as single and independent phenomena. And it is imperative to remember that since people will always be engaged in grassroots cultural production, cultures will cycle in and out of existence over time, with a novel and visionary and, at times, controversial character. This is culture's strength.

It is entirely possible that critics might charge that explaining why something *changed* is useful, but it is also easy to do. A better sociological model or theory would have a predictive capacity, one to forecast how and when the change might happen. While I believe that identifying these five forces in progress can assist us in forecasting cultural change, I am also aware that the explanation needs a clearer focus on the present and future. Chapter 5 zooms in on this matter by discussing the cultural work people do to control the present and future states of their music scene.

Finally, being able to use these forces of cultural change to explain other music scenes, cultural collectives, or social worlds would be a major accomplishment. However, something else to consider is the extent to which this explanation is useful in explaining music scenes, youth cultures, and social worlds outside of the United States. In other words, is the explanation offered here specific to the United States, or is its scope much larger? Chapter 6 begins to address this question by reporting on my fieldwork in London and Ibiza, Spain. It offers comparisons between EDM scenes in two nations, different from each other and distinct from the United States.

5

"Players and Their Tracks"

Types of Cultural Work in the EDM Scene

Adapt or Die.
—Everything But the Girl[1]

One evening in the fall of 2003, I was at the record store for Josh Wink's[2] *Profound Sounds V.2* CD re-release party. The store was filled with young males, many local or wannabe DJs who admired Wink and were happy to celebrate his success and get a chance to network with this rave-era icon and current international EDM superstar.

For a while, I hovered in the background watching Josh talk with his would-be protégés. With a bit of cajoling[3] by Rick, Paulie, and Cameron, I introduced myself. After Josh and I discussed his new CD and our mutual tastes in music, I asked him how he thought the rave scene had changed over time. Without hesitation Josh replied, "Restoration, preservation, and transformation." He told me about people today who wanted to return the scene to its roots; in other words, restore its authenticity. Others, he claimed, were concerned with simply holding onto it in its current state, while still others wanted to transform it, perhaps into something new or innovative.

Over the course of my study, I would find lots of support for Wink's characterization. Briefly, I discovered several forms of cultural work that scene insiders, especially stakeholders, engaged in to shape the culture and scene they loved. Their activities were geared toward both change and stability.[4] By the end of my data collection, I would reclassify Josh Wink's characterization into three major styles of cultural work: restoration, preservation, and adaptation. I found people, groups, and agencies engaged in actions to restore rave culture's authenticity, while others were busy preserving the EDM scene in its current, more compromised state. Still others were adapting or assimilating rave culture to the more commercial clubbing and mainstream music industries.

The purpose of this chapter is, therefore, to carry on the discussion of raves' alteration and decline by describing people's current activities in the EDM scene today that will likely shape it well into the future. I discuss the cultural work people do on a daily basis not only to keep a music scene alive but also to retain the identity and lifestyle it provides them. The effort they expend on this objective is, therefore, personally and collectively motivated. In addition, describing their actions should further inform how music scenes fare over time.

Understanding Cultural Work

Recently, William T. Bielby (2004) introduced two concepts useful in understanding the cultural work exercised by common people in music endeavors. The first is called grassroots cultural production and refers to the everyday activities people at the local level—for example, in the city of Philadelphia—do to produce their culture or lifestyle and the artifacts that comprise it. Examples would be producing new dance music, putting on weeklies, monthlies, and one-offs and flyering (promoting) events around town. Local DJs, event promoters, and music producers (stakeholders) most often engage in such acts of grassroots cultural production.

On the other hand, grassroots cultural participation refers to the daily, weekly, and so forth consumption of and participation in the music scene by people—loyalists, pretenders, spillovers, clubbers, and others—at the local level. Showing up at EDM events or logging onto a scene chat room are examples of grassroots cultural participation.

Throughout this book, I have focused on the experiences and actions of participants in the local Philadelphia scene. Some of the people I studied possess a lot of clout, stature, and resources, but most have relatively little. My focus on the everyday experiences of rank-and-file members of a scene represents a departure from many music scene studies. They have, instead, privileged celebrity artists and musicians and institutional actors, such as major music companies, radio stations, record labels, and so on.[5] Given this, my focus is mostly on grassroots cultural production and participation. However, I add to Bielby's concepts by articulating three different strains of that cultural work. I found that grassroots cultural production and participation can take the form of restoring a cultural entity to its perceived authentic state, preserving it in its current form, or adapting it to a mainstream, commercialized variant.

One more point of clarification is warranted. In order to understand the grassroots cultural work performed by people in the EDM scene today, we must again understand that EDM and rave culture are separate entities. A music scene houses certain styles or genres of music, the culture that develops around them, the events and venues that showcase them, and the people who participate in them. Historically, styles of music have emerged as underground art forms, typically accompanied by unique cultures. Some examples include jazz in the 1940s, punk in the 1980s, folk music in the 1960s, and hip hop of the 1980s.

Yet, over the long term, it is not always possible for music and culture to remain linked in the same way. At times, music retains its culture. Other times, its culture is compromised or traded for a different form during music expansion or development. The relationship between a scene's music and its culture has been a critical theme throughout this book, but the connection becomes even more salient when discussing the cultural work done to shape a music scene's future.

Elaborating on the connection between music and culture over time will likely contribute to music scene studies. For example, researchers often focus on developments in a scene's music rather than its culture, or they do not directly address the connection between them. For example, the common story about an underground music scene going commercial is one about a scene's music gaining popularity in the mainstream music industry, not necessarily its cultural traits, venues, and actors. Less often, researchers describe how the music-culture connection changes over time as the scene encounters external influences, like those articulated in the last chapter. When the highly respected music scholars Andy Bennett and Richard Peterson (2004: 4) write that "scenes are often regarded as informal assemblages, but scenes that flourish become imbedded in a music industry," they are talking about the path of a scene's music, not its music-culture connection.

What I have shown throughout this book is that the events and venues that house the current EDM scene showcase variable connections between dance music and rave culture. Dance music (e.g., house, techno, trance, and break beat) has expanded beyond the scene, due to some of the forces discussed in the previous chapter, for a broader appeal in society. Thus, the cultural work described here possesses different connections between EDM and rave culture. For example, I found that restoration-like work seeks a re-fusion of EDM with raves' cultural elements, while preservation has a much weaker commitment and ability to do so. On the other hand, adaptation pursues more of a separation of dance music from its cultural origins due to raves' negative public image and inability to resonate broadly in the mainstream. Exploring these varied connections between music and culture, with respect to the three forms of cultural work, should help advance sociological studies of music scenes.

Restoration

Jeffrey Alexander (2004) claims that a collective's cultural elements[6] can remain fused or connected when the collective stays simple and small. However, as the collective grows and becomes more complex—as did raves and rave culture—its components will become differentiated, segmented, and de-fused. It is also reasonable to expect that some might be abandoned or replaced.

This has been, as the previous chapters have indicated, raves' trajectory from their origins in the late 1980s to their peak in the late 1990s. Small and obscure acid house parties gave way to illegal rave massives in the U.K. and U.S. countryside. They grew to feature elaborate organization and many different styles of music, people, and identity markers. In today's post-rave era, the EDM scene is spread across a rave–club culture continuum with varying allegiances to its authentic roots or to commercial club culture.

The first form of cultural work I want to describe, then, is restoration, which involves activities geared toward returning the EDM scene to its rave-like origins. Restoration is fundamentally concerned with the authenticity of rave culture. Thus, this form of cultural work seeks to retain and strengthen the connection between the scene's music and the culture fashioned at its inception. In order to successfully accomplish this, restoration must, as Alexander (2004) argues, reclaim and re-fuse raves' music, cultural artifacts, principles, and styles that have been dispersed onto the modern rave–club culture continuum or abandoned altogether.

Restoration seeks such a re-fusion because the scene's most stringent loyalists and insiders believe that elements of the rave scene have changed for the worse since a perceived "high point" or utopia in the early to mid-1990s. Recall Jason[7] from Chapter 2's *weekly* vignette. My conversation with him revealed his dissatisfaction with the contemporary EDM scene and his longing for the rave culture of the past. Jim offered similar sentiment:

> Philadelphia used to be slamming. It was like which party did we want to go to, not is there a party going on. Now it's pretty much like there are a lot of little bars. I mean, I give people credit; they're trying to keep the scene alive in these little bars. But it's kind of what we've been restrained to.

Like other music scene studies[8] have found, insiders blame commercialism for corrupting authentic raves or social control by the oppressive state for decimating rave culture.[9] Restoration, then, attempts to reclaim or revive the past, that is, raves' more authentic form, to honor the cultural components of authentic raves: a PLUR-like ethos, the anticorporate and anticonservative ideology, grassroots organization, DJ equity, unconventional event locations, and underground music.

Restoration thumbs its nose at the stigmatization of rave culture. This cultural work, therefore, is a form of resistance. Those engaged in restoration work do not apologize for wanting to return to rave culture's authentic elements, including its deviant and stigmatized activities, for example, illegal drug use. Instead, such behavior is celebrated as defiance against state social control and public conservatism.

What constitutes restoration cultural work and agency? They include things like DJs playing underground music and rotating equally at massive parties in obscure or illegal locations. Party promotional materials—like flyers—might include rave-like identity markers (neon colors, anticorporate or government language or symbolism) and participants might sport rave fashion, wield glow sticks while dancing, and consume lots of drugs, especially ecstasy and other club drug favorites. Finally, events would seek to establish vibes anchored in the PLUR ethos or another intimate solidarity.[10]

Local-National Restoration: Music versus Culture

I encountered restoration work during my fieldwork. This discovery once again illustrates how local music scenes are linked to the national and international levels. For example, I learned about one case of national restoration at another Josh Wink release party, this time for his 2004 CD *20/20*. Wink's CD was a mix of acid house tracks and it was touted by local stakeholders and EDM industry heavyweights as a benchmark for a new trend back to the acid house sound of the 1980s. Wink's *20/20* CD was soon mapped onto a timeline published in *BPM* that predicted acid house's restoration.

In the April 2005 issue of *BPM*, Cristina Fisher proclaimed that "Acid is back!" As you'll recall, acid house music exploded in the United Kingdom in the late 1980s and birthed the Second Summer of Love (1988) and rave culture in the early 1990s. Thus, it would seem that by declaring "Acid is back," Fisher could be announcing a major act of restoration under way at the national and, perhaps, international levels.

But what exactly is being restored, and how does such a scene heavyweight like Fisher—with full authority of one of the leading EDM magazines in the world—measure such a return? A close look at her *BPM* article (which is a timeline of acid house's history) shows most cultural events or elements of acid house appeared in the late 1980s and early 1990s and that the post-rave era (from 2000 on) shows only musical restoration of the acid house "sound." In other words, Fisher's proclamation is based on the release of acid house music by well-known DJs—including Josh Wink—and the development of machines[11] and technology by software and electronics companies to produce it. She does not cite, at least in this article, any cultural restoration, such as identity markers, parties or clubs, or other cultural elements in acid house's return. Thus, while acid house music may have made a comeback in the post-rave era, it is unclear to what extent the culture that once housed it has done so.

The return of the acid house sound was not the only music-based restoration act I witnessed over the course of my study. There were other attempts to revive aspects of the rave era. One is illustrated in Figure 5.1. At this weekly, techno and the so-called classics, played by DJs who proudly boast not being superstars, constitute an act of rave authenticity. However, while the weekly party claims to be a "Throwback," the cultural markers on the flyer indicate it fuses rave-like music and DJ styles with commercial club culture traits, such as a legal superclub venue, sexualized images and language, and corporate sponsorship (e.g., the flyer is stamped by Coors Light).

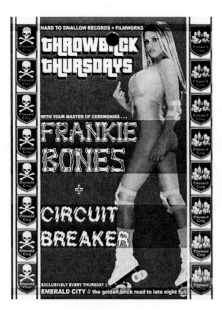

Figure 5.1 A restoration flyer.

Direct Observation of Local Restoration

In the very same issue of *BPM*, however, Fisher wrote in another article[12] about the return of underground parties[13] in major cities like Chicago, New York, San Francisco, and Los Angeles. She claims, "Underground parties in the US are on the rise once again as we look back to the passion that is underground: our music." Thus, if restoration of "authentic" rave culture is in progress, it comes in the form of the underground parties put on by promoters and club owners in these four leading EDM cities.

While it is difficult to gauge how successful or lasting these underground parties or the musical return to an acid house style is, one finding from my fieldwork is that such restoration work was scarce in Philadelphia, which is a smaller city with other music scenes, for example, hip hop, dominating the nighttime economy. I found very few underground, warehouse-like EDM parties in the Philadelphia area, although I was aware they occurred more often in major cities like those profiled in Fisher's piece.[14]

One such underground party occurred in the fall of 2004. It was put on by one of the founders of the U.S. rave scene to commemorate the September 11, 2001, tragedies in the United States. It promised to re-fuse and restore raves' cultural elements at the event, including the promotion of goodwill, an antigovernment theme, rave-era music, and a rave-era DJ lineup. Party promotional materials described it as follows:

The inexplicable tragedies of 9/11 remain a harsh reminder of how horrible mass murder is. Meanwhile, our own country continues to resort to terrorism in order to "fight" terrorism, which in turn spawns even more terrorism. But regardless of how horrendous the present has become, we must not forget the past. Stimulus Productions and *Ruby Nation* host a tribute event donating a portion of the proceeds to a 9/11-related charity. Firemen, police and EMS are honored guests and can party for free until 3:30 A.M. with three rooms of club-storming dance music. Brooklyn's rave pioneer Billy Franks headlines the night with a raw beat-down of bouncy techno anthems.

When I arrived at the event at Ruby Nation around 11:30 P.M., the club looked the same as it did on any other visit. Ruby Nation is one of Philadelphia's largest venues, and it is located in the city's superclub area. It has three rooms—one for a trance music weekly, a second smaller room for a mainstream hip hop weekly, and a third "backroom" for special events or one-offs. Because of this, Ruby Nation hosts very diverse crowds with unique styles and is managed unequally by club staff.

Briefly, the trance room (the second largest) was about half filled with white and Asian young adults wearing clothes by mainstream retailers such as Abercrombie and Fitch. The sizable dance floor was flanked by two massive bars that ran the length of two walls and were staffed by four bartenders. Two waitresses offered table service. Alcohol—mostly domestic beer—was being consumed heavily and people were dancing, chatting with friends, and chilling out on the sofas. One security member was positioned by the DJ booth.

The smaller hip hop room was packed and the room temperature was noticeably higher than in the trance room. It was populated by black, Hispanic, and white young adults, who were also drinking considerably, but more mixed drinks and imported beer. Like in the trance room, the hip hop occupants had ample access to alcohol at two bars with four bartenders, but their dancing and socializing were somewhat different. Dancing occurred in opposite-sex pairs, closely intertwined in slower, sexualized movement. Dancing in the trance room was more independent, fast, and asexual. In the hip hop room, conversation seemed to center on courtship, with females chatting with each other about males and vice-versa and men approaching women to talk, request a dance, or buy a drink. Club security was positioned at the room's three exits.

The back room, where the September 11 restoration-like event was being held, could not have been any more different than these two rooms. The walls were unpainted and the bar was small, portable, and poorly stocked and staffed. There was no DJ "booth" like in the other two rooms. Instead, a long, folding table holding DJ equipment (two turntables, two CD players, and a mixer) sat in the middle of an elevated stage. Dangling from the table appeared to be hundreds of power cords which the DJ had to carefully avoid and which looked to me like a fire hazard. Massive speakers cornered the front of the stage and made it impossible for those near them to communicate.

Inside this room were mostly white young adults, dressed in very casual clothes: t-shirts and jeans or cargo pants on the males and jeans and tighter tops on the females. Most were wearing comfortable shoes: sneakers, flats. They were drinking beer, water, and Red Bull while dancing in a typical EDM style (a few with glow sticks), chatting with friends, or watching the DJ spin obscure and hard techno. The room was the least crowded of the three and no security were on patrol inside it. Instead, a few roamed outside it in the corridor connecting all three rooms.

Over the course of the evening, I met and talked with the party promoters and DJs. A few were from New York City, where such underground parties are rather plentiful and do not have to coexist with other music scenes as often as do Philadelphia events. Other promoters and DJs I spoke with were from Philadelphia. They selected Ruby Nation for the event because it was well equipped and available for a party and they believed they would be able to pull off a rave-like vibe and style in this underutilized backroom. However, they realized by the end of the evening that conflicting vibes from the commercial hip hop and trance rooms, club management styles, and low party turnout would ultimately disallow that. They were disappointed with the night in large part because this restoration-like tribute for the 9/11 tragedy did not jive as they had hoped, like it might have in another location or at another period in time.

The Billy Franks 9/11 party had been billed as a restoration event, yet it took place in a commercial venue that forced it, and many other EDM parties, to coexist with dramatically different music scenes (e.g., hip hop) with very different cultural styles. Thus, while the party attempted to re-fuse some of raves' cultural elements, its success as an act of restoration was fairly limited.

The Restoration Challenge

From my fieldwork, it seemed as though rave-era stakeholders and loyalists were the most involved with restoration work. They were focused on restoring the culture of the scene, not simply the integrity of dance music's sound. In other words, much restoration work is about bringing back the culture of raves and what they stood for, not simply on privileging underground or white label music. For example, Casey, a long-time party promoter in Philadelphia, and I discussed trying to restore some elements of rave culture in his current breakbeat monthly. I asked him, "Do you want to try to bring things from the rave days into your events?"

CASEY: Some of the elements definitely.
TAMMY: Which ones?

CASEY: The uniqueness of it. When we had DJ Crush in the end of September, we did it at Cousteau's. I don't know if you've been to any of the Cosmos parties that Downtown Productions did there. There are trees and a beautiful fountain there. The atmosphere is incredible and I was bringing a crowd there that hadn't really experienced it before and people were just amazed. Like with the DJ and the atmosphere and just the whole night. People were asking me and like other people like "Does this happen here all the time? If not, where can I go to like get this again? Where can I go to hang out with this type of people, such a very diverse, open crowd?" I don't know it's hard to pinpoint what it was that made it that way but that's what I wanted to re-create.

Casey is discussing getting back to some of the nonmaterial aspects of rave culture, like the vibe of the parties and their ethic of diversity celebration or tolerance. But later in our conversation he also discussed a return to the more organizational aspects of rave culture, such as DJ equity and a rejection of the superstar phenomenon, which the September 11 party also attempted. Casey told me:

The guy [DJ] I had in November and October from Australia, like they don't have agents. They have this one guy that does their management, you know, it's not a huge organization. They're all working together. It's very grassroots. That's what we need more, to rebuild this thing [authentic rave culture]. Like get off your soapbox, get off your high horse, you're not a freaking superstar. I mean the electronic music industry is still so young. I think it's still trying to find itself. You went from the raves you know, and then all of sudden like what happened was people said "Wait a minute this is now a business." The DJ fest skyrocketed. The cover charges to get into the parties skyrocketed. And then this and that skyrocketed and all of a sudden it's an industry rather than a culture.

Restoration work most often occurs at underground parties. Party organizers fuse authentic identity markers, grassroots organization, and PLUR-like ethos into their events. This earns underground parties the most rave-like classification on the rave–club culture continuum (see Chapter 2). Corporate raves and some music festivals also showcase restoration-like cultural work, but they often come up short in re-fusing and restoring rave culture because of the breadth of people who attend them (see Chapter 3) and their reliance on corporate sponsorship. While officials tend to label corporate raves and other high-profile one-offs as modern-day raves, the work to put them on is very different than the authentic raves from yesterday. Grassroots cultural work has been replaced by collaboration between EDM promotion groups or companies, busy marketing their brands.

Preservation

A Los Angeles–Philadelphia Connection

William, a key informant of mine, has a Saturday night weekly at a superclub, Club Noir, on Summerfield Boulevard. As a daytime plumber and father of three, William has been a dance music loyalist since the rave era. He started out as a bedroom DJ and worked his way into local gigs via an unwavering affection for New York–style progressive house music and his talent to spin it. He has spent the past few months building his night's reputation, especially among the area's Asian (mostly Korean and Chinese) population, as one of the best progressive house events in the city. This is a notable accomplishment since the club itself, Club Noir, sits next to one of Philadelphia's largest strip or "men's" clubs and has been troubled by deviance-related complications. In fact, there was a fatal shooting in the club's hip hop room two weeks prior to my visit. Since then, local EDM chat rooms hosted threads debating the scene cultures of house and hip hop and whether this killing would shut down Club Noir or William's weekly.

For his Halloween 2004 Saturday night, William invited a West Coast DJ friend of mine, DJ Nicole, to co-host his weekly. Both Nicole and William are progressive house aficionados, and they looked forward to an opportunity to trade off West Coast and East Coast styles. Since progressive house was my favorite genre, I too was extremely excited to hear them spin together.

I met Nicole two years earlier on www.clubradio.net, during my initial discovery of dance music. I wrote to her after listening to several of her mixes. She immediately became a key informant, teaching me about scenes on the West Coast and her national and international experience in dance music and rave culture.

Nicole and I arrived at Club Noir around 11:00 P.M. to find it packed with about eight hundred[15] mostly white college students from one of the local universities. They had rented this private nightclub for a Halloween party. The students were dressed in costumes and consumed massive quantities of alcohol at the two-hour open bar. I saw males and females carrying two and three bottles of beer at a time.

Nicole and I struggled through the crowd, kicking beer bottles and side-stepping vomit,[16] on our way to the DJ booth. The scope of the students' beer consumption can be gauged by the fact that the club's beer supply was depleted in one hour. I had never seen anything like this before.

By the time Nicole and I reached the DJ booth, we realized William was not spinning at all. Instead, a resident DJ[17] was playing a commercialized blend of oldies, hip hop, and house music. After introductions, I asked William what was happening and why he was not spinning. He told us the club owners asked one of the club residents to spin the college party. William just looked at me and shrugged his shoulders in a kind of "what-can-I-do" fashion. I felt terrible for him as I could see his discomfort with being powerless over his own night. I also started to worry that Nicole's guest appearance would be jeopardized and that the West Coast–East Coast collaboration might not happen. However, after a short while, William asked the other resident DJ to step aside and Nicole took over at the decks. William told her to play what was in her record box even though it was dramatically different from what the club's resident was playing for the students.

Like many other DJs I've met, William and Nicole believe turning people on to music they would not normally hear—enlightening them to new and underground sounds—is their responsibility. With William's support, this is what Nicole began doing immediately. The crowd below responded well to the transition from the Commodores' "Celebration" to the dark, heavy basslines on Nicole's white label records. This pleased us. We interpreted the students' reactions as support for our belief that people will welcome noncommercial dance music if they are exposed to it. Perhaps the meeting of East Coast–West Coast styles would take place after all.

Unfortunately, a Club Noir manager pulled the plug on our progressive dreams. About twenty minutes into Nicole's set, he ordered her off the decks and told the club resident DJ to resume his commercialized fusion. Nicole was stunned and William embarrassed. An argument evolved between William and the club manager, with Nicole and myself quizzically standing by. The manager insisted the college students contracted to hear music they could "recognize" and did not want obscure house music. William argued instead that they seemed pleased with Nicole's West Coast progressive house sound. The club manager pulled rank and Nicole stepped aside.

The college party crowd did not even notice the change in music. From what I could tell, they were like the clubbers, spillovers, and pretenders profiled in Chapter 2. They were at Club Noir to drink, dance, and court the opposite sex, not to hear West Coast–East Coast styles of progressive house music.

So, Nicole, William, and I hovered by the DJ booth until about 1:00 A.M., when the college party started to wind down. As the drunken students boarded their buses, the usual weekly crowd began to filter in. Nicole jumped back on the decks and we noticed immediately an appreciation for her sound. From the dance floor, several people looked up to the DJ box and waved approvingly.

After an hour or so, William took over and Nicole and I walked around the club. Club Noir is yet another late-hours club that combines dance music with commercial hip hop. It has been a necessary but unhappy marriage. The friction is due to the culture clash between the two scenes, which is easily visible between the club's two rooms. For example, Nicole and I noticed very large men—mostly white, but some black—in the back hip hop room. They were wearing athletic attire and gold chains over massive chests and arms. They stood around the small dance floor's perimeter watching the mostly white females dance to highly sexual hip hop music that at one point instructed them to "Put it in your mouth, your mother-fucking mouth. Swallow, bitch, swallow." This was a dramatic contrast to the larger room where William's weekly was located. The people there were smaller, dressed club chic, and danced in couples or independently to lyricless music at a much faster pace.

The Preservation Quagmire

This experience epitomizes the vulnerable state of preservation work and the relative powerlessness of those who attempt it. William engages in heavy grassroots cultural production to increase the availability of the progressive house sound in Philadelphia. To do so, he must coexist with another scene (i.e., commercial hip hop in the club's back room) so the club's owners can maximize profit. At any point in time, William's desires and activities can be thwarted by club staff or even the "perceived" tastes of certain clubbers. During my visit with Nicole, it was easy to see that William does not have the luxury to restore a past culture or even the ability to bring in some of its elements. He fights very hard to preserve the integrity of his sound—the music he wants to play and that his regulars have grown to love. He ceded control of his music on this particular night so he could retain his weekly—he knows he cannot piss off his more powerful club managers. But he does not dream about restoring the culture that birthed his love of dance music in the first place. That aspiration was abandoned a while ago.

The preservation mode of EDM work is not nearly as ambitious or optimistic as restoration. It accepts the more diminished rave culture and the waning popularity of the current EDM scene. Its goal is to hold onto what it has and freeze it in its current state. This means that most preservation-like work is preoccupied with keeping EDM events alive so people have regular opportunities to participate in local EDM scenes, for example, to hear and play the music. Consequently, preservation is preoccupied with consumption, or grassroots cultural participation. Grassroots cultural production or re-fusing or de-fusing rave culture is not and cannot be prioritized.

Preservation work is troubled by a very tenuous relationship between music and culture. The primary reason for this is financial pressure from club owners. The constant burden of filling a club or bar in order to secure or retain one's party forces those involved in grassroots cultural preservation to sacrifice culture, at times, in order to maintain public access to the music they love. Because of this, raves' cultural elements are not a priority. There is little concerted effort by those trying to preserve the scene to re-create the vibe and symbolism of authentic rave culture. Parties and events are geared more simply toward bringing a specific musical style to an audience and, most importantly, toward generating enough revenue so that club owners will continue to house them. Since local DJs and promoters have great stakes in these parties, they feel the most pressure to succeed. During our interview, Suzanne, a former raver and current DJ, described this:

> Back when the clubs were fuller and the economy was better, it was more who could play the best shit and who could really make every-body dance. And that's really what it [rave culture] was about at its purity. Now it's kind of like who can bring the most people out, who can bring all the girls out that are strippers or whatever. Because there's no money in it, so they had to do it, the clubs had to start doing that. The DJ is now pressured to fill the club. And if they don't, their night is cut, it's gone.

Casey added:

> The club owners and the bar owners . . . they want numbers, they want them now, they don't care how you get them.

Alexander (2004) has noted that when cultural actors possess little power, they are forced to fuse authentic and commercial interests. In fact, cultural consumers possess a lot of collective power. The ability to perform certain types of cultural work is highly dependent on consumption patterns of modern-day party people. Thus, stakeholders must, to some extent, find a balance between the music and culture insiders and outsiders want. So, even though Casey aspires to throw unique events that might restore some of rave culture, he admits having to settle for preservation-like goals:

> We've always tried with "Discobreakz" and "Rock and Glow" to just mainly promote fun. In fact, we were really careful to not even promote the music or break beat per se because we understand the state of the electronic music scene. So you know, the attendance at these events is typically considered down. You know we're not packing clubs on a reg-ular basis.

From my observations and conversations, it seems as though weeklies epitomize preservation work. The weekly EDM party is a huge obligation for those who put it on. Weeklies happen every seven days, operate on low bud-gets, and are extremely vulnerable to clubber turnout. And it does not help that people take them, and the people who put them on, for granted (see Chapter 2). These things constrain cultural producers. Monthlies also feature preserva-tion work; however, due to their relative scarcity in comparison to weeklies and their more ample resources, they can engage in some restoration-like activities. If actors restricted to preservation work desire a different course, chances are they will move toward adaptation, for it will deliver more people and subse-quently more money.

Adaptation

EDM is global movement with one language: good music.

—An unknown participant at the Club Culture panel,
2004 Miami Winter Music Conference

This statement came during a heated discussion among EDM insiders at a panel during the 2004 Miami Winter Music Conference. I sat in the audience and took notes on this two-hour debate about underground authenticity versus commercial expansion and sell-out. The speaker was trying to convince the panelists—scene heavyweights (including major club owners, representatives from large promotional groups, and national EDM magazine editors)—about the importance of remaining true to rave culture by connecting the cultural aspects of the scene to its music. His campaign fell on the deaf ears of the more powerful panelists: club owners, industry representatives, and leisure industry officials. Their one concern was widespread commercial success for EDM stakeholders.

Adaptation work epitomizes the transformation of an underground music scene into a commercial enterprise, from a culture into a conventional industry (Negus 1999). It usually involves a marginal cultural entity transforming, in fundamental ways, to match, mimic, and embrace a more mainstream or commercial form. More original cultural components—ethos, organization, norms, behaviors, and symbols—are easily exchanged for mainstream variations. Recall from Chapter 2 how the organization of some EDM events is adapted to fit or mimic the clubbing industry. The following paragraphs discuss other instances of such cultural exchange.

Before getting into them, it is important to consider Alexander's contention that when a cultural entity attempts such adaptation, it often possesses no strong commitment to authenticity. In other words, music scenes might transform without regard for their authentic cultures. The path they take depends, in large part, on members' perceptions about how the scene's culture will resonate with the masses. In fact, many of the stakeholders I spoke with or heard speak believe mainstream adaptation is a good thing, a logical step in EDM's evolution. Typically, these were people with more success, power, and resources. Less powerful types, and largely local actors, often viewed adaptation as negative.

Adaptation work does not, as Alexander (2004) noted, always honor the connection between a scene's cultural elements. Rather, it takes an instrumental approach to them: adaptation retains the connection if it works commercially. If a music scene's culture—aesthetic, ethos, behaviors, or lifestyle—does not resonate outside of it, cultural change or substitution will follow in order to permit music's development. If, on the other hand, a music scene's culture is honored outside of it and by a much broader audience, its cultural elements will be retained as its music develops. Still, adaptation will pick and choose among which aspects of culture to retain or re-fuse, as stakeholders doing adaptation work will forge ahead with that which sells in the mainstream. I found at least two major types of adaptation at work in Philadelphia and the larger national U.S. EDM scene: the integration of EDM into the commercial music industry and EDM's cultural makeover.

Integration of EDM into the Commercial Music Industry

At the national level, the most popular DJs and music producers busy themselves with adaptation work, such as getting their tracks onto satellite radio, into video games, or used as ringtones for mobile phones. Superstar DJs increasingly work to secure a place on television via making videos for MTV or participating in TV commercials or cable lifestyle shows.

Philadelphia superstars like Josh Wink, King Britt, and Dieselboy have been successful in these endeavors. For example, during a weeknight of fieldwork in 2003, I stumbled onto a TV commercial set outside the record store. House-music expert King Britt was filming a car commercial. While the crew filmed, I stood around with my EDM buddies looking on and waiting until Liquid opened for a party. There was a lot of excitement about this among the local fans and DJs and it was easy to see and hear how people were inspired by their more famous Philadelphia comrade.

Many local DJs and producers, like those I was hanging out with during the King Britt commercial, wanted to grow artistically and support themselves full-time in some aspect of the EDM scene or dance music industry. For them, this required following the activities of others in the music industry. As electronic musicians, they must adapt to the music industry in both minute and substantial ways. This kind of cultural work is individually oriented, rather than more collectively focused on restoring, preserving, or advancing a larger rave or EDM culture.

Given this cultural sacrifice, it was no surprise to find still others who believed the integration of underground dance music into the U.S. music industry was problematic. Music scene scholars and cultural sociologists have long reported on the real and perceived consequences of this transition. At issue are things like musical integrity and artistic freedom. Tony, a techno DJ and key informant, articulated this complaint:

> The quality of the music just disappears when major production companies get behind a DJ. Party people and the general public consume the mainstream stuff. Ravers and unknown DJs search for underground stuff, produce and remix their own stuff and thumb their noses at mainstream production companies.

A consistent concern I heard from insiders like Tony was that DJ artists would lose their musical integrity with the transition to the mainstream music industry. Other insiders were also concerned about the loss of such cultural elements as the PLUR ethos. While other music scenes studies[18] have discussed the threat to musical integrity with commercialization, one unique thing about rave culture and dance music is that the ethos of PLUR or anything similar is especially difficult to preserve via adaptation since it is dramatically different than the business ethic of commercialization. So the threat to cultural integrity may be especially acute for EDM as it approaches mainstream adaptation.

EDM's Cultural Makeover

Gaining commercial success and mainstream legitimacy for dance music, and even aspects of the EDM lifestyle, was also attempted via what seemed to be a kind of cultural "makeover." Simply put, adaptation required changing EDM's image from its rave-like origins to more conventional club culture styles. Specifically, actors trade rave culture's antimainstream, asexual, and nonmaterialistic image for one that is more sexualized and status based. In short, adaptation work required adopting the cultural forms and identity markers conveyed in mainstream media such as commercial radio and MTV. Pursuing adaptation separates EDM from rave culture. It does this in hopes of gaining legitimacy and increased popularity for dance music.

A good example of this cultural makeover came from the direct observation at a large club—Liquid Dreamz—once famous for hosting raves and servicing the EDM scene. Early in his training, I asked Phil Kavanaugh to observe an event there. His field notes illustrate the modern commercialized vibe (e.g., highly sexualized), style (commercial chic), and behaviors (drunkenness and courtship) at an event hosted by a long-time EDM DJ vested in expanding his night to the mainstream:

> From the moment I entered the club at 11, I saw overtly sexual dancing, although no one was on the stage. The place was a meat market and the vibe was intensely sexual. Everyone was dancing in that close, hook-up, grinding style, and there was simulated humping going on as well. There were slicked-back ponytails on some males with open-collared shirts. Others had styling gel in their hair. The women were dressed to show cleavage and wore short skirts. The vast majority of people were on the ground-level dance floor. It was very hot in the club, especially after 12:00 A.M., when the club was extremely crowded. I noticed some females dancing sexually with one another on stage, to the delight of both the crowd and the DJ, who commented approvingly. The DJ told them that the girl on girl action was coming later and that they had to slow down. In all instances, everyone was following the orders of the DJ. He was controlling the party. He would call people up on stage, and then tell them to "get the hell off the stage." In every

instance it was females who were summoned to the stage. The DJ would say things like "I want to see some big ass boobies up here right now. If you got big old boobies get up on the stage." The club gave free shots at midnight. I was on the dance floor when the DJ announced this, and I fought my way up to the bar to observe it when it was announced. I saw mostly males walking up to the bar and getting shots poured down their throats out of a bottle by a sexually provocative-looking female who was standing on the bar. Most males bought more shots after they got their free ones.

During my fieldwork, I heard people at the local, national, and international levels discuss a substantial revision of the EDM image (collective identity) and aesthetic (fashion, rave props, and other identity markers) that many believed were damaged by rave culture's hedonism and the stigma associated with it. The makeover would be something that resonated more broadly with the American public. Hip hop was invoked by many as a model[19] to adapt, while traditional rave clothes, props, and styles of drug abuse were to be abandoned.

Big parties, like superstar one-offs, music festivals, and, at times, corporate raves are especially likely to adopt a commercialized hip hop style, especially in Philadelphia, in order to secure enough attendance to profit from the event. This was discussed in Chapter 2. Casey explained:

> Downtown Productions and those guys, they have a little more commercial appeal than I do and that's by choice. Downtown really promotes an image you know. They really promote an image and I'm not necessarily into that and that definitely will affect how well I do financially in this business.

At a more national level, scene heavyweights worked with large-scale designers to market clothes to young people. For example, at the Miami Winter Music Conference in 2004 and 2005, Armani Exchange used EDM to sell revised rave-like fashion to young consumers in a new lifestyle campaign. Their clothes were casual and comfortable, but also club chic, trendy, and quite expensive. Other major fashion designers like Diesel, Armani, and Paul Frank target the new dance scene as well.[20]

Mike P. expressed his sentiment about the relationship between lifestyle campaigning and EDM culture:

> Like now we see companies like Gap and MTV catering to us and we're seeing how pop culture has reshaped itself around our culture, the underground dance scene.

Another example of this cultural makeover and lifestyle campaigning is the spinning of EDM live at retail stores. A few of the DJs in my study had gigs at local Adidas and Nike stores in corporate attempts to attract new customers and sell merchandise. The DJs told me they were paid in merchandise, not in cash.

Still another aspect of this adaptation-inspired cultural makeover was outright denigration of drug use by scene stakeholders. The passage of the Rave Act weighed heavily on the minds of the stakeholders with whom I talked. Many believed that drug use at EDM events threatens their livelihoods as DJs, promoters, club owners, and so on. This is because media portrayal of EDM in the United States has emphasized drug use, resulting in a negative reaction toward drug use by scene stakeholders. They worked to separate the scene from drug use.

In short, adapting the EDM scene to the commercial music industry and contemporary pop culture required an emancipation of dance music from rave culture and a cultural exchange toward something less peripheral and more commercial. The new cultural form would meet young Americans where they were technologically, physically, and stylistically located, and in so doing, it would begin alienating those subscribing to past rave ideals.

The Role of Politicking in Music Scenes

No matter the type of agency or cultural work employed, the people I spoke with over time claimed "politicking" in the local EDM was required to achieve their objectives. During my research, I discovered two types of EDM politics: external, societal politics and scene-based or industry politics. External or societal politics pertain to the culture's leftist, anticorporate, or antigovernment ideology. Rave culture and the EDM scene have not taken an activist role in bringing about the kind of societal change they desire. The previous chapters and other research have shown, instead, that such externally based political ideals are more an ideology that defines an alternative lifestyle or scene, not a subculture or political movement with direct public protests against corporate America or government agencies.

The more pressing type of politics, and the type I want to describe in this chapter, is internal, social-networking politics among scene stakeholders. These politics are about negotiating the scene for a desired outcome. In short, DJs, promoters, or anyone else wanting employment in the scene constantly engage in social networking activities to achieve their goals For example, securing nights at clubs and getting people to support your event means you have to attend other people's events as well. Art told me:

> Everyone has their own clique that comes out to each other's night. It's like "I'm not going to go to that night because so and so is promoting, I'm going out to this night. That's our boy."

There was a sense among the people I talked with that they had to go to support other stakeholders' parties if they expected the same in return. To get

weeklies, monthlies, or any DJ gig, a fair amount of networking was also required. While the EDM chat rooms in Philadelphia exercised some control
over this, the record store seemed a major force in local scene politicking. Mike
P. was a local DJ during the rave era who worked for several years at the record store. After a brief falling out with the club's owner, Cameron, he told
me how his disconnection with the record store impacted his DJ-ing and scene
involvement:

> Cameron and I had some disagreements and at some point we just
> parted ways. He asked me to not work there anymore, so in a sense I
> was fired. You know, I don't hold that against him. But then afterwards,
> I stopped being known. I mean, I still had some residual 611 power, but
> eventually, you know, it caught on to everyone that I was no longer part
> of 611. I got so discouraged with the scene. I really didn't buy records
> anymore and I didn't go to parties.

Respondents and key informants were also very cautious in maintaining
good relationships with rival promoters and club owners. No matter if they
were trying to restore rave culture, preserve their party, or adapt to something
more commercial, no one could afford to make many enemies in Philadelphia's
small EDM scene. Casey told me a story that illustrates this sentiment:

> Oh man. One time, my friend Gus Lamont was promoting one of his
> parties outside a different club and one of the security guys, who was a
> friend of mine at that time, took his flyers and threw them on the side-
> walk. I heard about it afterward. You know, Gus talked to the club
> manager about that and was like, "You don't do that, man." Basically,
> you keep a positive relation with the promoters. It's very important in
> clubs. Even with somebody who promotes for the rival, you never know,
> they might do stuff for you later.

Marianne was very active during the height of Philadelphia's rave era and
had tons of experience and perspective to share. Like William, Marianne
worked her way up the DJ ladder to achieve a fair amount of local stature. Her
recollection of the past provides a clear example of the connection between
agency and politicking in the EDM scene:

> Every night I was on the street handing out flyers. I would go to the
> distributors on Mondays and buy records and deal with all the distribu-
> tors and DJs. I was always dealing with their agents or with the DJs
> directly and like dealing with concepts. What is the concept of this
> party? We need to have a new framework and like everybody is doing
> this but we have to do it different because we don't wanna get caught
> up in that and we've got a whole different idea of what a party should

really be and it's really more than just the DJ. We've gotta create an atmosphere and figure out the message we're gonna convey. And so it was like if I wasn't DJ-ing, I was working at the record store. If I wasn't working at the record store, I was promoting parties or at home signing contracts and faxing shit and talking to people about what they need, making sure we had the right mixer and like the right alcohol. Who's going to pick them [DJs] up at the airport? And then when I wasn't doing all that I was partying, having a great time, hanging out and supporting other people's parties.

Conclusions

In this chapter, I sought to further inform raves' transformation by understanding the cultural work that people, mostly stakeholders, engaged in to shape their little corner of the current EDM scene. I found three major types of work: restoration, preservation, and adaptation. Each showcased a different connection between music and culture, signifying that music scenes may not always possess a constant or unified link between the two over time. Instead, the fate of music's cultural connection or of a culture's or lifestyle's attachment to music will vary depending on the types of cultural work performed by those having stakes in them. Thus, since this chapter is about grassroots cultural agency and since people are the ones who perform it, much of the power to shape a music scene, or perhaps any other cultural entity for that matter, rests with them.

We have also learned here that when people attempt to restore a scene's authenticity or to re-fuse its culture to an original state, they are prioritizing the cultural and collective identity part of their experience rather than simply musical or artistic components. Still, they likely prioritize these things because of their refusal to separate art from culture, for example, EDM from rave culture. For them, all must be restored or re-fused even if it is highly unlikely to happen in the complicated and highly commercialized clubbing industries of today.

On the other hand, when people seek to widen the appeal or accessibility of their music or art, or when they seek music's emancipation from its underground or peripheral state, they will follow the route of cultural adaptation, seeking to become part of the mainstream music industry. Adaptation features either a retention or trading of authentic culture, depending on financial return and mass endorsement from popular culture. By trying to adapt to the commercial music industry, EDM stakeholders, for example, prioritize their individual growth as artists or entertainment professionals and deprioritize their cultural connection and shared identification with rave culture. Commercial adaptation reflects, more closely, the capitalist growth pattern: as small cultural entities grow into something much larger and more complex, opportunities for individuals will lure them away from cultural authenticity with economic independence and social recognition.

Between these two forms of agency lies a middle ground: cultural preservation. It has not been well articulated in past music scene research and does not fit nicely into the ideas of cultural sociologists like Bielby and Alexander. Perhaps this is because preserving a cultural entity in its current state—in order to prevent it from going too commercial and because one sees authentic restoration impossible—reveals vulnerability while clinging to optimism. In a world where nothing stays the same for long, trying to hold onto some aspects of a music scene's authenticity, while larger forces are at play in changing it or stamping it out altogether, requires lots of hard work. Thus, preservation is a difficult and unappreciated line of work, even though it may be much more common.

Finally, it should be noted that no one exclusively engages in restoration, preservation, or adaptation. The cultural producers and consumers I talked with and observed employ these three forms of cultural work off and on over time. At times, they might attempt an act of restoration and see it become one of adaptation; for example, it becomes a new commercial trend to "restore" the acid house sound. Many will use a restoration tactic to help preserve or reenergize a scene. Thus, these forms of cultural work are not mutually exclusive.

6

EDM as a Vibrant Global Scene

It's a very open culture. People will accept you for who you are. You don't have to be anyone different. It's quite liberating actually. There are very few environments in society now where you can experience that.
—Sophie, twenty-nine-year-old London EDM loyalist

Sophie's opinion about the contemporary EDM scene in London is a significant departure from what the people I talked with in Philadelphia said about the current EDM scene and from the conclusions reached by U.S. scholars. I found her sentiment quite prevalent in London and in Ibiza, Spain, among people from many nations,[1] during my trips there in 2004 and 2005. In addition to the considerable popularity of dance music and the wide variety of parties that celebrate it, it seems the ethos of acceptance, diversity, and liberation is also alive in EDM scenes outside of Philadelphia and the United States. Even David Ireland, the publisher of *BPM* magazine, told me in a 2005 e-mail:

> The American scene is rather small as the style of music here is much different, much like the general attitude of the American consumer. America is all about greed and success and the European mentality is a little more communal and laid back. Americans love hip hop and ballad rock. The EDM scene in Europe has also always been more fashionable.

There is also something more fundamental about Sophie's comment that warrants attention. She and the other people I spoke with view the modern EDM scene as a legitimate cultural entity with an appealing collective identity. As discussed in Chapters 3 and 4, people in Philadelphia used to see raves this way; however, they less often do so presently.

Scene participants are not the only ones in London, or even the United Kingdom and Europe, who see raves and the EDM scene in this fashion. A rich academic tradition has, from its inception, adopted a similar stance. Scholars from the United Kingdom and Europe have, for many years, viewed youth subcultures and scenes, like raves, punk, Goth, and rock, as legitimate cultural collectives by which to advance core sociological ideas.[2] Such work began with studies by Mike Brake (1985), Stuart Hall and Tony Jefferson (1976), and Paul Willis (1977) at the Centre for Contemporary Cultural Studies (CCCS). They maintained that class conditions, that is, economic alienation among the working class, helped spawn important youth subcultures (e.g., Mods, Rockers, Teddy Boys, punk) that pursued societal resistance largely through deviant activities and alternative lifestyles. Some studies of raves fit into this class-based, structural perspective. It claims that members of the working class who participated in raves showed symbolic resistance of mainstream capitalist societies by adopting behavior that challenged the status quo (Tomlinson 1998).

Other research adopted a more evolved subcultural approach that portrayed raves as a hedonistic and deviant subculture (i.e., one that involved excessive drug abuse), albeit one that permitted escape from the trappings of contemporary capitalist society (Knutagard 1996; Melechi 1993; Redhead 1993, 1995; Reynolds 1999; Rietveld 1993; Thornton 1996). Some of the most recent studies of raves and EDM culture (Bennett 1999, 2001; Malbon 1999; Muggleton 2002) also fit comfortably within this more "raves as postmodern subcultures" perspective. However, this work downplays raves as a site for drug use in favor of addressing the intersecting issues of locality, change, music trends and newly emerging music genres, peer networks, and style (see Anderson and Kavanaugh 2007 for a review). The point here is that the U.K. cultural studies–oriented work reinforces the idea that raves' primary offering was cultural, something more meaningful than mere deviance and hedonism, just as Sophie and other respondents I met in London claimed.

In fact, when we look east of Philadelphia and the United States, we see EDM's proliferation and prosperity in the United Kingdom and Europe. How can such remarkable differences exist between the United States and other nations? In the United States, raves have been reduced to a public health threat and a matter for the war on drugs. Yet, they mean something quite different in the United Kingdom and Europe. What explains this?

In this chapter, I begin to address this and other questions by comparing the Philadelphia scene to that in London and Ibiza, Spain, two of the most dynamic EDM locations in the world. These comparisons give us not only opportunities to understand regionally influenced differences in the life spans of music scenes but also a chance to learn more about culture, identity, and social change. My fieldwork speaks directly to local scenes in London and Ibiza, rather than to the entire United Kingdom or Spanish mainland. Research by others, however, enables me to both broaden and qualify my findings to other cities and towns therein.

London

Most enthusiasts of EDM and rave culture view England as one of the scene's past and present capitals. Raves and the acid house sound emerged at underground clubs in London and Manchester and in the countryside across the United Kingdom.[3] And when early EDM pioneers like Paul Oakenfold, Danny Rampling, and Pete Tong (all British) took the sound to the so-called White Isle,[4] they helped make Ibiza, Spain, into a global EDM vacation resort with a uniquely British style and following. Today, several of the scene's leading magazines—*XLR8R, DJ Magazine, International DJ, MixMag*—are produced and published in the United Kingdom and are among the best-selling EDM magazines in the world. Moreover, the leisure magazine *Timeout London* lists pages of electro, house, techno, drum and bass, break beat, and multigenre EDM parties every week. A simple perusal of these listings reveals parties ranging from highly commercial events to new rave styles.[5]

My own understanding of London's EDM prominence took shape early in my project via www.clubradio.net and the many DJs I exchanged e-mails with there. No matter their country of origin or residence, most discussed London and the United Kingdom as a central EDM location and where new trends in music, parties, and lifestyle practices were fashioned.

When I found 611 Records in Philadelphia, the DJs there similarly spoke about the London scene and others scattered across the United Kingdom. They told me that local DJs often played in London or some other part of England. Others longed to do so one day. When they talked about London or the United Kingdom, their stories shifted from complaints about being music scene underdogs in Philadelphia to confidence and pride in the U.K. scenes.

In several ways, Philadelphia was connected to London and other parts of the United Kingdom. For example, many local DJs had professional contacts in the United Kingdom and often flew across the pond to spin. A few others collaborated on record labels with other EDM stakeholders in the United Kingdom. Furthermore, local DJs and promoters, who put on events in Philadelphia, often brought U.K. DJs to play at events in the city. Through all of this, it became clear that I could not only better understand the Philadelphia EDM scene with a research trip to the United Kingdom but also enhance my knowledge of the scene's more global significance.

Participants' Profile

Table 6.1 provides a very brief overview of the people my students and I interviewed in London. They were young adults, for the most part, ranging in age from twenty-one to fifty-one. They were slightly younger, on average, than the Philadelphia pool. Thus, the demographic makeup of the London pool offers an interesting opportunity to compare the scenes with respect to the generational schism discussed in Chapter 4.

TABLE 6.1   BREAKDOWN OF LONDON STUDY PARTICIPANTS'
            DEMOGRAPHIC CHARACTERISTICS

Race/Sex	Loyalist	Stakeholder	Clubber	Total
White Male	2	5	4	11
Asian Male	0	1	0	1
Black Male	0	1	0	1
White Female	5	1	0	6
Total	**7**	**8**	**4**	**19**

While prior work[6] on the rave scene documented a more diverse race and ethnic pool of ravers and EDM clubbers—in the United Kingdom as well as in the United States—the respondent pool is disproportionately white and male.[7] This has to do with some practical constraints I faced in doing fieldwork in London.[8] As such, the race/ethnic and gender composition of my respondents may not be representative of the London scene. While mostly white, the nineteen respondents were from cities, towns, or villages scattered across the United Kingdom, not simply London. One was a U.S. citizen who had relocated to London to work in the dance music scene.

In other demographic respects, the London pool was similar to the Philadelphia pool. Most were raised in middle-class families and typically retained their socioeconomic locations as adults. Twelve completed an undergraduate degree at a U.K. university (one of these also had a master's degree in computer science), four had completed some college, and the others had high school diplomas. When I interviewed them, most were working full-time in the service, retail, computer technology, and management fields. Others were piecing together several part-time jobs amounting to full-time employment. Their annual salaries ranged from 12,000 pounds[9] to 80,000 pounds per year. The eight stakeholders typically juggled full-time, day employment with nightly EDM work. Only two, Jack and Kevin, were fully self-sufficient in the EDM scene. They piece together jobs as DJs (live at clubs and virtually on Web-based radio stations), EDM magazine columnists, record label owners, and music class instructors at local universities.

Like the Philadelphia group, the London pool was heterosexual and single. One female was a parent and one other was married. The London respondents were not religious; in fact, they typically reported growing up around religion but being turned off by its rigid doctrine. They believed organized religion was restrictive and intolerant—like the Philadelphia pool believed. They preferred to be spiritual instead. Raves and some EDM events, in addition to drug use, facilitated their spirituality.

Rave–Club Culture Continuum

In London, I initially relied on *Timeout London*[10] magazine to identify events or parties for direct observation and respondent recruitment. Later on, as the interviews unfolded and as I met people in the scene, I learned about other types of parties not listed in *Timeout*. I also gathered lots of party flyers from local retail stores and from the parties[11] I attended. These sources revealed a variety of modern-day EDM events into which raves had transformed. Some were similar to those I found in Philadelphia, while others were different. In general, there was more diversity among London's EDM parties. My fieldwork revealed eight major types: squat parties, underground parties, music festivals, monthlies, weeklies, club nights with superstar DJs, branded parties (including massives or corporate raves with numerous arenas or tents and multigenres of music), and summer boat parties. The breadth of these parties indicated that while the authentic rave scene was over in London, and perhaps the entire country of England, there was some evidence of its return (restoration) as well as considerable success in reshaping and expanding it into more commercially viable entities (adaptation and innovation). In short, EDM music and its culture and lifestyle were thriving in the United Kingdom, evolving into a bona fide part of the leisure industry.

Given this, the rave–club culture continuum described in Chapter 2 would require expansion to capture the British scene in at least three ways. First, some of the London events were different in form and style than in Philadelphia. For example, underground and superstar DJ parties varied in organizational style and had some other cultural meanings assigned to them. Second, branded parties came in a few varieties of which only one could be viewed as a corporate rave. Third, there were at least two different types of events in London that were not present in Philadelphia: the squat party and the summer boat party. They were at opposite ends of the rave–club culture continuum. The following paragraphs describe these unique parties in London.

SAME PARTIES, DIFFERENT STYLE

In London, I found underground parties and superstar one-offs to have very different organizational styles and cultural compositions than their Philadelphia counterparts. The greater size, popularity, and dominance of the London EDM scene permitted the creation and support of more variation in events.

Take, for example, the classification of underground parties, which I located on the rave side of the rave–club culture continuum. In London, people talked about *underground clubs and venues* that faithfully served the scene rather than a few venues that occasionally hosted *underground parties*.[12] As you will recall from Chapter 2, underground parties in Philadelphia often had no set location. They were put on sporadically or with some regularity but not usually at nightclubs considered to specialize in "underground" parties only. The Philadelphia scene was simply too small and not popular enough to allow that. In London, however, people discussed a sort of "underground tier" of clubs, not just events, which served those desiring a departure from commercialized venues and parties. Underground clubs in London had a similar feel or vibe and attracted a comparable crowd, that is, mostly self-described insiders, as did the underground parties in Philadelphia. The following entry from my field journal offers brief comparison of the differences between parties at underground clubs versus those at more commercial ones:

> June 13, 2004—The people I talked to last night were more hopeful when describing the scene's meaning. To them, it's light and happy music—fun and inspiring. And they danced, danced, danced. Dressed to the nines—most of them—this was the "Tinsel Town" party—a high-end club event that smacked of Studio 54 in NYC. They told me trance was too hard, too serious, too dark, something they did when they were younger. Grindstone was a "dirty" underground trance scene. On the contrary, "Tinsel Town" at City Lux was a glamorous, happy event that one could take more pride in and that more closely resembled mainstream culture.

In Philadelphia, superstar one-offs were one-time parties featuring the EDM scene's most famous and best-respected DJs. They were held at some of the city's largest nightclubs and populated by all kinds of party people: insiders and outsiders. They were at the commercial end of the continuum.

One of the most compelling things I found in London, which was immediately evident in *Timeout London*, was the sheer volume and presence of superstar DJs at London parties on a weekly basis. Several EDM-oriented clubs (many of them quite large and famous) had world-renowned DJs playing every Friday and Saturday night. At times, several well-known DJs played at different clubs on the same night, making it difficult for fans (including myself and the undergraduates) to choose events to attend. For example, on our first weekend in London, *Timeout London* listed several of the world's top 100 DJs spinning at various clubs on Friday and Saturday night. These included Benny Benassi, Tall Paul, Fergie, David Seaman, Nick Warren, Darren Emerson, Way Out West, and Above and Beyond, to name a few. As indicated in Chapter 2, superstar DJs played rarely in Philadelphia.

London's clubs seemed to have the economic power and EDM cultural capital to bring in such talent. And given the crowds we saw at events, concerns about finances or profits seemed unlikely. In fact, DJs and fans repeatedly told me that the London scene was competitive: fans demanded excellence in DJ performance and DJ competition for gigs at parties or clubs was intense.[13]

THE RANGE OF BRANDED EDM PARTIES

EDM party "brands" are much more prevalent in London than in Philadelphia, and they seemed to take on more variable forms as well. While I did not have the opportunity to learn about all of the varieties, at least three caught my attention. The first was similar in nearly all respects to the corporate raves I described in Chapter 2. They were professionalized raves catering to young clubbers. They featured many elements of authentic rave culture and much of its

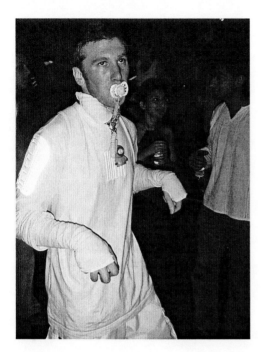

Figure 6.1 A cyber boy (candy kid) at a corporate rave in London, 2004.

organizational form. These brands or corporate raves differed in at least two respects from those in Philadelphia: (1) their reputations were widely known, well beyond the local area, and (2) they occurred often over the course of a year and traveled to numerous villages or towns in the United Kingdom. The following is an excerpt from my field journal on one of these parties:

> There were five rooms of music and each had numerous DJs that traded off every hour. Big talent was there and also lesser-known DJs, local stars in the UK. I realized that because each played only one hour, it made the time pass more quickly for me. I looked forward to the next one and felt relieved that my misery would end soon if I didn't like a particular one. There were booths that sold rave accouterment. Neon everything. So, glow sticks were common on the dance floor as well as neon jewelry (plastic) and clothes. There wasn't much club chic here. The crowd looked mostly working class or not well-off. There were lots of cyber kids there—candy kids as we call them in the states, especially in the hard house room. The dancing is more like jumping around and cheering with hands in the air. I have pictures of the cyber kids and they ranged in age—up to late 30s, but most were in early 20s or late teens [see Figure 6.1].[14]

There were also branded parties with a more commercialized character that were viewed as some of the premier EDM events in the world. The Cream and Godskitchen brands are two among them. Each is a cross between a music festival, corporate rave, and superstar one-off. For instance, they are outdoor parties in remote locations (typically in warmer weather) and feature numerous tents by genre with long lists of superstar DJs regularly trading off on the hour or so. Parties like these produce CDs to commemorate the event, which are globally available at such commercial retailers as www.amazon.com, Tower Records, and HMV music stores.

A third type of EDM branded party was the superstar DJ's weekly or monthly club night. Like those discussed in Chapter 2, weeklies and monthlies were hosted by a DJ and offered largely for scene insiders. In London, however, such nights were put on by superstar DJs—many ranked in the top 100 DJs in the world—who typically used London as their base or home.[15] Even though the local Philadelphia DJs "named" their weeklies and monthlies too, there was considerably more cultural significance to a superstar's named weekly or monthly in London.

NOVEL EXTENSIONS TO THE CONTINUUM'S
TWO POLES

Two other types of parties, which merit their own classification on the rave–club culture continuum, are squat parties and boat parties.[16] I would classify them at opposite ends of the continuum since squat parties are modern-day raves and boat parties are elite commercial club events.

The name *squat party* comes from the illegal occupation of abandoned properties by EDM enthusiasts for modern-day raves. Typically, the term *squat* is associated with the homeless, as they "squat" or illegally occupy abandoned properties for housing. I first learned about squat parties from Emily, a rave diehard whose preference for squat parties ran deep. She described them as

> parties put on by the sort of people that are putting themselves out to keep the music alive, to keep the beat going, to keep the party going. And in London there is a massive scene of that, of people just coming up with some of the most interesting venues you have ever seen. I mean we have squatted parties in Bishops Avenue, the most expensive roads in London. And they [organizers] find out the venues and then put on the parties. They have to put some money up front towards the generator and stuff, but at these squat parties, you have not been asked to pay anything apart from what you consume and do while you are there. People go to a lot of effort for these parties. They are really just having it, you know, they are just absolutely partying and dancing and "cocking a snew," I suppose, at the commercial side of the industry. I would say there are some situations where I feel uncomfortable in the squat party scene, but for the most part, they are fun and safe.

Emily describes a grassroots organizational style of squat parties, true to raves[17] from the past. She also mentions noneconomic motivations for the party (no cover charges) and a purposed boycott of the commercialized scene ("cocking a snew" at it). Thus, squat parties feature classic rave organization and cultural elements. Emily described considerable drug use at squats, especially hallucinogenic drugs (LSD, ecstasy). She gave me the name of a squat party promoter and I chatted with him about them at a London pub. He also claimed the squat party was a conscious attempt to restore rave culture.

On the other hand, the EDM summer boat party appeared to be the complete opposite. Boat parties are usually held in the summer in London and elsewhere in the United Kingdom. Those in London travel along the Thames as a sort of pre-party (6:00 P.M. to 10:00 P.M. on a Friday or Saturday) or after-party (Sundays from 6:00 A.M. to whenever) event. They are attached to superstar DJ nights at some of the best-known London clubs. The event's main act, a superstar DJ, is typically on board to spin a bit and meet and greet the lucky clubbers. It was my understanding that the DJ's guest list for the cruise usually left little room for regular clubbers to get on board. These parties were expensive and they sold out very quickly.

It was easy to classify the boat party toward the commercial end of the continuum and a major departure from authentic raves. The venue, exclusive yachts, epitomizes big business and extreme wealth. Planning for the event likely took much effort and cooperation between promoters, club owners, and business people. And since the clubbers on board were a more exclusive bunch, the cultural elements of raves (identity markers, ethos and vibe, etc.) were abandoned for a more flamboyant club chic.

Collective and Personal Identities

In general, there were remarkable similarities between respondents in both London and Philadelphia regarding EDM-related collective and personal identities. Briefly, London respondents recalled the rave era collective identity in much the same way as did those in Philadelphia. They defined it as being about togetherness, mutual respect, belonging, peace, tolerance of diversity, and antigovernment. In London, however, there was a much stronger sense that the rave-era ethos and collective identity were alive in the modern EDM scene, especially at squat parties, underground clubs, or some branded parties (depending on the party's vibe).

COLLECTIVE

The sense of EDM we-ness that the London respondents discussed was centered on community, tolerance and celebration of diversity, and an overall concern for humanity. While they did not invoke the phrase PLUR,[18] their description of the scene's ethos was consistent with it. Benjamin described it to me:

The idea being in that sense of community and that kind of "wanting to be there for somebody else" even if it's in the small piddly unimportant things, like giving someone a drink of your water bottle because their bottle has run out; giving someone a menthol because they want a menthol cigarette, whatever it might be. You know, you are not giving someone 20 quid or a loan of 10,000 pounds to set up a business, it's obviously very different. But nevertheless, the thing that underlies that in giving a cigarette or whatever, our world would be such a better place, it's such a cliché to say, but I think our world would be such a better place.

Chloe, a former raver and current EDM DJ, described the rave-era collective identity in England as a way to break down racial barriers between people and provide a sense of belonging to outcasts:

I was brought up very suburban, very white, and so I hadn't really met many black people until I went there [raves]. And I met black people and found it broke down barriers really. Everyone sort of, everyone was in that place, and it was just about the music, and having a good time. There were no politics or racism in there at all. That's probably why it was so life changing for me, you know? Because, I'm glad. It's sort of like, I met black people in that environment, instead of listening to my parents, you know. I mean, my parents aren't racist anymore, but their generation, it wasn't integrated like it is now. And I think raving had a lot to do with that . . . bringing people together. It was just like a sense of belonging with people. You just feel like "one" with everyone who is in the room.

Like Chloe, several respondents told me about protesting their families' racist beliefs by spending time with blacks at EDM events or by liking black music—its soul and passion were opposite to the repressed emotional state of their families and the national culture created by the Thatcher and Major governments. Others I spoke with talked about the continued presence of this collective identity and solidarity in London's modern-day EDM scene. For example, Joshua describes the warmth and connection he and his sister feel at modern EDM parties:

It's [the EDM scene today] really special and the first time that you go to that sort of place, and whether you're taking drugs or not, I think you realize that. My sister is completely straight down the line. She's very different than me. She never does any drugs and probably never will, but she cares about the scene quite a lot. She felt that sort of warmness of the scene so I think there is something special about that sort of atmosphere and that's why it's nice to go to those sort[s] of places and to meet those people.

The continued endorsement of such a collective identity in London and at least some parts of British club culture likely explains U.K. scholars' continued consideration of rave culture and the EDM scene as a meaningful experience or a bona fide sociocultural entity rather than a simple drug subculture or scene. But since many music scenes, each having unique collective identities, were also popular in the United Kingdom, how is it that the people I talked with became involved in this particular one?

PERSONAL IDENTITY AND PATHWAYS TO EDM

The people I interviewed reported three main pathways into the EDM scene, which were consistent with those among the Philadelphia respondents. Rave and EDM scene involvement was viewed as (1) a solution for personal alienation in adolescence; (2) a way to bypass other scenes with more rigid gender norms, heightened sexuality, and aggressive vibes and behaviors; and (3) an effort to further expand adolescent hobbies or their interests in and love of EDM and computerized technologies. The discovery of consistencies in personal identity between the Philadelphia and London respondents shores up the concept's importance in understanding individual pathways to music scenes (and perhaps other social groupings) and to, perhaps, broader matters in cultural sociology.

Take, for example, Jack, a stakeholder and one of the first people I interviewed in London. He is the oldest respondent in the study and, perhaps, the most widely experienced in the past rave and current EDM scenes. After he spent nearly an hour describing his current EDM work, I asked Jack how he got involved with EDM. He told me:

Back in the day, we were, my parents loved us and we knew that, but they didn't really show any emotion. My mother was very Victorian in her lectures towards life and still is, even though she's in her nineties now. But I mean, a very deep woman and very hard to understand. You couldn't get inside her head at all and you were lucky to get inside her heart. And we weren't really told that we were loved as kids, and I don't know why, I didn't rebel as a child at all. We were good kids in the terms that we didn't cause my parents problems with the police or with the neighbors or anything like that. But we weren't a close family, and because of my passion for music (I started when I was sixteen or seventeen), my friends would ask me to play at parties. And that seemed to fill the void.

Harry, a stakeholder, also described the outcast/personal alienation reported as a common rave and EDM pathway in Chapter 3. He told me about his love of dance music as a way to escape the stress of family divorce and school routines:

But I think also I found education very stressful to deal with because I didn't have, at the time, I was quite rebellious. It was at the age of fifteen, sixteen, I started getting into the music side of things as an escape route. Because fifteen or sixteen is sort of when the family thing [parents' divorce] was becoming quite difficult, the realness of the situation, and that was when I first got into the music scene heavily. You know, I went clubbing at fifteen or sixteen.

Ten respondents reported gravitating to rave culture and the EDM scene for personal, alienation-related reasons. The EDM scene and raves functioned as an alternative community where they could gain a sense of belonging and respect for who they were and what was important to them.

A second common pathway taken by both the London and Philadelphia respondents was agreement between personal values and scene vibes regarding gender and sexuality. With near unanimity, the London respondents described the vibe at EDM parties and their collective identity as more androgynous and desexualized; the scene did not prioritize hooking up. This was desirable to them, as it was to the respondents in Philadelphia. Megan, a Generation Y insider, told me:

I think people at the house nights or whatever, I find that a lot of people are not on the pull[19] and such; it's not like a meat market, because they are there for music. But that is what their intention is to go there and have a good time, dance for seven hours straight, buzzing [being high on drugs] and have a good time. But it's not a meat market, it's not a[n] "on the pull" kind of thing.

Specifically, EDM parties and the venues that showcased them were typically very different from those in other music scenes (e.g., garage, R & B, or hip hop). Jack expressed his views about genre-based differences, for example, highlighting what he dislikes about hip hop:

I could never get into hip hop. To me, it was too raw. I know it's wrong for me to say and I do like my music raw, or rough around the edges, almost unfinished, but it [hip hop] was the wrong sort of raw. It had attitude. It didn't embrace love, peace, and happiness. You can take a crap record, with the most unusual, awful, or most horrible lyrics under the sun about hos and pimps and bitches and whatever, and spend three-quarters of a million or so on a video with women walking around with their chests hanging out, wearing skirts, you know what I'm saying? I'm not a prude, don't get me wrong, but why should you have to walk around like you're attending a nudist convention just to sell your music?

However, the more commercial EDM parties could often be quite sexually charged as well. In a conversation about music, gender, and sexuality, Benjamin discusses differences between more commercial EDM parties with the more underground ones he attends:

TAMMY: In Philadelphia, women have often said to me they don't necessarily like trance and techno, but sometimes they go out to those nights because they want a break from the sexual tension elsewhere.

BENJAMIN: That was one of the things that I was interested in and appreciated as well, like one of those assets of this community, that it [sexual tension] wasn't an issue. And if I wanted to try and make a move on a girl, then great, but I didn't have to and there's no pressure. There is no big deal about it, whatever. I love that. It's very liberating like that. . . . I went to those kind[s] of cheesy crap commercial dance clubs when I was younger as a beer boy or whatever you might say. I went to meat markets; I didn't go because of the meat markets, I went because I was going with my eight, nine, ten blokes[20] from school, my mates from school. Yea, I had a mate who pulled one hundred[21] girls in one night apparently. Stupid, pathetic, typical kind of machismo or bullshit that I don't have much time for.

The respondents' attraction to EDM parties because of their more muted gender and sexuality traits and practices could be another example of how the EDM scene and its unique culture provides an attractive "other" social space, lifestyle, and collective identity for those who do not subscribe to the larger society's conventions regarding gender and sexuality.[22]

The third pathway for four other respondents, all males, was their attraction to raves and EDM parties via a technological fascination with EDM's production and sound. Similar to some of the Philadelphia respondents, several London respondents were musically trained as children. They played instruments and classical music or grew up in households with a strong musical presence. In addition, they had computer- and science-related hobbies and most worked in some computer-related job now as adults. These background characteristics influenced their attraction to dance music in late adolescence or early adulthood.

Lewis is a good example of this pathway. He is a computer database programmer for a well-known technology company earning a good salary—the second highest in the sample. He was raised in a loving household by a father who worked as a school teacher and a mother who was a nurse and into classical music. He told me his childhood hobbies were "astronomy, electronics, science-type things." Lewis currently plays the violin in two orchestras in London and checks dance music CDs, especially trance, out of a local library on a weekly basis. While talking with me, he compared classical and trance music that revealed a motivation for EDM scene involvement:

I don't know why, but I get the same sort of rush from trance music, and the kind of classical music that I like, which is from the classical period, Mozart, Beethoven, Schubert, and maybe Bach and Handel a bit earlier. I put them pretty equal in terms of how much I like the music, or the effect it has on me. And some people ask me, "Well, how can something so repetitive as trance music be in the same league as classical music?" I don't think it's repetitive. I think that's one of the things that makes trance stand out, say, against techno, that it is evolving over time. It's a constant beat, yeah, but there's something changing all the way though.

Explanations for Raves' Transformation

Authentic raves of the late 1980s and early 1990s seemed largely a thing of the past in London. Yet their evolution into the leisure industry had left London, and perhaps all of the United Kingdom, with a more vibrant EDM scene than that found in Philadelphia. *In other words, raves (their form or cultural traits) have transformed in both Philadelphia and London, but that change has been accompanied by scene decline in Philadelphia and scene expansion in London.* London's EDM parties are scattered heavily along the rave–club culture continuum with signs of successful restoration, preservation, and adaptation everywhere.

As in Philadelphia, I asked people what explained this change. Two familiar reasons were offered. The most common was about commercialization, pertaining to raves' partnership with legitimate nightclubs in London. The other had to do with legislative control—specifically, local ordinances for noise and gathering, the 1994 Criminal Justice Public Order Act and the Section 8 amendment[23] in 2001 to the Misuse of Drugs Act—which attempted to control raves in much the same way as the Rave Act (2003) in the United States. In short, the London respondents believed commercialization (legitimate nightclubs) altered raves' authentic culture and organization in critical ways and that government policy tried to eliminate the culture altogether. Thus, the London respondents also cited two of the most common explanations of raves' changing, which have also been used to explain declines in other music scenes, cultural entities and social groupings. Megan, a young EDM loyalist who had never attended a classic rave, discussed commercialization as a corrupting force of the scene:

> MEGAN: It's not as exciting, I think, anymore. I would love to go back in time and to have been to some raves. It was still freezing cold but . . .
>
> TAMMY: So there was a certain excitement about raves?
>
> MEGAN: Yea. I think you have to be really into the whole scene to go out to them. I think you will find a certain sort of person there, and now, clubs, it's so commercial out there. I think a lot of DJs are

trying to make things too commercial. They are trying to make more money out of it instead of for the love of it.

Financial interests, of course, inspire the commercialization trend. This was discussed in earlier chapters and has also been raised by numerous music scene studies and classic cultural theorists.[24] It is not difficult to grasp the profit potential of EDM parties. Their "extended hours" organization increases the size of their market and permits individuals to consume more goods (beverages, drugs, etc.). While in London, I learned several clubs had twenty-four-hour alcohol licenses. Other clubs were open nearly around the clock. The following is a field journal entry about a corporate rave I attended at a large nightclub near Trafalgar Square. It reveals the profit potential for clubs, which helps explain their continued hosting of EDM parties:[25]

Blue Sky had its doors open from 10pm last night [Friday] until 7am today [Saturday]. Then, it will re-open at 1pm for a lesbian party and will stay open til 9pm, when it kicks everyone out and re-opens at 10pm, only to run until 7am on Sunday. It is hosting another party Sunday night. I talked with a male employee who said they [employees] are expected to stay all night Friday and then go home at 7am Saturday but return by noon. He was just going to crash at the club. So the club gets to stay open for business nearly around the clock due to EDM parties' style and organization. I wonder if these hours and work requirements encourage staff to use amphetamines or cocaine?

As was the case in Philadelphia, people in London had mixed feelings about rave culture's commercialization. Some believed clubs "civilized" the rave era, expressing similar views as those in Philadelphia: raves' coming indoors to legitimate clubs was desirable because clubs had better equipment and were cleaner and safer. On the other hand, rave-era loyalists like Emily thought this partnership ruined the scene and culture. She criticized it while recounting a story about a recent club outing:

We were all treated like animals. The bouncers were rude and invasive. They had nothing to do with the scene whatsoever and yet they totally dictated the scene from the moment you got there. They were brisk, they were just . . . I mean they were violating people, they were just doing such invasive searches of drugs on people, and blatantly, whenever they would find drugs on people, they were blatantly keeping them for themselves and laughing in people's faces. And so by the time we got into this club, there were guys all standing around the walls looking down, intimidating, and it was a horrendous evening because the two cultures [rave versus commercial club] clashed. They charged about ten to fifteen pounds to get in and, you know, nobody felt free.

The social control of rave culture by numerous levels of government was also cited as an important transforming factor. Hill (2002) discussed non–drug-related social control of raves from the enforcement of gathering and zoning codes and noise ordinances in the English countryside during raves' early days. Both the Philadelphia respondents (see Chapter 4) and some London respondents recalled this type of social control. For example, when I asked Daniel, a former raver, why the rave scene changed in London, he told me:

> I think it's more red tape, and, you know, it's more political than anything. In the old days, you used to be able to set up a rave word of mouth, hold it in a field. Now, there is more red tape. You've got to get licenses, you've got to get the blessing and grants of the local council, local area police have got to be involved in discussions from very early on and right up to it. And it's so much that a promoter would have to go through now, to put on one of those big raves, that, you know, they just grew tired of the bureaucracy of it really.

Shifting the rave location to legally owned and properly licensed nightclubs eliminated these grassroots organizational obstacles. Hosting events in nightclubs was simply easier and less risky. A consequence of the shift, for some like Emily, was that nightclubs robbed the scene of its authentic culture. However, the loss of very young EDM fans—which was cited as an important consequence of commercialization, complicated by generational schism in Philadelphia—was less of a consequence in London since the drinking age for club admission was eighteen, lower than that in Philadelphia.

Several London respondents also believed that drug-related social control at the national level also levied a blow to rave culture. This matter has been discussed by Bennett (2000, 2001), Collin (1997), Angela McRobbie (1994), Reynolds (1999), and Thornton (1996). Chloe told me:

> A lot of the scene died as well, when they added the criminal justice bill.[26] That put an end to raves really, because then it had to be in clubs. You know, it all had to be licensed, and they were basically taking away your freedom. That's why now, as the DJ, that's why I like to use a lot of the old music, to try [to] educate people about what it [raves] was really like, you know? A lot of youngsters today that are going out to clubs, it is like, they wonder what it was like for us in the late eighties. They have a certain amount of awe, knowing it will never be like that again.

But while the people I talked with believed that drug-related social control helped to stamp out authentic raves and transform rave culture, we found drug use at club-based EDM events prevalent with often lax attitudes about it among security.[27] For example, some of the students and I went to an underground club the first weekend of our London study abroad. We stayed at the party from about 11:00 P.M. until 4:00 A.M.

It seemed the entire event revolved around drugs. It was the most drug use and drug-defined interaction I had seen since I commenced the project. For example, the students told me either that they were offered drugs several times throughout the evening or that others asked them if they had any. The clincher to this was when Damon found a powdery substance in a bag on the floor and a clubber told us to give it to a bouncer. I gave it to the bouncer and asked if this was what I was supposed to do. The bouncer replied, "Yes, or keep it for yourself."

The concern of law enforcement, anywhere, might be about drunkenness and drug use in public spaces, that is, outdoor raves or EDM events, rather than that taking place inside privately owned businesses or dwellings. While it was true that outdoor EDM parties had diminished with formal social control, London's clubs seemed filled with illegal drug use. Official data and reports (see www .homeoffice.gov.uk/drugs and *Focal Point* 2005) in England showed drug use rates, especially ecstasy, at nightclubs substantiated my observations.[28] In comparison, ecstasy and other club drug use is down considerably in the post-rave era in the United States. One explanation for the differences between the United Kingdom and United States could be nation-level policies and public sentiment about drugs and alcohol but also cultural ideals and practices regarding leisure. This brings us back to the model of cultural change described in Chapter 4.

Why EDM Thrives in London: Confronting the Model of Cultural Change

If authentic raves are largely over, why has EDM continued to thrive in London and not in cities like Philadelphia and, perhaps,[29] the rest of the United States? By thriving, I mean London's EDM scene continues to have a very visible presence in popular culture and the leisure industry and remains a music and lifestyle of choice among a significant portion of a locale's population. As indicated at the beginning of this chapter, EDM is far more popular and dominant among young people in British cities like London than it is in U.S. cities like Philadelphia. It is a leading music of choice among young Britons, which is one of the biggest differences between the two locations. Therefore, an analysis of scenes in London and Ibiza, Spain, permits further assessment of the model of cultural change. In short, does the model hold up in music scenes outside of the United States?

One way to assess this is to consider that the five forces of change identified in Chapter 4 (generational schism, commercialization, cultural hedonism or self-destruction, formal social control, and genre fragmentation) might operate differently from one location to the next. Remember that scene alteration was accompanied by decline in Philadelphia but expansion in London. Thus, a music scene's changing in one direction or another may depend on the degree to which the five forces are stymied or enhanced.

WARDING OFF GENERATIONAL SCHISM
VIA INCREASED DIFFERENTIATION

My fieldwork provided some evidence that a generational schism, between Generations X and Y,[30] in London helped change rave culture and the EDM scene but did not threaten their overall viability. One obvious reason for this is that the admission age for nightclubs in London is eighteen,[31] three years younger than in Philadelphia. This permits broader access to venues that play EDM. As noted in Chapter 4, strict enforcement of twenty-one-year-old policies in the United States helped stymie recruitment of younger participants, for example, Generation Y.

According to the London respondents, the main reason for the lesser threat of generational schism in London, however, is that people seemed to age into and out of certain types of music and parties over time. For example, older ravers were said to have aged out of the rave scene and into the higher-class, commercial house music scene; others preferred smaller, less flashy parties with people they knew. Younger participants seemed to prefer big rave-like parties. And the London leisure industry—both commercial and underground—provided plenty of parties for everyone. Jack told me:

> I mean there are people who would be probably my age, but would still be listening to drum and bass, but, you kind of grow up through it, and you progress, you progress as a group. A lot of people are around about thirty to forty in the areas where I play house music.

The people I spoke with also told me about the London scene's ability to retain significant portions of these cohorts using some of the strategies discussed in Chapter 4.

To begin, the EDM scene in London appeared to be more differentiated, which allowed it to appeal across a wider range of people. While the Philadelphia scene was differentiated by genre of EDM, the London scene was differentiated by age and socioeconomic class as well as by music genre. I did not observe these types of age and socioeconomic class distinctions in Philadelphia. The London respondents repeatedly told me, for example, that the vocal, soulful, and progressive house scenes were more for the mature, middle-class clubber, while the hard house and trance scenes were for younger "blokes and birds" from the working class. As in Philadelphia, drugs also varied by scene, which the *Focal Point* (2005) report also noted. For example, in London, cocaine was the popular drug of choice at many soulful, vocal, and progressive house parties populated by wealthier and older clubbers. Trance or hard house events featured a lot of ecstasy use. Daniel told me:

I'm working class, but if I would put music into classes, probably house would be middle class, but sort of U.K. garage and stuff like that would be more working class. They are, in a way, a grade below. You've got people who are older in the house scene, almost more mature. They've kind of probably been through the whole drug scene, already done it. And now, it's kind of like, they just want to go out and have a night, they'll have a few drinks, but they're probably already done with drugs. Whereas I feel U.K. garage attracts a lot of younger people like eighteen to twenty-five, which is more the, you know, the higher end of the drugs that will probably be taken at their age, than what they are later on.

To further illustrate these ideas, we can compare two very different DJ stakeholders from the London pool: Oliver and Chloe. Oliver is a Generation Y university graduate who currently earns a high salary from a job as a mortgage banker. He got into the EDM scene—specifically, house music—via his middle-class friends a few years ago and, consequently, missed the whole rave era. Oliver attributes his current success as a DJ to starting out with middle- and upper-class clubbers, spinning at their private residence parties. Today, he knows people at London's most popular EDM clubs and has started to accumulate a fan base. He spins or parties every weekend and consumes a lot of cocaine with his house music mates. According to him, he does this without consequence. Oliver told me his future is in banking and that DJ-ing was a hobby he planned to abandon in a few years.

Chloe, on the other hand, is an older raver from the past, now trying to establish herself as a DJ. She is from a working-class background and was exposed to EDM, she told me, via the working-class rave scene, where she consumed lots of ecstasy and still does so, albeit much less often. Chloe did not attend university and currently struggles to support herself and her child. She pieces together low-paying gigs at small clubs, part-time retail work, and some public assistance (housing allowance) to get by. Chloe wants to make music a career and she is taking small steps to make that happen.

The differentiation of subscenes by class and age, in addition to musical genre, may permit the continued participation of a broad range of people over time.[32] This is something I noted in Chapter 4 as necessary to ward off population loss from generational schism. For example, people in London aged out of one subscene (e.g., trance or hard house) and into another (e.g., house), whereas those in Philadelphia seemed to age out of EDM clubbing altogether. Thus, the differentiation of London's EDM scene into age- and social-class–stratified and genre-based subscenes has, perhaps, permitted older ravers (who are now more conventionally embedded) to stay involved as they have grown from financially strapped and rebellious ravers into better-off club connoisseurs. This finding suggests that while Generation X ravers in the United States may have aged out of EDM scene participation, the parallel cohort in London seemed to have aged into another part of it. This is not surprising in a nation where dance music is so popular and where rave culture has successfully adapted to the mainstream leisure industry. Such conditions allow greater subscene differentiation and the reestablishment of collective identities and cultural styles consistent with various social-class groupings.[33]

NATION-SPECIFIC STANDARDS OF CULTURAL HEDONISM AND OTHERNESS

A second explanation for rave culture's successful adaptation into London's leisure industry has to do with differential standards for cultural hedonism and "otherness." Simply put, the Londoners I interviewed and interacted with at club events had more lenient views about drugs and placed greater value on alternative lifestyles and the identity markers that signified it (Thornton 1996).

For example, what was defined as alternative fashion in the United States did not seem so strange in London. This was noticeable not only in the clubs but on city streets daily. In London, there are numerous neighborhoods that cater to alternative lifestyles. For example, in SoHo, Covent Garden (Neale street, specifically), and Camden Town there are many independent clothing, record, and paraphernalia stores that cater to EDM and various other scenes. This is also true of other cities across the United Kingdom. In contrast, Philadelphia has, perhaps, one street (i.e., South Street) that appeals to alternative lifestyle and fashion, but it is not EDM oriented and is dominated more by the skater and graffiti cultures. Thus, the so-called other identity markers of the EDM scene that many Philadelphia clubbers rejected or grew out of seemed to be more popular in London. They were not as "other" there.

Undoubtedly, some will point to patterns of drug use between Philadelphia and London clubbers as an explanation for the EDM scene's greater success in London. This would be consistent with the public-health, drug subculture approach U.S. scholars use to understand rave culture.[34] But this is an oversimplification. My work shows the importance of other non–drug-related explanations for EDM's decline. Moreover, the drug experience in rave culture is much more culturally embedded than prior work has indicated.[35]

To begin, drugs were viewed very differently by the people I spoke with and observed in London; they redefined what was hedonistic or deviant. For example, during my fieldwork, I found drug use to be more prevalent in and a more acceptable part of the overall EDM lifestyle, no matter the subscene. There was simply a greater tolerance for drug-related leisure and a greater respect for leisure in general.[36] People were far less ashamed to discuss their own consumption patterns and they openly bought, sold, and used drugs at EDM events. In short, people understood that EDM parties and the EDM lifestyle were closely tied to illegal drug use, but this connection was not stigmatized to the degree that it was in the United States.[37] For example, after observation of people at EDM events and casual conversations with them there, as well as interviews with the respondents, I began to see an ecstasy use pattern of about two to four pills per night at a rate of half a pill for every forty-five minutes or so.[38] Of course, many people did less, while others much more. Megan explained this consumption pattern to me during our interview:

> TAMMY: How much E do you consume at parties?
> MEGAN: It depends because sometimes if I'm driving, and I shouldn't drive when I'm drunk, so I will do a half pill if I'm driving. But if I'm not, then four or five in an evening.
> TAMMY: Whole tablets?
> MEGAN: No. I only do half at a time.
> TAMMY: So it's only two total?
> MEGAN: I will have four pills. I will buy four or five pills and I take half at a time.
> TAMMY: So you are taking them what, one every half hour or hour?
> MEGAN: Every forty-five minutes.

I also witnessed the pattern Megan reported at a party outside of London. I wrote about this in my journal:

> July 10, 2004: There was considerable drug use at last night's party. For example, I saw two young white guys—early 20s—taking one pill after another about every 45 minutes or so. They were drinking Smirnoff Ice, instead of water, and were smoking like crazy. Everyone here smokes a lot. Clubbers are thinner too.[39]

I also witnessed plenty of people experiencing ecstasy-related side effects (nausea and vomiting, sweating and dehydration, and varied states of unconsciousness), yet few of these were defined as "consequences" by those who experienced them or who witnessed them.[40] In a journal entry after a corporate rave, I wrote the following:

> July 2, 2004: When I left the corporate rave at 3am, I saw a guy lying on the street outside. I suspect many more were in a similar situation, but I couldn't stay much longer. I was just too tired. I also saw open drug dealing, visible drug consumption, [and] active drug seeking and I heard open drug discussion.

My interviews also revealed some of the same side effects I reported in previous chapters among Philadelphia clubbers: short-term memory loss and depression, missed work, draining of funds, and so on. Yet, the London respondents did not interpret these as having the same kind of a deleterious effect in their lives as did the Philadelphia respondents. Finally, several of the fifteen respondents had to reschedule their Monday or Tuesday interviews because of "illnesses" that surfaced after a weekend clubbing.

Thus, despite the prevalence of drug use and the scope of physical and mental consequences, few people perceived it as surpassing the threshold for cultural hedonism and otherness. Perhaps one reason for the seemingly different standards for drug-related cultural hedonism between London and Philadelphia is the overarching approach to drug matters in the United Kingdom and the United States and the normalization idea that Parker et al. (1998) discussed. Briefly, the United States wages a war on drugs with a zero tolerance policy about drug use and strict penalties for infraction. The United Kingdom, on the other hand, has had a history of treating drugs as a medical problem, where reducing health-related consequences of drug use[41] is prioritized over criminalizing users. While problematic drug use remains medicalized in the United Kingdom, there has been a recent shift toward criminalizing recreational use, especially with club drugs (Measham 2006a, 2006b; Measham and Moore 2008).

VARIATIONS IN FORMAL SOCIAL CONTROL

In Chapter 4, I noted that two kinds of social control by the state—enforcement of local gathering and noise ordinances and state- and federal-level drug laws—helped transform rave culture and contribute to raves' alteration and decline. For example, the punitive U.S. approach to drug use chilled the promotion of raves and nightclubs' hosting of EDM events via rave- and ecstasy-related legislation. The stigmatizing public relations campaign that accompanied these legal changes would eventually sour the U.S. public on the whole scene.

During the period of my study (2004–2005), a different approach seemed to operate in London. Historically, the United Kingdom has employed a public health and public safety approach to illicit drug use, which has likely helped the scene flourish due to a greater lenience toward drug use. The U.K. goal was to reduce the physical, mental, and social costs associated with drug and alcohol misuse. Thus, ecstasy- or cocaine-using clubbers were considered people to be protected, not arrested. This approach may soon, however, become a thing of the past (Measham 2006a, 2006b; Measham and Moore 2008).

Still, the more harm reduction approach employed in London and the rest of the United Kingdom likely reduced the negative impact government policies and actors had on a music scene. When government policy treats drug use as a medical problem, promoters and club owners may not be discouraged from putting on rave-like or EDM events because they worry less about being arrested or closed down.[42] Also, the harm reduction approach does not employ a derogatory public relations campaign about the illegal drug use taking place within a music scene and the people who participate in it. On the contrary, it is proactive in disseminating to the public lots of prevention-based education about drugs and their potential consequences. Because of this, much drug-related stigma is avoided. With drug policies defined this way, the state and its formal control agencies may act to facilitate a scene's thriving rather than controlling it.

While in London, I saw the medical approach in action. For example, I saw London club staff looking out for clubbers' health in numerous ways. First, several clubs had "house-keeping" employees scouring the club throughout the night to collect bottles or broken glass. This activity, I learned, was to protect clubbers from cuts and bruises, which were the main type of injury at clubs. The floors were kept fairly clear of items that could injure.[43] In Philadelphia clubs, I seldom saw club staff walking around gathering up bottles on the floor. To me, it seemed as if U.S. clubs viewed customers as a business liability, while London clubs seemed more concerned with their safety.

A second illustration of the medical approach came from a conversation I had with a security guard, Andrew, at one of London's most famous EDM clubs. I befriended him one night and he met me a week later for a two-hour interview. When I first saw Andrew at the club, he was standing along the wall near the entrance of the club's main room. I asked him why he was standing there and he told me his job was to make sure no problems cropped up. During our interview, I asked him to explain what he meant. He said it was his job was to make sure that people who looked like they were sleeping were actually sleeping and not in a coma. He told me he is very busy on weekend nights checking on such "sleeping" clubbers.

Curious, I asked him what he would do if someone was actually in a coma, not just sleeping. He told me he would take them to a rest area in the club and call down the medic, who was on site, upstairs in the club. Think about the dramatic difference between Andrew and the hostile bouncer I profiled in Chapter 4, who booted the troubled Asian couple out of the techno party. Andrew's job was to protect the clubber's health, whereas the Philadelphia bouncer's was to reduce the club's legal risk and financial liability.

Lessons from London

There were some important similarities and differences between London and Philadelphia that substantiate many of this book's themes and premises regarding the cultural transformation of the EDM scene and related conceptual matters. To begin, my London fieldwork revealed that the continued popularity of a music scene permits its growth in numerous directions, including the restoration of its authentic state (e.g., the squat party), a healthy preservation at accessible and diverse events (e.g., a tier of underground clubs and events for all ages, social classes, and genres), and cutting-edge adaptation or evolution to more commercial variations (e.g., world-famous branded parties, regular access to superstar DJs, and high-end luxury events like the summer boat party) that help expand its appeal. This greater variation in and popularity of EDM events and the music's widespread endorsement by young clubbers has acted not only to empower this cultural collective to withstand the test of time but also to flourish in numerous forms that appeal across various social groups.

Perhaps another key to understanding EDM's enduring popularity in the United Kingdom lies in the concepts of identity—collective and personal. Despite the tremendous variation in parties and differentiation among the clubbers who attend them, the substance of the rave-era collective identity continues on in London. While music, dance, and drug use attract and unify people, the continued linkage between collective and personal interests within a scene is likely, also, facilitated by external forces outside of it. With the assistance of past government policies, a nationwide value on leisure and diversity, and relaxed standards about what is "other" or deviant, the London EDM scene has been able to overcome the five potential threats to its viability.

A point of caution is, however, warranted. Since my fieldwork in 2004, drug control policies in London and the rest of the United Kingdom have toughened up against casual drug use and clubbing. A punitive shift in policies is currently under way (Measham and Moore 2008), which may ultimately impact EDM scenes in London and throughout the United Kingdom in much the same way as it did in Philadelphia. Punitive social control strategies might further professionalize EDM scenes, stigmatize the lifestyle and people who engage in them, and hinder the recruitment of new participants. These are some of the ways social control weakened raves in Philadelphia and, arguably, the United States. If such policies do not work in this fashion, then other forces beyond those discussed here must be considered. Since scenes cycle in and out of existence over time, we can be assured of ample opportunity to assess this matter in the future.

Ibiza, Spain

Perhaps the clearest benchmark of the great global diversity in raves' alteration can be found in Ibiza, Spain—an entire island organized around the EDM scene and post-rave culture. While other music scenes might enjoy greater influence and popularity, none I know has completely claimed an island, city, or town in the way that EDM has stamped Ibiza. Exceptions include Manchester (Redhead 1993, 1995) for EDM and raves, the blues tradition in Chicago (Grazian 2003), or the country music lifestyle in Nashville (Peterson 1997). This was at least one reason to consider a research trip to Ibiza, but I soon learned about others.

Shortly after we arrived in London, for example, people began telling us that Ibiza (the third largest of the Balearic Islands[44]) was a central part of the United Kingdom summer EDM scene and that we "had" to go to there in order to fully understand what we were studying.[45] Clearly, their collective sentiment indicated that the local London EDM scene and others in the United Kingdom were also translocal and global in nature; that is, they were tied to scenes in different geographical locations. U.K. clubbers, DJs, and other stakeholders made Ibiza a normal part of their summer activities.[46] Magazines, record and CD stores, and travel agencies posted advertisements for "cheap" Ibiza package deals that catered to U.K. clubbers, especially those favoring house music. So, on a warm Sunday morning in July 2004, the three undergraduate research assistants and I boarded a plane at Gatwick airport for a 7:00 A.M. flight, and a one-week research trip, to what some fans believed the premier EDM location in the world.

On our flight were mostly alternative-looking young adults, dressed casually. They looked as if they had not been to bed yet from the night before or had just rolled out of it prior to boarding. They were weary-eyed, yet excited. Shortly after takeoff, most of the passengers—including my undergraduates—fell asleep for the two-and-a-half-hour flight.

We arrived in Ibiza around 9:30 A.M. and stepped into an airport crowded with what seemed like hundreds of other clubbers. Glancing at signs held by tourist company staff, we followed the hefty crowd outside toward a line of charter buses—the airport transport part of the package deal—that would take us to our hotel in Playa en Bossa—the clubbers' beach. On our drive, we passed billboards (see Figure 6.2) advertising branded parties—weeklies with superstar DJs—mostly at what I would later learn were the "Big 8" clubs.[47] The people on board cheered, gasped with awe, and applauded as we drove by signs showcasing their favorite DJs.[48]

The bus dropped us in central Playa en Bossa, a seemingly "touristy" part of the island. The streets were lined with souvenir shops, retail CD and clothing stores, restaurants, and entertainment activities (bike and scooter rentals, boat trips and tours, and small theme parks). At 10:00 A.M., most of these places

Figure 6.2 Billboards in Ibiza, 2004.

were either vacant or closed, which posed a bit of a problem. We could not check into our hotel until 12:30 p.m., and we were hungry and cranky, having been up since 4:00 a.m. to make our flight.

Thankfully, our package deal included lunch vouchers for one of the only open restaurants. So, the students and I walked in and sat down for breakfast. The menu items were printed in four languages: Spanish, English, French, and German. The service staff spoke Spanish and a little bit of English, enough for my non–Spanish-speaking students to order pizza, burgers, and Cokes.

By the time we checked into our hotel, a DJ had begun spinning at the famous Bora Bora[49] beach, which was directly below our hotel room; no exaggeration. We settled into our run-down, dormlike accommodations—which cost my research grant a lot of money—and relaxed to the DJ's ambient-atmospheric mix until about 2:00 p.m. The students eventually fell asleep, so I went down to the beach and lay in the sun with other clubbers in a very "spring break"–like atmosphere.

In talking with other sunbathing clubbers, I learned many were on week-long holidays from various European countries. Most of them told me they planned to attend the Manumission party slated for later that night (Monday) at the world's largest nightclub, Privilege. I had heard about this party many times before.[50] It was described to me as one of the biggest, most outrageous parties on the global scene. An estimated ten thousand turned out for it every Monday night and paid the U.S. equivalent of $65 for a Cirque du Soleil–like EDM party spectacular where DJs spun records in a swimming pool. The party started at 11:00 p.m. and would end at 6:00 a.m., with the official carry-on (after-) party at Space from 6:00 a.m. to 6:00 p.m. Tuesday.

So, I bought tickets for the event and left the beach party around 6:00 p.m. to try to nap in my hotel room. After all, I had been awake since 4:00 a.m. Unfortunately, the nap did not happen. The Bora Bora beach party was going full-tilt, playing progressive house music since midafternoon—and it was scheduled to go on like that until midnight. People outside were cheering and trucks were stocking restaurants and collecting garbage. Plus, Playa en Bossa is very close to the island's only airport. Planes flying overhead contributed to the noise.

About fifteen hours later, I returned to our hotel room from the Manumission party and a few hours at the Space carry-on party. I had now been awake for more than forty hours, with brief and intermittent naps and no drugs[51] but lots of caffeine and Red Bull. I realized then that I would not be sleeping much this week. But then again, people did not come to Ibiza to sleep. They came for the music and to party in one of the world's best EDM hot spots.

A Snapshot

The Ibiza EDM scene represents, perhaps, one of the clearest, most successful, commercial adaptations of an underground music scene to mainstream dominance. The once-grassroots-organized rave scene—a spin-off from Ibiza's hippie days[52]—has been transformed into an EDM-oriented tourist industry controlled by professionals who wish to carve out a livelihood from the millions of yearly island visitors. Their market is comprised of two main groups. The first are European and U.K. families who come to the island during the summer months for the warm weather, beautiful skies, and spectacular beaches. They consume Spanish culture and native Ibizan (who are locally called Ibencencos) history in Evissa town and Dalt Villa (the walled city). They tend to rent in hotels and villas in the quiet parts of the island, away from clubbing hot spots. Increasingly, party promotional groups and local government officials attempt to lure more families and older professionals to the island for non-EDM leisure. In Dalt Villa, for example, there is an annual jazz festival in July, and the International Gay and Lesbian Film Festival stops there as well. In addition, groups like Balearic People, for example, have started live concert series featuring Spanish musicians. These events are often marketed toward young families and older professionals, not just EDM clubbers.

The second and larger group of tourists is EDM clubbers and enthusiasts from all over the United Kingdom, Europe, and elsewhere. Their holidays to Ibiza have financed the island's growth, its infrastructure, and most aspects of life there. While places like Mykonos (Greece), London, and Berlin also attract lots of EDM tourism, nothing compares to Ibiza. It has reigned not only as the premier EDM capital since the early rave days but also as one of the top spots for European leisure. Clearly, Ibiza (like London and, perhaps, the rest of the United Kingdom) represents a case of raves' alteration and expansion rather than decline.

Clubbers' Profile: The clubbers we surveyed on the island seemed a fair representation of those we saw or met at parties. They were multiethnic and white, hailing from places such as Holland, Australia, Germany, the United States, various towns and villages in the United Kingdom, and several nations in southern Africa and Central America. They ranged in age from eighteen to the early thirties, with an average age of twenty-four to twenty-five. Most were employed full-time, but several of the younger respondents were unemployed college students currently in undergraduate, graduate, or professional programs.

Most had been EDM fans for a long time: from four to more than ten years. Some had experienced the early rave scene, but most had not. They told us they liked dance music because it was happy and energetic, fostered a sense of peace and community, and enabled them to relax and dance. They listed house music (progressive, Latin/Balearic, and soulful versions) as their favorite genre but also liked techno and trance. Between 2004 and 2005, I noticed house music was increasing its dominance on the island, which was consistent with the respondents' favorite genre. While on holiday in Ibiza, they planned to dance, socialize with friends or meet new people, consume alcohol and various illegal drugs, and simply enjoy the island's spectacular weather and beauty.

Stakeholders' Profile: The ten stakeholders I interviewed in 2005 were demographically different from the forty people we surveyed in 2004. For example, they were much older, on average. Two were in their late twenties (DJs), four in their thirties (three DJs and one employee for a promotion company), two in their forties (co-owners of a promotional group), and another two (one a DJ and the other an EDM professional) over fifty years of age. They were all long-time dance music enthusiasts and most had ample rave experience. In fact, their participation in the early rave scene led many of them to the island in the first place. Once there, they were bitten by the Balearic bug and set up residence in Ibiza or returned every year for the summer season.

The younger stakeholders (six of the ten) were current DJs in Ibiza. They played at after-parties, opened main acts at large nightclubs, or hosted their own events at smaller clubs on the island. Each came to Ibiza every summer to financially support himself or herself in the EDM scene and to enjoy its lifestyle. They had varied success in doing so. Like other DJs I talked with in Philadelphia and London, they pieced together several club gigs with other kinds of work to get by. All desired to produce music and advance their careers in the EDM scene. So, in the off season,[53] they fled to Brazil, Spain, and various European sites to continue their EDM professional work.

Nearly every DJ I have spoken with over the course of this project, including these six, told me that playing in Ibiza was like living a dream and something that would earn them a lot of cultural currency within the greater, global EDM community. But while it might be easy to focus on the positive aspects of the DJ lifestyle, I learned about personal turmoil and short- and long-term consequences from my conversations and correspondences with DJs. I noted some of these in Chapter 3 (e.g., failure at interpersonal relationships and financial insecurity), but in Ibiza, the problems seemed more magnified. For example, all of the stakeholders I spoke with, not just the six DJs, told me about continued sleep deprivation from working the twenty-four-hour EDM lifestyle. It harmed their health, impaired their judgment, and often led to the consumption of drugs, especially amphetamines and cocaine, in order to function or cope. They were often able to avoid the lure of drugs at the beginning of the season but fell into troublesome patterns by its end. This was one of the only reasons they appreciated leaving Ibiza in October. It prevented more lasting habits and related complications.

FORCES OF CULTURAL CHANGE

Ibiza's history as a music colony, its current status as an EDM mecca, and its local EDM-dominated economy, social organization, and culture likely enabled it to overcome several of the forces that killed off raves, described in previous chapters. For example, the island had an Association of Discotecas, a coopera-tive of large club-owners, who worked with several government agencies to promote the island's EDM industry.[54] This resulted in little interference or control over the EDM lifestyle. In addition, while security at Ibiza clubs is very tight at the door, it drops off dramatically inside the party. Security acts to control movement into and out of the club, not the clubbers' behaviors. This means they often turned a blind eye to drug use.[55]

As in London and the rest of the United Kingdom, standards for drug use or other hedonistic activities were far more relaxed than those in the United States. Like those in the United Kingdom, Ibiza's laws about drug or alcohol consumption (e.g., see the International Center for Alcohol Policies 2002) are not nearly as restrictive as they are in the United States. Moreover, there ex-isted very little drug-related stigma among the clubbers, stakeholders, and is-land professionals or residents with whom I spoke. So the cultural hedonistic force that helped the Philadelphia rave scene self-destruct seemed irrelevant here. In fact, an Ibiza EDM holiday was, by definition, supposed to be hedonistic![56] The 2005 feature film *It's All Gone Pete Tong* does a good job capturing island life and EDM party decadence. The crowds, activities, and parties depicted in the movie are like those I saw on both my trips.

This does not mean that Ibiza clubbers did not experience consequences from their hedonism or that drug and alcohol use did not cause problems on the island. It simply means these consequences had alternative meanings and were dealt with differently than in the United States.

For example, while in Ibiza in 2004 and 2005, I witnessed lots of drug use and talked with many people about their own consumption patterns while there. Unanimously, they told me they used more drugs than usual while club-bing on the island.[57] For instance, one night I was sitting with two young men from Scotland, in a small funky house room, inside one of the island's Big 8 clubs. One of my new friends asked me how I found the ecstasy on the island. I told him I could not comment on it. Then he told me he found the pills quite lovely here and that while he normally takes five to seven a night, he found he was doing quite well on just two. So I asked him if that meant he would do fewer than normal and he replied no, he just looked forward to having a better high doing his usual amount. In 2004, three people the students and I be-friended at our hotel had gotten so sick and run-down on ecstasy by the week's end that they could not leave their hotel rooms. One man from England told us his friend ate seven tablets one night and that he himself was on his eleventh straight pill and had been awake for two days.

The people we surveyed told us they not only did more drugs than usual while visiting Ibiza but that they did drugs they normally would not do. For example, people who normally drank alcohol and smoked weed might indulge in ecstasy or cocaine while on the island. Most attributed their drug use to the island's party climate and the general expectation of what one does on holiday.

Clearly, rave-era styles of drug use remained part of the EDM lifestyle in contemporary Ibiza despite the change in the scene's organizational form and culture from its Brit-influenced origins in the late 1980s.

Closing Thoughts

As a modernized club culture mecca, Ibiza seems positioned to carry on as a
utopian EDM haven for tourists all over Europe and, perhaps, the world. The
clubbers we surveyed were extremely optimistic about the EDM scene's continued growth and popularity not only in Ibiza but also in other parts of the
world, especially Europe. They were confident about continued musical innovation that would help keep them vested and active in the scene. For example,
the Ibiza Rocks party features U.K. guitar bands. Balearic People, a major island leisure company, also hosts live concerts that are more family oriented.

The stakeholders I interviewed were hopeful as well. None had plans to
abandon DJ-ing or promoting parties. On the contrary, they talked only about
more work and career advancement in what they described as a trend toward
EDM's greater commercialization and global popularity. They outlined the
kinds of musical innovation they saw on the horizon for EDM's future. This
included increased genre-specialization via new types of branded parties, a
continued return to certain genres anchored in the past, including acid house
and electro (1980s-like sounds and songs remixed to a faster beat), and a shift
toward live DJ performances.

Clearly, Ibiza's ability to adapt to, ward off, or invalidate the five forces of
cultural change explains its successful alteration and expansion from an early
rave colony to a global EDM hot spot. But Ibiza's success in keeping EDM alive
is not just about the successful commercialization of a music scene. It is also
about its ability to preserve and restore other periods or forms of the scene.
After all, Ibiza houses a viable underground scene for those who do not like
posh, pricey superclubs with famous DJs. It offers a tier of smaller clubs with
greater intimacy and specialization for lesser-known DJs and their fans or
friends. And it provides space and opportunity for industrious stakeholders and
loyalists who desire throwing new versions of raves, psychedelic and Goa
trance parties in open island fields and large house music parties in caves.
Similar to London, then, the Ibiza EDM scene has been able to conquer potential cultural threats and grow in all three directions of restoration, preservation, and adaptation.

In the meantime, the fate of Ibiza as an EDM clubbing mecca may follow
from how it handles growing tensions between U.K. business people's demand
for an alcohol-based pub cultural style versus local Ibencencos' and Spaniards'
desire for a more native chic. For example, during my 2005 visit, all of the
stakeholders I spoke with had an opinion about the development of a new highway that would transport clubbers from Evissa (Ibiza's "center city" with many
historical landmarks on the southeast side of the island) to San Antonio (hub

of pubs and taverns on the west side). The pub owners on the west side, who catered to young Brits on holiday, wanted the highway to more effectively transport Evissa visitors to the west side for drink specials at the smaller bars and taverns. Many native or Spanish business people were against the highway because they believed it would disrupt the island's beauty and laid-back culture. They also did not want to encourage more drunken debauchery on the west side. Local Ibencencos, especially those with few resources, had mixed feelings because building the highway would provide some off-season employment.

The tug of war between Brits, Ibencencos, and Spaniards over Ibiza's culture and industry seems destined to grow. Time will tell who comes out ahead and what factors explain the victor. As of now, it looks as if the Brits are losing their grip on the White Isle. In the 2006 season, the world-famous, British-produced Manumission party that I attended in 2004 and 2005 was shut down. So, in the final chapter of this book, I offer some speculations about other scenes in the future as well as review the book's major themes.

Twenty-First-Century Scenes, Sounds, and Selves

The cultural transformation of a music scene is a process of considerable importance to academics, music enthusiasts, and the general public. This is because a music scene's *culture*, *identity*, and *lifestyle* can matter a great deal to all kinds of people. Yet, scenes, like the music itself, are certain to change over time. This has been as true for raves or the EDM scene as for more popular scenes, including rock, hip hop, and others.

Consider the recent release of Nas's hip hop CD, *Hip Hop Is Dead* (Def Jam Records 2006). Nas's CD title suggests that he, a first-rate MC, thinks America's hip hop scene is in trouble, or at least in serious transition.[1] In the 2006, year-end issue of *Timeout New York*, Nas and journalist Jesse Serwer[2] talked about the death of hip hop in New York City—how commercialization, the development of new subgenres, and social control have contributed to hip hop's transformation. Nas thinks "repairing hip hop" to its previous state will provide "hope" for its future. Is Nas's CD the same kind of restoration cultural work that EDM's recent return to the acid house sound, discussed in Chapter 5, was? If so, then some people must believe that musical innovations can restore a scene's authentic culture and identity.[3] But does innovation work that way, or does the restoration of a music scene take much more than that?

Serwer is not optimistic about Nas's objective. He claims that the newer, southern-based subgenres of hip hop—crunk, bounce, and trap—resonate all too well with the "national mood," as they are club centered, repetitive, and sexually suggestive. In other words, Nas's call for musical restoration may not bring back the authentic culture for which some hip hop artists and fans long.[4]

The financial lure and social appeal of the cultural mainstream may be too powerful for that.

This recent example of a music scene in transition, one very different from raves and EDM, substantiates the importance of this book's subject matter, including its core questions about how and why music scenes change over time. Here, I have discussed what original cultural forms are carried forward or left behind as a music scene changes and how ordinary people, as well as powerful ones, become involved in this transformation. The purpose of this final chapter is, therefore, to review the book's main points and use them to contemplate the future of other music scenes, as well as other social groupings.

Rave Culture Recap

The story told here is one about a music scene that originated with a birth cohort (Generation X) that came of age during the 1980s' conservatism. It is about what happened to rave culture internally as it attempted to persist and change over time into what has become the modern-day EDM scene. The book also explored how this alteration was linked to scene decline and social change.

I have used the concept of scene to help understand raves' alternation and decline. Scenes with unique cultures can foster social change by establishing a new lifestyle that people can adopt and negotiate. When people participate in this scene, they become involved in shaping the social world that matters most to them. This is the type of social change discussed throughout this book. While it may not inform the pursuit of social or political movements (as seen in the subculture approach), it is important to understanding daily interactions, lifestyles, and identities of its participants. Over time, scholars have used music scenes to articulate important sociological concepts and ideas, including deviant identity, social control, youth resistance and countercultural identity, collective identity (e.g., race and nationality), and social change.

The Rave–Club Culture Continuum and In-between
Cultural Space

Understanding the transformation of any music scene or other cultural collective first requires describing how the EDM scene and rave culture changed over time. In other words, what were raves like at their origins, and what is left of them today? Chapter 2 answers this question. Briefly, raves have evolved into six basic types of events that are currently wedged somewhere between authentic rave culture and commercialized clubs. In London and Ibiza, Spain, there are even more varieties along this continuum. Two important points follow from the continuum.

The first has to do with what defines a cultural collective. A music scene, and perhaps other collectives and social worlds, has several cultural components by which participants establish or gauge authenticity. These elements include ethos, social organization, identity markers, norms, and behaviors. At a generic level, then, these five cultural traits will be useful in assisting researchers in studying other types of collectives and social worlds, for it is easy to see them at work in punk, Goth, rock, or hip hop. Consider the last. Today's underground hip hop scene, an evolution of yesterday's Old School style, boasts an ethos ("keeping it real") of a hard-knocks life with African American–centered social and political consciousness, behaviors (e.g., tagging or graffiti, seen by many as deviant), identity markers (baggy pants, tattoos, gold jewelry, Timberland boots), and a social organization (open block parties or events at underground clubs with MC-ing) related to its ethos (Watkins 2005). By understanding the cultural elements in any scene or cultural collective, we can learn about what is important to people and the nature of the connections between them and more public or institutional actors.

Yet another important lesson from Chapter 2 is that the space in-between perceived authenticity (e.g., original raves or today's underground or squat party) and commercialism (e.g., corporate raves, superstar one-offs, or branded parties) is a fruitful area for research on identity, types of cultural work, and the relationship between alternative social worlds and conventional society. The rave–club culture continuum provides insight into grassroots cultural work by everyday people as opposed to professionalized endeavors by business people. By describing the content, style, and organization of these events and the work people do to put them together, we gain further understanding of the relationship between society's mainstream and its periphery and powerless and powerful people, puzzles that sociology has wrestled with in many different areas over time. From this study, we learned that there is a lot of important social and cultural space between authenticity and mainstream commercialism. Future research ought to explore this under-studied terrain.

Collective Identity

Chapter 3 provided additional information about music scenes by documenting group or collective identities and various personal pathways to the rave and EDM scenes. The chapter began by discussing the collective identity of rave culture and how it had changed over time. Philadelphia's rave identity was anchored in the PLUR ethos—peace, love, unity, and respect—while that in London centered around something very similar. In addition, the collective identities of the past rave and current EDM scenes incorporated other "alternative" ideals that distinguished them from the cultural mainstream, including the celebration of more androgynous and asexual gender identities, norms, and behavior. In this respect, the past rave and current EDM collective identity remains in opposition or resistant to those situated in more mainstream social groupings. Before reviewing individuals' connections to EDM's collective identity, I want to point out a few insights about collective identity that can be gleaned from this study.

Song lyrics have been an important focal point for scholars writing about music, collective identity, and social change. Given this, how can the relatively lyricless dance music and the scene's lack of a direct call for social action render it capable of possessing a collective identity that would attract and connect people? In other words, what else do people rely on to establish collective identity when language is relatively absent?

From fieldwork in Philadelphia, London, and Ibiza, I showed this can be achieved by at least one form of ritual activity, dancing, coupled with a love of music. This is what united me with strangers at a club in Ibiza and what many others told me consistently connected them to the rave and EDM scenes over time (see Chapters 3 and 6). Sociologists have noted that ritual activity can be a powerful force in establishing collective identity and that language is not always required to do so. Alexander (2004: 527) has argued, "Ritual effectiveness energizes participants and attaches them to each other, increases their identification with the symbolic objects of communication, and intensifies the connection of the participants and the symbolic objects with the observing audience, the relevant 'community' at large." Many kinds of physical activity or action, not just ritual behavior or dancing, may work to shore up solidarity and define group identity. In short, coordinated and purposed group activity of all kinds motivates and unites.

Personal Identity

This brings us to individuals and their motivations for participation in scenes, celebration of unique cultures, and attachment to collective identities. A key point throughout this book is that music scenes provide identity solutions and desired lifestyles for those involved in them. Sociologist Sarah Thornton (1996: 164) observed, "Taste in music, for youth in particular, is often seen as the key to one's distinct sense of self. Youth, therefore, often embrace 'unpopular cultures' because they distinguish them in ways that the widely liked cannot." Thus, when we try to understand the future of cultural collectives—like music scenes—it might be wise to begin with such questions as, who do people want to be and how do they want to spend their time? Surely, culture and media industries have stakes in the answers to these questions, but so do many others, like government officials and agencies, parents, friends, schools, and employers, and stakeholders, artists, fans, and clubbers.

History has shown that many people will identify with the commercialized U.S. mainstream and its post–Civil Rights cultural value on image, materialism, and heightened sexuality. As this book has shown, these are values that run opposite to rave culture and the EDM scene. In a skit from his debut show on *Comedy Central*, comedian Dave Chappelle provides a good example of the mainstream identity. In his now-famous faux Mitsubishi car commercial[5] skit, Chappelle is seen driving his car. Seated beside him is a white woman dancing a version of the pop-n-lock to the classic EDM track "Days Go By" by superstar

DJs Dirty Vegas.[6] Chappelle is outraged by her, so he pulls over and throws her out of the car. Looking at the camera, he cringes and tells the viewers that music like that "makes his penis soft." She is replaced by a curvy black woman who dances provocatively in his car to hip hop. A smile returns to Chappelle's face and he is portrayed as being all right with the world.

From Chappelle's skit, we are reminded about the importance of music in shoring up identity. Chappelle's skit could be read as a rebuke of rave culture's and the modern EDM scene's more androgynous and asexual style and an endorsement of modern hip hop's more sexualized one. The current dominance of hip hop in the United States likely indicates Chappelle's skit about music and identity resonates more closely with the U.S. mainstream.

But while many young people may adopt this mainstream identity script, there will also be others who opt for something different or for what many may view as "other." These are people like Lucy, a DJ in London, who longs for more socially and politically important meaning from her music scene involvement. She told me:

> When I was in Croatia DJ-ing, I definitely got a sense of that, "being a post war state." I sensed a lot of the young people were really kind of delving into their creative sides and their art as a sort of refuge of all the bullshit going on politically. I definitely see that in some places in the world, but I don't necessarily think we are like that. In the U.K. and the U.S., I don't think we are that tuned in on stuff like that, unfortunately.

Or they are people like Michelle, who participate in music scenes for human connection and to cope with a problematic past that rendered them outsiders. During our interview, she told me:

> Yeah, just to be able to be accepted, you know, was great. Growing up and moving from place to place . . . it's hard to mesh well with other people. Eventually I started to just kind of build up this wall around me where I didn't really get to know people. Raves were a nice change because [they] connected me with people from all over the place.

In Chapter 3, I reviewed three pathways (alienation and alternative scene appeal, avoidance of gender and sexuality-based ideals, and musical and technological fascination) into the rave and EDM scenes, which were shared between respondents in Philadelphia and London (see Chapter 6). These pathways begin to document how individuals get linked up with a scene and embrace its collective identity. They are, therefore, an important way to understand the link between the individual and the larger society and culture in which he or she is located. No matter the pathway, belonging to something greater than the self defines and connects people in fulfilling activity.

Scenes, especially alternative ones, offer great appeal for people who were marginalized early in life and, for one reason or another, come to view themselves as outcasts. Such outcasts confront an interesting question: why change myself to fit the mainstream when I can find an alternative scene that fits me nicely? Fitting into such alternative spaces can be very empowering, for in developing their alternative world, these outsiders may affect the larger world as well. Even if they do not inspire social change, they remain happily entrenched in the peripheral enclave and busy themselves with shaping it. This is the very essence of the sort of social change discussed in this book: the ability of everyday people to change the world that matters to them most, the scene they identify with and live in on a daily basis.

Participant typologies emerge within many cultural collectives to establish scene authenticity or to facilitate understanding for participant involvement and scene change. Such classifications are common in everyday life and can be especially informative to topics in sociology. People tend to always designate "insiders" (i.e., loyalists, stakeholders, and hustlers) who occupy more core positions, as well as others more peripheral to the scene (i.e., clubbers, pretenders, and spillovers). These ideal types represent the variable connections people have to a music scene. When a scene's insiders categorize others involved in the scene (i.e., create ideal types), they are making statements about authenticity and defining norms for style and behavior.

How do we identify the insiders, marginal members, and outsiders of social groupings or cultural collectives? Our first tendency might be to think of insiders—especially loyalists and stakeholders—of any music scene as those who are highly committed to the scene's central activity (e.g., music and dancing) and outsiders as those who are less committed or are indifferent to it. At another level, however, the insiders of any nonconventional social grouping might be those who have shared experiences of marginality and "otherness" to mainstream culture. This more fundamental experience with alienation may explain continued identification and commitment to the "alternative" as much as artistic tastes and preferences.

Do these ideal types, both those at the core (loyalists, stakeholders, and hustlers) and those on its edges (clubbers, pretenders, and spillovers) have parallels in social groupings other than music scenes? Are they useful for understanding participation, commitment, and involvement in other social worlds? Perhaps. Certainly, all social groups get off the ground from hardworking loyalists—those most committed to the group's purpose, form, and activities. With expansion and success, stakeholders evolve and set the legitimating process in motion. Their honorable intentions can be facilitated or undermined by hustlers, who also use the group to secure financial or other personal gain. Finally, all social groups need potential recruits (i.e., clubbers) and may attract the disingenuous (i.e., pretenders and spillovers). Thus, while some of the names of these ideal types might not seem applicable outside of club culture, they may have substantive counterparts in other scenes. These categories provide useful ways for understanding the connections between a group's collective identity and individual attachment to it. Further exploring these links promises to be a fruitful area of sociological study.

Forces of Cultural Change

Understanding the raves' alteration and decline also requires examining the external forces that shaped its course. Chapter 4 identified five such factors: generational schism, commercialization, self-destructive hedonism and deviance, formal social control, and genre fragmentation and the development of subscenes. Earlier analyses have examined the effects of two factors, commercialization and formal social control. For example, rave-related drug legislation did not have the all-encompassing impact that researchers and respondents have given it; instead, local enforcement of public gathering and noise ordinances and the chill effect from potential, not actual, drug law enforcement nudged raves toward partnership with legitimate clubs, which provided momentum to the scene's commercialization. In any case, social control (of any kind) and commercialization were only two factors shaping raves' trajectory.

Perhaps the most powerful force was the schism between Generations X and Y in the United States, which was less a factor in London. An important finding here is that birth cohorts are not just groups of people born at certain historical moments. They also have strong cultural dimensions, including ideologies, values, tastes, identities, and styles. Scenes and, perhaps, other cultural collectives are defined by their host generation. In order to persist over time, they must adopt cultural and organizational styles that permit both continued involvement of their base group and the recruitment of others. They must also keep a close watch on potential intersecting forces that might indirectly exacerbate generational schism. Raves and the more modern EDM scene have not been very successful in doing this in the United States but have been far more successful doing so in London and Europe.

When people discuss the commercialization of a music scene, they often refer to artists forfeiting creativity and autonomy ("selling out") or to how other stakeholders transform cultural traits and customs for music industry commodities. The commercialization debate is less often about what happens to a scene's cultural elements, its collective identity, and its alternative lifestyle. This book has showed that commercialization compromises music scenes' culture, identity, and lifestyle. It compromises them or abandons them for a sort of commercial and conventional adaptation. Consequently, when people shift their attachment from the marginal to the conventional, all aspects and components of scenes and their cultures are jeopardized, not simply their art or cultural products. And make no mistake about it, such a shift is desired by many music scene participants with outcast roots. S. Craig Watkins (2005: 157) quotes hip hop mogul Russell Simmons saying, "The hip hop community takes pride in growth. They love big. Not cool, small and alternative. Hip hop aspires to own the mainstream."

For those with more modest goals, the life span of a music scene requires a very careful balancing act between opposition and convention. While an underground music scene must resist the lure of the mainstream in order to preserve its authenticity, it cannot allow its opposition or otherness to cripple it. Thus, another novel and powerful determinant of a music scene's long-term existence is the degree of its cultural deviance. Simply put, there are limits to how "other" or hedonistic a scene can be. When norms, behaviors, and styles cross the invisible hedonistic line, the scene loses people and dies. To prevent this, scenes must adopt forms that will guard against self-destruction and that will return respect.

Finally, there is another aspect of a scene or collective that raises the potential for cultural change. It has to do with size and diversity. As a music scene grows and encompasses more music diversity—a barometer of its success—it runs the risk of fragmenting into smaller entities because of participants' desire for musical specialization, intimacy, and homophily. The musical diversity at raves (e.g., drum and bass, hard house, trance, and techno tents or rooms) symbolized raves' cultural ethos of PLUR. But with the expansion of all genres of EDM, the proliferation of DJs and events, subscenes soon developed that specialized by genre. This created opportunities for loyalists and other fans to support a favorite style rather than having to "put up with" many different ones at large raves. Genre fragmentation, therefore, gave people a choice between supporting a diverse collective or participating in something more singular and taste specific. Minicultures or subscenes soon developed around these genres, and today they boast unique identities, lifestyles, and behaviors. For some, the alteration of a collective into smaller, more specialized scenes is desirable and an indicator of the larger scene's success. This pattern of expansion has characterized many music scenes over time as well as other types of social groupings or cultural collectives. Such change is considered common in modern, advanced nations where people desire access to what they like.

But as Alexander (2004) has pointed out, the cultural elements of the collective may or may not be carried forward into these smaller cultural enclaves. In fact, this study has shown that not only are a scene's cultural elements traded or redefined during the process of transformation, but people's willingness to honor a larger ethos and collective identity may also suffer. Today's EDM landscape is cluttered with subscenes that have not only their own styles, music, norms, and behavior but also cliques and perhaps tribes that maintain taste-defined boundaries for identity and membership. Some antagonism between people from different subscenes has become well established, and this compromises the larger goal of diversity acceptance as well as the endorsement of peace, love, unity, and respect.

The explanation for cultural change articulated in Chapter 4 is valuable for the sociological study of music scenes in several respects. First, it identified five forces that explained the alteration and decline of a music scene. These forces are not solely about culture and economics, a common narrative in the sociology of culture (Dowd 2004a, 2004b). They require consultation with literatures on deviance and social control, and youth lifestyles and collective identity. Moreover, three of the forces (generational schism, cultural hedonism and self-destruction, and genre fragmentation and subscene development) have been under-studied previously while the effects of commercialization and formal social control have been somewhat overstated—at least with respect to raves. *Rave culture*, then, identifies five important and nuanced concepts to help guide the future on scenes and other collectives.

Second, the explanation is also important because it highlights the interconnections among the five forces in explaining scene alteration and decline. This is likely to make future research challenging but also necessary and potentially even more valuable. Some of the most compelling findings can be gleaned from the relationships among the five forces, which when traced carefully can show the centrality of some forces (i.e., generational schism) over others (commercialism and formal social control).

Finally, by considering two types of "outcomes" (alteration and decline), this explanation gets into the "black box" of scene change, that is, what kinds of change are addressed. That three of the five forces produced scene alteration and decline while the other two produced only decline provides further evidence of the centrality of each force and offers a road map for future work about either scene alteration or decline. Again, future work is also needed to shore up the pathways between the concepts, and the two types of change studied require enhancement before a formal theoretical model can be stated.

Cultural Work and the Future of the EDM Scene

The split between EDM as an art form and rave culture is important in this book. It became especially important in Chapter 5 where I expanded upon Bielby's concept of grassroots cultural production by discussing three types of cultural work stakeholders do to secure EDM's present and future. They include restoration (returning to an authentic state), preservation (a compromise or holding pattern), and adaptation (assimilation or "evolution" into mainstream forms). These three forms of cultural work do not equally prioritize a scene's music and culture. While all three attempt to honor EDM's sound (its music), two (adaptation and preservation) are prepared to sacrifice its cultural elements. For example, restoration values musical integrity (a reliance on underground music or that produced outside the mainstream music industry) and a return to a more authentic rave culture. Preservation often finds itself divided between music and culture. It strives for underground musical enlightenment but often must adopt a more commercial sound. This "compromise" hinders its ability to honor the scene's authentic culture or even a more modernized variation. Finally, adaptation mostly strives for the increased popularity for EDM, which can involve leaving behind many of the scene's cultural elements.

In all three instances, it is the culture of the scene, not its music, that is most vulnerable to the cultural work expended. Thus, cultural work is challenging. Everyday music consumers often make cultural work, especially preservation and restoration, even more difficult. This is because people often care less about culture and collectives than they do about their own tastes or aspirations. This brings me to the future of music scenes. What lies ahead for some contemporary scenes, and how will they be impacted by external forces?

Twenty-First-Century Scenes, Sounds, and Selves

In the closing section, I want to briefly consider the applicability of this book's findings for the future of three music scenes: the EDM scene, gay circuit parties, and mash-ups.

The EDM Scene

Over the course of my fieldwork, I have seen several new developments in the EDM scene that are attempting to chart its future. Some of these innovations are adaptation oriented, especially where DJs, producers, and music are concerned. For example, the production, performance, and sound of EDM increasingly resemble those of a live rock band.[7] There is a sense that a DJ once could get gigs and rise to popularity based on his or her expertise in spinning other people's music live at raves or burning his or her mixshow onto a "compilation" CD. But soon, DJs found themselves pressured to produce original music in order to advance and establish themselves in the scene. The production of original music by EDM DJs led to the "artist album," which was distinguished from the compilation CD. Artist albums contained original tracks produced by the DJ. Tracks on artist albums are generally shorter, and they may or may not be mixed together. This newer form makes them more conducive to the commercial radio format.

Today, artist albums are produced largely by superstar DJs, who are under tremendous pressure to put out new artist albums and compilation CDs on a regular basis. Even compilation CDs are becoming more labor intensive to produce as newer technologies in music production, sampling, and mixing tempt DJs to use new ways to layer existing tracks for new sounds.

But just when the standards for EDM's tangible products would change, so too would those for live performance. For example, when I first started attending EDM parties, it was common to see DJs spinning vinyl records or using CD mixers. Today, many use laptops and other computers to piece together samples live (on-the-spot) into new music just as a saxophone player or hip hop MC might freestyle a solo. A difference is that the live electronic DJ is freestyling all night long or for many hours. This is labor intensive, but the novelty of it and its artistic value often draw an audience that promoters and other stake-holders long for.

In my studies, I have seen such live performances alter the interaction of clubbers with the DJ. On several occasions in Philadelphia, Miami, and Ibiza, I have seen a DJ detach from the audience in order to focus on his computer screen and I have seen clubbers standing still on the dance floor watching, not dancing to, the DJ's performance.

It is developments like these that make me pessimistic about the return to or preservation of rave culture's ethos and collective identity even though I am enthused by the musical innovation and believe that EDM will continue to develop. Like many of the people profiled in this study, I long for the continued coupling of a scene's music with its more collective cultural elements. How-ever, signs in the United States point to continued musical innovation via new genres of EDM (e.g., electro, techno funk) but not necessarily rejuvena-tion or celebration of the scene's culture. In places like London and Ibiza, EDM scenes seem destined for a different course. There, both the music and the cultural aspects of the EDM scene are better situated to survive into the future.

There are some glimmers of hope for EDM culture in the United States. Some of the city's subscenes are thriving among committed groups of loyalists and stakeholders. For example, the Philadelphia techno scene is relatively small, but very hot, with frequent and unique parties by Funkshun, a small underground promotional group that puts on weekly, monthly, and one-off par-ties throughout the city. Moreover, some of these subscenes host weeklies, monthlies, and superstar one-offs that, at times, support social causes or chari-ties. Not all events operate for business purposes only. And EDM scenes in the United States will likely be influenced by sociopolitical involvement of EDM stakeholders elsewhere. Consider Paul Van Dyk's[8] participation in the 2002 Rock the Vote campaign. He campaigned heavily in the United States for an MTV-based get-out-the-vote effort. On October 1, 2006, Van Dyk was awarded a medal of honor by the government of Berlin for his accomplishment and dedi-cation to dance music and social issues. At the ceremony, Van Dyk claimed, "When I started DJ-ing, electronic music didn't really involve itself with wider social issues. I felt that the energy within our culture is so strong that it could be put to wider use." Countless other superstar and lesser-known DJs have also adopted socially conscious practices and activities. Thus, EDM's link to liber-alism and social justice may continue even as its image and lifestyle move in a more commercial or mainstream direction.

Gay Men's Circuit Parties

Closely related to the EDM scene is the gay male circuit scene. Using the terms outlined in this book, circuit parties are large, superstar one-offs featur-ing EDM (mostly progressive and vocal house). They are attended mostly by gay men. The name *circuit* comes from the practice of gay men traveling to cities for such parties throughout the calendar year. These highly commercialized events are synchronized to prevent competition and maximize turnout. Gay men are said to "do the circuit." The parties last all night and feature lots of drug use, especially ketamine and crystal methamphetamine. In these respects, circuit parties are like early raves. However, unlike raves and the modern EDM scene, circuit parties are highly sexualized and feature lots of promiscuity that has caused considerable public health concern in the United States.

Circuit parties are a modern-day innovation of an "out and proud" gay culture. Their predecessors date from the early twentieth century, when gays and lesbians gathered socially at tea dances, that is, late-afternoon and early-evening events held at private homes or clubs of wealthy socialites. People waltzed or danced the polka rather than pulsating to today's latest house music. Gay bars in major metropolitan areas in the 1950s and 1960s followed and became central to a more public gay culture because they promoted shared and positive identity, enabled community building and political activism, and spawned gay-oriented neighborhoods. Gay bars soon became entwined in the Civil Rights movement of the 1960s, including the post-Stonewall protests.

Disco exploded in the 1970s as Americans prioritized leisure activities—and leisure suits—in an era of heightened liberalism. This new cultural phenomenon stormed the urban landscape and is a direct precursor of today's gay nightlife scene, including circuit parties. Disco allowed gays and lesbians to establish a more open homosexual identity, one that celebrated same-sex love. It was also hedonistic, valuing physical attractiveness, up-tempo dancing, sexual adventure, and excessive drug (especially stimulants like cocaine) and alcohol use.[9]

The gay circuit scene is a modern offshoot of disco's death. Once hugely popular and profitable, however, it is showing signs of transformation and decay. At issue is the sexual and drug-related hedonism of what society considers a very dangerous group: gay men, especially HIV-positive ones. Circuit parties are notorious for a great deal of largely unprotected sex and the ingestion of large quantities of alcohol and other toxins. Certainly, the scene is not all drugs and sex, but many studies[10] show that substance abuse is high, equaling or surpassing levels during the height of the rave movement. Another major issue is crystal methamphetamine, ecstasy, and Viagra use with increased HIV and syphilis prevalence, all of which are prevalent at gay male circuit parties.

In 2004 and 2005, I volunteered at a couple of Philadelphia's gay male circuit parties and witnessed lots of hedonism and risky behaviors. However, the most compelling thing I saw was the age range of the crowd: they seemed much older than the typical clubber or insider I saw at routine EDM events in the city. I gauged the men's ages at these two circuit parties between about thirty and sixty-five. There were very few young gay men at these two circuit parties. I asked party promoters, other gay volunteers, and some gay men I knew from my study about this, and they told me that the circuit crowd was aging and that young gay men either could not afford to attend them (their high prices are a consequence of commercialization) or were turned off by the scene's "de-cadence," especially its drug use (Dennis, a young gay male respondent, mentioned this in Chapter 2). Nationally, circuit parties continue, but their attendance seems to have peaked for the moment. Their vulnerability to what looks like a generational schism, excessive hedonism, and high-end commercialization seems be hurting the scene and may act to further cripple it in the future. However, like many other profitable cultural commodities, circuit parties might be "made over" into a different experience designed to attract a younger population.

Mash-ups

Currently, the dominating music scenes in Philadelphia are hip hop and commercial Top 40, with salsa and mash-ups close behind. I want to briefly profile mash-ups here because many of the EDM respondents and informants I interviewed, and many of the clubs that used to host EDM parties, are now involved with the mash-up scene. Mash-ups are events where DJs spin dramatically different genres of music together. For example, a mash-up DJ might play a hip hop track and follow with a rock or reggae track. A very good mash-up DJ might play two very different types of music at the same time. In other words, he or she might layer some hip hop lyrics over a rock or pop song. The goal is to "mash" together very diverse sounds that would not normally mix.

It is not difficult to see that mash-ups would appeal to EDM fans. There is musical diversity at mash-ups just as there was with raves, and there is lots of technological expertise, which also attracted many to EDM. The culture of mash-ups also has things in common with rave culture and the current EDM scene. The events celebrate diversity. In fact, the mash-ups I have attended have been more racially diverse than most EDM parties I have witnessed.

There are also aspects of mash-ups that may fit them better to the U.S. mainstream than raves and might bode well for the scene's future. For example, currently there are few mash-up superstar DJs, so events tend to be less expensive, even though mash-up DJs are very talented and well respected, like Philadelphia natives Hollartronix.[11] Also, mash-ups are an alcohol-based culture, not a drug-oriented one, and bouncers and club owners have told me that mash-up clubbers do not really cause them any problems. Finally, the image or style of mash-ups resonates well with the mainstream. The hipster style of dress is marketed by major retailers like Urban Outfitters, who, incidentally, have sponsored mash-ups in the city.

Given this, it looks as if mash-ups will likely continue being popular in Philadelphia and elsewhere. There are signs that mash-ups are growing nationally and internationally. Branded mash-ups now travel between U.S. cities, and some EDM superstar DJs are now delving into mash-up music and mix CDs.

In short, mash-ups seem to have what it takes to persist as a viable scene in the future: musical diversity and innovation coupled with a user-friendly culture that many can enjoy without significant consequence.

Closing

We cannot take for granted that the cultural components of music scenes will always prevail or be preserved, restored, or even valued. Nor can we assume that the cultures that emerge around other art forms or social issues will, either. Culture, ideology, and identity are strong, yet susceptible to many social forces with ample uncertainty. While this book showed that five forces (generational schism, commercialization, self-destructive hedonism and deviance, formal social control, and genre fragmentation and the development of sub-scenes) helped transform rave culture and may also work to impact others, surely they are not the only forces of change at play. At least one other major force, technological advance, routinely changes both music and culture.[12]

> *iPods and the five minute culture.*
> —Elite Force (tech funk DJ)[13]

Technology has changed music's production, its form, and, perhaps most importantly, its dissemination and consumption. The culture of a music scene and its collective identity and lifestyle are not automatically affected by technological advance, but its music often is. For example, consider the iPod and the revolution in music distribution and consumption that is sweeping the nation and, perhaps, other parts of the world. Could empowering individuals to download particular songs they like fundamentally impact how musicians, including DJs and producers, do their work? It has already done so. Will downloading tracks level yet another blow to music scenes? That might just depend on the genre of music and the particular scene in question. My forecast is that the EDM scene—and even EDM itself—could be especially hard hit, at least in the immediate short term, by the impeding war over personal digital assistants and music devices of all kinds.

Recall that the rave DJ's and the EDM mixshow's genius lay in the seamless fusion of tracks into an electronic symphony that transported the listener to another place. A symphony by Beethoven or Bach worked in the same way. Individual EDM tracks were, consequently, given meaning by their connection to others in a DJ's set. Raves, fans, and clubbers jumped on board and let their electronic captains transport them to awakenings, ecstasy, and acceptance. How will these journeys fare with the advent of iPod-like devices and the downloading of single tracks? Downloading mixshows to an iPod or similar device is currently possible, but few are available at the iTunes or other Internet music stores.[14] Can enlightenment be achieved by shopping iPod's music store or Beatport.com's .mp3 files? Can a culture's ethos be captured by a single track? Will those who download songs at their computers feel peace, love, unity, and respect with others who download the same songs? Probably not. Scenes and collectives will likely suffer, since the rest of their cultural components may be left behind as their music evolves. Artistic vision may also suffer a blow. Philosopher Alan Kirby (2006: 36) recently argued,

> The downloading and mixing and matching of individual tracks on an iPod, selected by the listener, was certainly prefigured by the fan's creation of compilation tapes a generation ago. But a shift has occurred, in that what was once a marginal pastime of the fan has become the dominant and definitive way of consuming music, rendering the idea of an album as a coherent work of art, a body of integrated meaning, obsolete.

When the tech funk DJ Elite Force called iPods a five-minute culture, he was lamenting the trend away from the EDM mixshow and album to single five-minute tracks. What he loves about mixshows and quality books is their ability to transport him to a better place with deeper meaning. Music consumption that is driven by individual selection of "preferred tracks" obstructs the vision the EDM DJ tries to convey to us via his or her mixshow journey. Recall David Alvarez from Chapter 1. Is his objective hampered or facilitated by the iPod?

However, outfitted with the latest technology[15] and caught up in a tsunamilike trend, twenty-first-century young Americans may increasingly ignore cultural meaning, collective identity, and human connection in their desire to custom-fit the world to themselves. So what will happen to people like Lucy and Michelle who want music and its culture to provide sociopolitical awareness, belonging, and connection? Maybe they will remain on the outside or, perhaps, alone in their own little worlds, shuffling tunes on their iPods to dreams about the lives they really want to live.

Appendix

The Ethnographic Approach

Loic Wacquant (2003: 1466) recently defined ethnography as "social research based on the close-up, on-the-ground observation of people and institutions in real time and space, in which the investigator embeds herself near (or within) the phenomenon so as to detect how and why agents on the scene act, think and feel the way they do." In general, ethnography is the systematic investigation of phenomena within the environment in which they occur. Ethnographies often include talking and interacting with common people located in settings of interest, such as prisons, schools, jazz clubs, or EDM events. Beyond this, ethnographies today are highly variable (see Holstein and Gubrium 2003 for a discussion of these styles). The one I conducted and report on here fits this description.

This book derives from three years of intensive ethnography; it draws on several kinds of data about a wide range of people and events that constitutes the EDM scene between 2003 and 2005 in Philadelphia. In-depth interviews with diverse groups of scene participants (respondents and key informants) provided testimony or narratives about rave culture and the modern EDM scene. In addition, direct observation of EDM events by me[1] provides another source of information. While these two types of data comprised the bulk of my fieldwork, I also collected a lot of additional information via other channels. Some of these included collecting event flyers, casually interacting with people at record stores several times a week, weekly visits to EDM Web sites and chat rooms, regular purchasing and reading of five leading EDM magazines,[2] and ongoing e-mail communication with people I met over the course of the project. The information discussed in Chapter 6 reflects a similar approach employed in London (June and July of 2004) and in Ibiza, Spain (seven days in July 2004 and ten days in July 2005). Before describing the details of my data collection in these places, I want to review a few important points about my overall approach.[3]

These data, and my strategies in collecting and analyzing them, combine two contemporary approaches in ethnographic methods: peopled ethnography (Fine 2003) and autoethnography (Anderson 2006). Both are modern variations of qualitative approaches originating in the past (see Adler and Adler 1987; Glaser and Strauss 1967; Merton 1988). To begin, a peopled ethnography seeks a conceptual understanding of the phenomena in question and is theoretically purposed rather than simply offering detail on a particular phenomenon (see also Snow et al. 2003 on this point). For example, my early conversations with key informants—including those I had in virtual space with DJs on clubradio.net—raised questions about cultural change, collective identity, and grassroots cultural work. From the start of this project, I realized that, in addition to describing the current EDM scene, I would need to draw on the sociological literatures on culture, scenes, collective and personal identity, deviance, and drug abuse.

Peopled ethnographies build on existing research (Fine 2003). Over the months of my data collection, I read many studies of music scenes, raves and drug use, and other youth scenes to find concepts and ideas I might need to address in my project. Especially helpful were the culturally based ethnographies of rave and club culture in the United Kingdom and Europe. While I also drew on studies of social problems (i.e., illicit drug use) in the United States, I found this work less useful because my early informants and respondents talked about their rave and EDM experiences as cultural matters, not simply as experiences in deviance or with drugs. While the more culturally oriented literature on raves and EDM documented their rise and peak in the mid- to late 1990s, there have not been many studies exploring what happened after raves peaked. Thus, I view my study as a way to carry on the conversation about raves and the EDM scene.

Peopled ethnographies also study individuals and small groups where they are located (Fine 2003). The interviews I conducted, with both key informants and respondents, were with people active in the EDM scene. In Chapter 6, I report on those active in scenes in London and Ibiza.[4] The people I talked with had diverse ties to and motivations for interaction in their respective scenes; they ranged from those who occasionally attended EDM events to more loyal fans and diehards from the rave era. They included both low-level and higher-level stakeholders with varying amounts of fame and clout.

Peopled ethnographies also often collect data in multiple research sites (Fine 2003). Classic ethnographies more often examined only one place (such as Laud Humphries's *Tea Room Trade* and William Foote Whyte's *Streetcorner Society*). Thus, they were primarily studies of particular settings. The questions that interested me were broad and would not be well served by a study of a particular club, bar, festival, rave, or EDM event. They required extensive fieldwork across numerous sites: interviews with many people, direct observation of lots of EDM events for several hours each, and attendance at conferences, seminars, and forums. My fieldwork provided me with detailed information on EDM scenes in London and Ibiza, Spain. Moreover, through my experiences in and conversations with people in these locations, I also learned about scenes in Baltimore, Los Angeles, New York, Washington, D.C., Miami, and San Francisco as well as Panama, Brazil, Germany, Belgium, Calgary, and much of the United Kingdom.

Finally, the analysis reported here relies heavily on elaborate field notes, a final characteristic of peopled ethnographies (Fine 2003). During my study, I amassed more than 600 pages of handwritten notes from the interviews alone, in addition to approximately 750 single-spaced electronic pages of interview transcripts. I also took 100 pages of electronic, single-spaced notes from my direct observation of club events in Philadelphia. Ultimately, the hours of informal interaction at the record store, surveying of Internet sites, reading of EDM magazines, and other activities were simply too many to count. And it is impossible for me to accurately count the number of e-mails I exchanged with respondents and key informants. I used three different computers during this project, and I tried to retain e-mail communications in a separate mailbox directory. However, even though each of these computers has more than 1,000 notes in each directory, many exchanges have likely been deleted or lost during routine computer operations. When I use the word *fieldwork* in this book, I am making a general reference to all of these materials.

Data "tallies" in London included 200 handwritten pages of field notes (interviews and direct observation), 50 single-spaced electronic pages of field notes (interviews and direct observation of EDM events), and 300 single-spaced electronic pages of interview transcription. Data collected in Ibiza, Spain, were recorded largely in written notebooks in both 2004 and 2005, accounting for about 300 pages of field notes.

The vignettes from EDM events in Chapters 1, 2, 3, 5, and 6 follow a second ethnographic strategy, autoethnography. Autoethnographies are those conducted by investigators who are both observers of and participants in the scene in question (Merton 1988). Occupancy of this "dual role" usually results in the researcher becoming a sort of insider to the scene she is studying. This is something I first described in Chapter 1 and have revisited throughout the text. There are five main aspects of autoethnographies. They include that the investigator (1) has a known status as both a complete member and researcher, (2) demonstrates analytic reflexivity (i.e., how her dual role might have influenced her own findings), (3) has a narrative visibility of herself in the text, (4) has an ongoing dialogue with study participants beyond herself, and (5) has a commitment to theoretical analysis (Anderson 2006). Each of these five characteristics was discussed throughout the book but especially in the vignettes from direct observation. Additional attention to these matters is given in the following text.

Interviews with Respondents and Key Informants

Today, qualitative researchers use many styles of interviewing (Holstein and Gubrium 2003). My approach fused more modern characteristics with those from the past. I conducted face-to-face, in-depth interviews—lasting about 1.5 to 2 hours each—with the twenty-seven respondents. In London, I conducted in-depth interviews with fifteen respondents who were similar to the Philadelphia group (see Chapter 6). They lasted, on average, the same amount of time as those in Philadelphia.

The in-depth interview guide[5] included semistructured and open-ended questions about the respondent's background, living situation and lifestyle, involvement and commitment to the EDM scene and interaction therein, and experiences with drugs and other types of deviance. Thus, the respondent interviews were more structured than those done for many contemporary studies. However, by revealing and discussing my own biography and attachment to the scene and by encouraging respondents to discuss what they believed relevant or to elaborate on things they thought important, portions of the interviews were more interactive and power between myself and respondents was more shared. This also followed the principles of autoethnography. In short, the interviews sought to balance my own questions with respondents' ideas about what was important to them.

Respondent interviews took place at a private office in the record store, at a coffee shop nearby, or at my flat in London. The interviews followed an informed consent process (approved by my university's Institutional Review Board) and were tape-recorded for later transcription by an undergraduate research assistant on campus.

No set interview guide was utilized with key informants or stakeholders in Philadelphia, London, or Ibiza.[6] Questions and discussion were based on their knowledge, position, or expertise. Thus, I did not obtain detailed personal information from them since the reason for talking with them was to obtain their expertise on scene happenings. This resulted in variable key informant interview content and length. I did ask each a few basic background questions (see Chapters 3 and 6 for a description).

Key informant interviews were generally not tape-recorded, and they did not require locations that were as secluded. Again, there was less need for privacy due to the focus on their expertise rather than their personal lives or experiences with sensitive topics like drug use, so most key informant interviews could be conducted at restaurants or coffee shops.

Finally, in 2004, my students and I administered short surveys to forty sunbathing clubbers on our hotel beach, Playa en Bossa, which is the clubbers' beach. I did not repeat this in 2005. Instead, I conducted "expert" interviews with ten scene stakeholders on the island (see Chapter 6 for more detail).

Recruitment

Many qualitative studies use ethnographic mapping to identify locations of interest and where the social world in question is located. From there, sampling tends to proceed along a few different lines. Two are respondent-driven sampling (RDS models) and live recruitment (see Heckathorn 1997). I believe that when coupled together, such recruitment can reduce selection bias and improve the study's reliability.

Recruitment began with ethnographic mapping to identify people for the Philadelphia component of the study. This involved identifying an area or location where lots of subjects could be found and beginning recruitment therein. In this case, recruiting respondents and identifying key informants for this study began at the record store where I met people enmeshed in the Philadelphia EDM scene and learned about events and parties in the city. From there, recruitment took two pathways.

The first was a respondent-driven model (RDS model), which relied on using respondents or informants to recruit others for the study. Early on, employees at the record store—Rick, Tony, Doug, William, Chris, and Jon, as well as Cameron, the store's owner—acted as both key informants and respondent recruiters for interviews. Two were paid an hourly fee for such referrals, interview setups, and weekly reports in scene happenings. The people they referred to my study subsequently referred still others, and so on. The theory behind this approach is that bias will be reduced as respondent networks fan out to those whom researchers may or may not have been able to identify. Still, issues remain. Bias can persist if early contacts are situated within the same social networks, and the RDS model requires lots of time and very large sample sizes before the researcher can get outside original networks.

The tables on respondents' characteristics in Chapter 3 show that I ran into some of this bias, as my sample overrepresents scene insiders, who were linked to the record store employees. Live recruitment during direct observation was an alternative recruitment strategy, one that permitted me quick access to unrelated respondents. It helped reduce selection bias by discovering new respondents or opening up new networks of respondents. There are, however, problems with live recruitment. To begin, most people did not want to talk about anything academic or "serious" while at an event or club, so rejections were common. Some were also suspicious of my requests, for interviews, live at clubs. My age contributed to this suspicion. I was older than many clubbers in Philadelphia and, therefore, sometimes viewed as out of place. This suspicion was greatest at the more commercial events with big crowds where few people knew me. It was less the case at more underground spots, where people recognized me, but recruiting live there would likely yield more of the same pool I got from store employees. Still, I was able to recruit about eight people live at EDM events. I paid them $20 to refer others, giving me five additional respondents.

Key informants were identified with similar techniques. Most were recommended for their expertise, credentials, experience, and availability. As I learned about the local scene and the people active in it, I started asking my key informants to help secure others for interviewing. They were happy to do so.

For the most part, recruitment and interviewing were easy and quick and nearly everyone I approached agreed to talk with me. I managed to identify and interview the twenty-seven respondents in about six months. Interviews with key informants unfolded over a longer period of time. There was such excitement about the project and eagerness to assist me from key informants that at times I simply could not keep up with the fieldwork given my class schedule and other professional and personal responsibilities. For example, in October of 2004, I wrote in my field journal:

> It is Friday morning and I've decided to catch up on some journaling for the past few weeks. I have been doing lots of interviewing—typically three to four per week. The schedule is kicking my butt and my attempts to keep up with it are costing me more than 70 hours per week. I cannot maintain this pace long, as doing so would result in something else having to suffer—like my teaching.

This heavy workload is partially what justified the addition of Philip, a graduate student, toward the end of data collection. I needed assistance to keep up with the work and wanted a fresh set of eyes and ears about the scene. Also, near the end of my ethnography, I received a larger grant from the National Institute of Justice to study the differences and similarities between Philadelphia's dance and hip hop scenes with respect to substance abuse and crime. The data collection requirements of that project were also demanding.

London recruitment was more challenging (see Chapter 6) and followed a slightly different convention: snowball sampling (Glaser and Strauss 1967). Snowball sampling is a common way to identify respondents for qualitative interviewing. It is conceptually like RDS models but is not formalized with financial payment. It relies on respondent referrals; that is, one respondent provides the name of another, for possible interviewing. Half of the London participants were recruited this way, that is, from an initial contact I made via clubradio.net. The others were identified at club events and on a busy house music Web site or chat room.

The stakeholders I interviewed in Ibiza (2005) were referred to me by Balearic People (BP). The length of my stay in 2005 disallowed the recruitment of a more representative sample of island stakeholders. Consequently, this is a shortcoming of my fieldwork. Still, the ten stakeholders had worked many years among them on the island and with different promotional groups at many different clubs and bars. Thus, they offer a good snapshot of the island scene.

The forty clubbers surveyed on the Playa en Bossa beach in Ibiza (2004) were recruited by the students and me live, with no respondent referrals or assistance from island stakeholders. There is no way to assess how representative they are of island clubbers. Still, our goal was to get some sense of who holidayed in Ibiza for the EDM scene. Our surveys were brief (took about fifteen minutes each) but thorough. We gave people five euros each for them. Please see Chapter 6 for more information about them.

Direct Observation of EDM Events

As indicated in Chapters 2 and 6, my data collection also featured direct observation of about thirty-three EDM events in Philadelphia and ten events (a total of fifty hours) in London in 2004; seven events (a total of forty hours) in Ibiza in 2004; and six parties (a total of twenty-five hours) in Ibiza in 2005. Direct observation is a complicated, difficult type of data collection. Perhaps more than any other method, it requires a careful balancing of securing information on prespecified items of interest with an ear for novelty, spontaneity, and the unanticipated. Attending to these things requires standards, flexibility, and competence on the part of the investigator. The ethnographer must learn to cede or regain control during what can be chaotic interactions. I found achieving this balance at EDM events very challenging, and eventually so did Philip and other students I employed on the project.

The nightclub is like other settings in some respects and very different in others. Nightclubs have formal and informal norms and codes of operation. We enter them knowing what to expect, yet most of us hope to, and often do, encounter the unexpected as well. Because nightclubs and bars are leisure spots, heavily defined by courtship, sexuality, appearance, and drinking expectations, they are difficult to consider as places of social science research. It is tricky to remain sufficiently detached to document and discover activities and patterns. Here, I describe how I met some of these challenges.

To begin, the selection of events for direct observation followed from key informants' and respondents' referrals, as well as promotional flyers posted at the record store or distributed at other events, and from Sean O'Neal's column "DJ Nights" in the *Philadelphia City Paper*. These sources identified a range of EDM events in the area, including events held during weeknights and on weekends (lasting different amounts of time) in bars, lounges, nightclubs, warehouses, galleries, and festival grounds. Some were genre-specific events, while others had a multigenre presence.

The selection of events for observation in London and Ibiza was similar, although key informants played a lesser role in referring me to events since my networks there were much smaller. In London, I drew heavily from the weekly leisure guide *Timeout* to select direct observation events. Several major cities across the globe, including U.S. cities like Chicago and New York, publish a *Timeout* for residents and tourists. London's *Timeout* had weekly listings of EDM parties by genre (techno, house trance, drum and bass, etc).

In Ibiza, club events are easy to identify because they are the island's major tourist attraction and the basis for the local economy. There are billboards everywhere announcing parties and lots of local magazines that do the same. In 2004, I attended events with strong reputations and DJs I admired. These were all held at the largest, most prestigious clubs on the island. In 2005, I broadened my observation to lesser-known events and clubs because I needed diverse representation and the number of my contacts on the island had expanded. Taken together, the events and clubs in my London and Ibiza observations are representative of the EDM scenes located therein. The exception to this is an underrepresentation of squat or illegal parties in London and Ibiza. I was simply not networked well enough nor had I spent enough time in either location to identify and visit them.

The purpose of the direct observation was to obtain information on the culture of EDM as it unfolds live. Direct observation also helped generate new thoughts and ideas not previously considered or foreseen. While observing, I noted characteristics about the event's setting (physical and structural conditions, security, crowding, use of space, cleanliness, and physical evidence of drug or alcohol use), the demographic makeup of event attendees, identity markers, and patterns of behavior and their consequences as they unfold over the course of the evening. While most clubbers were likely only concerned with participating in event activities, as an autoethnographer or observer-participant, I had to also record events and conversations. I agree with Patricia A. Adler and Peter Adler (1987: 10) that this often made my fieldwork "near[ly] schizophrenic in its frenzied multiple focus."

I took notes while at the event on small notebooks[7] and later typed up a second, more interpretive version on my computer. These second "cuts" permitted sociological elaboration on what I witnessed and heard, the tracking of patterns and development of concepts, and personal reflections on how, perhaps, I was affecting my own data collection and how it was affecting me. I used the same note-taking strategy during the interviews.

The following is an excerpt from my computer field journal. It is a second cut of notes taken live during observation in June 2004 in London. It focuses on the personal impact of observation on me:

> It is 2pm Sunday afternoon and I just woke up. Last night and this morning, I was at one of London's most posh nightclubs—a guest of DJ S. He is a contact I made via the PF chat room—which is dedicated to those in house music in London. I stayed at the club from 11:30pm Sat evening until 5:45am today. Basically, I closed the club. This is the first time I have done that. Staying until 6am is hard. There is a big differ-

ence between 4:30am and 6am, at least to me. This night-time culture is surreal. You go out at the end of one day and stay out until the beginning of the next day. You arrive when it's dark and leave when the sun's out. And if you want to sleep, you piss away the best part of the day— the morning and afternoon, an especially evil crime in the summer on lovely days like today. Yet, I was invited to an after-party at a gay club that would last from 6am until 2pm. I have not yet been able to last or make it to an after-party. I cannot stay up that long. The caffeine fails me and the "sleep capital" gained from earlier naps has been spent a while ago. Of course, drugs aren't an option. My feet were so swollen last night. My eyes were dried out with my contact lenses pasted to them. I lost yet another pair of lenses last night. It was too painful to keep them in, so on the dance floor I tossed them.

Analytic Strategy for Making Sense of the Data

One of the defining features of ethnographies and other qualitative methods is their ability to produce current, thorough, and indigenous accounts. In other words, qualitative approaches are superior in capturing more comprehensive, detailed, personal accounts from the people under investigation. This quality, ultimately, burdens the ethnographer with managing and analyzing mountains of information.

Qualitative data management and analysis are formidable tasks. My experience has been that effectively doing them requires ongoing analysis throughout the project rather than waiting until data collection has ended. It also requires being flexible enough to change (i.e., interview questions, observational criteria, venues, etc.) as the fieldwork requires and as my presence or status as a researcher evolves over time. This kind of analytic reflexivity is congruent with the autoethnographic approach.

For example, early in this project I adopted a comprehensive style of note-taking (Wolfinger 2002), which included writing down as much as I possibly could about what I saw or heard. I took notes "live" during the interviews and while observing events[8] and then typed up a more interpretive second cut later at home on my laptop. This strategy allowed me to capture more information initially and then elaborate on it sociologically and personally soon thereafter. In the fall of 2004, I wrote in my journal:

> The interviews are going well. This week, I did three and have another scheduled for Sunday. I am still hearing new things from respondents— especially about the local scene.

Later on, as I began to see patterns and hear similar things, I shifted toward a style of note-taking that coded unique things during my fieldwork. So, by the beginning of 2005, I wrote:

I am taking notes during interviews, but I'm not writing everything down as I used to. This makes the interview more interactive but it may also increase my dependence on tape transcribing. I am looking for an undergraduate student to transcribe tapes right now and will have to see who applies. In the mean time, I have hand-written notes about the interviews, but will not spend the time typing them up electronically since I have them and the eventual electronic transcript. This means that when I start writing the book—or get ready to do so—I will have to comb the notebooks first to make a list with novel themes and ideas which emerged from specific interviews. Then I can use this list in the analysis and writing.

Nicholas H. Wolfinger (2002) calls coding the novel and unique aspects of fieldwork a "salience-hierarchy approach." It is an advance of classic ideas about reaching saturation (i.e., hearing the same thing over and over again) using a grounded theory approach.[9] In other words, at a certain point in data collection, when the researcher starts to hear a lot of the same things, he or she shifts to keeping track of new things mentioned in interviews or witnessed during observation instead of writing notes about everything learned.

Establishing this kind of salience to novel information eventually produced many of the concepts, typologies, and other patterns written about in previous chapters. An example of this is the discovery of insider and outsider identity types. Attention to novelty within these two types eventually produced even more detail (i.e., the various kinds of insiders and outsiders) that enriched the concept and further specified personal and collective identity within the modern EDM scene. Therefore, shifting from the comprehensive style of note-taking to a salience-hierarchy approach embodies the traditional canons of reaching saturation via a grounded theory approach (Glaser and Strauss 1967).

Beyond the analysis that followed from two stages of field note–taking, my analysis followed fairly standard practices in qualitative research. Once the field notes and interview transcripts were keyed electronically, I used Word Perfect to produce a vocabulary or thesaurus of words that commonly appeared in the interview transcripts or observation field notes. From this list, I began systematically coding the electronic materials. I used Atlas.ti to do some of this. It is a qualitative analysis program commonly used by social scientists. However, my continual reading and rereading of the transcripts and field journals in Word Perfect also permitted coding of text portions.

Reflexivity

Throughout this book, I have addressed some of the core principles of the autoethnographic approach, including reflexivity. To reiterate, reflexivity is about ascertaining the effects the researcher might have had on the project, for example, the respondents' accounts and live interaction with people at club events and the record store. In short, how did I influence my own data, information, and findings? While no researcher can be aware of all of the ways in which she influenced her findings, reflexivity simply asks that we consider the possibilities. A few come to mind. They have to do with my age and my professional status as a professor studying the scene.

In Chapter 6, I noted that participants in the current EDM scenes in London and Ibiza seemed older to me on average than those in the U.S. scene. As such, I believe that I was perceived as more "out of place" in the Philadelphia scene than in the London or Ibiza scene. I also felt more out of place in Philadelphia's EDM parties, especially the corporate raves. At one, a young man I passed stopped me and said, "Oh, you're kinda good-looking for an older lady."

My perceived age discrepancy with the Philadelphia participants was especially the case before others began viewing me as an insider. I could sense that some people questioned my attendance at events and likely kept their distance from me. I even heard through others that some believed me to be a Drug Enforcement Administration (DEA) agent or some kind of law enforcement officer. Certainly, this hampered my live recruitment of respondents, but it did not impact the notes I took at the events. More often, I just blended into the crowds and scampered off to a bathroom stall to jot down my observations.

My age and professional status had another kind of effect in the interview situations. There is no doubt that some people put on their best face when chatting with me. Being part of a book project was exciting to many and they wanted to be identified in it. Their hopes for "fifteen minutes of fame" changed when I told the respondents that I would use pseudonyms in the book and explained the importance of doing so (anonymity and confidentiality). By the time the long interviews were over, most respondents had become, by their own admissions, quite open and honest. My use of modern interview techniques (Holstein and Gubrium 2003) to establish shared identity and to diffuse my own power helped facilitate this outcome.

Considering how my own feelings about and experiences in the EDM scene influenced my work is difficult as well. Make no mistake about it: I love EDM and many aspects of rave culture and modern underground parties. It saddens me that such a music and culture are not more widely embraced in the United States, and this is a reason I like traveling to the United Kingdom and Europe. Many other music scene ethnographers have felt the same way about their work. Ross Haenfler (2006) and Lauraine LeBlanc (1999), for example, gave us very personal accounts of their involvement in the sXe and punk scenes from a very early age. Like theirs, my sentiments about the music scene I studied reflect those I interviewed, met, and interacted with. Obviously, this subject is important to me, since I spent five or more years studying it. Yet, my enthusiasm for and commitment to the EDM scene did not prevent me from seeing the obvious: rave culture has significantly declined in the United States and been reshaped into something more like everything else.

Finally, I want to revisit the issue of my abstinence from drugs as a potential impact on my data and findings. It has been mostly other scholars, not scene participants, who have questioned whether I can "truly" understand or represent the rave experience if I did not take drugs over the course of my project. This challenge emanates from an essentialist standpoint (Barrett 2001), where one has to "be" one of the groups in question in order to report effectively on it. It is also one about authenticity, but it reduces authenticity to one's drug use. In other words, when people challenge my findings based on my abstinence from drugs, they are essentially reducing the rave experience to drugs. I do not buy this, and I think that this book and my article with Phil Kavanaugh (2007) effectively show that raves were about much more than drug use.

More importantly, my lack of drug use likely had little effect on my findings simply because very few people knew that I was not taking any. My experience has been that most people do not know or care if you are on drugs. This is especially the case during direct observation. Let me give an example. At a party in Ibiza in 2005, I was talking with a young DJ and producer about his work and desire to succeed in the scene. I told him about my project and he became very excited. After about thirty minutes or so, he handed me an ecstasy pill and a mix CD as tokens of his affection and, perhaps, as a gesture of solidarity. I thanked him but told him I was going to chill for now and not take the pill, since I was headed back to my hotel room soon to catch a few hours' sleep before another party. He smiled at me and slid the tablet into my pocket. We then headed to the dance floor where we stayed for another twenty minutes or so.

I also doubt that I could have adequately performed the tasks of direct observation had I been high on drugs. My sobriety brought me clarity and enabled me to focus my attention on the subject matter. By altering my state of consciousness, I would have compromised by ability to document what was going on at the parties or understand what people were telling me. On the other hand, taking stimulants during fieldwork might have enabled me to stay up longer and attend more after-hour parties. The after-hour parties are something I pay less attention to here. My inability to stay up for them is one reason for this. Still, respondents told me about many during the interviews, enabling me to discern notable patterns.

In the interviews, respondents often asked me about my own drug use at raves and otherwise. I was honest with them about my abstinence, and they seemed to respect that. My admission to abstinence had the effect of increasing the interview's focus on other matters relevant to the rave experience. It likely also made some people defensive about their drug use. As a result, some respondents likely played down their own drug use because they were talking with someone who did not imbibe. I think that this modest underreporting of drug use is one of the only ways in which my own abstinence from drugs might have impacted my findings.

One last point is about how I chose to include myself in the text. I wanted to make this book about the people, places, and events that I studied, not primarily about my own experiences in doing the research. I wanted to write a text that privileged people and the scenes I studied, not me, the investigator. Yet, I include myself in the narrative at numerous points to be consistent with the autoethnographic approach (L. Anderson 1996).

Of course, the ethnographer always impacts the phenomena and people he or she studies, and I am no exception, as just discussed in the section on reflexivity. During interviews, a lot of impression management goes on between the parties involved. All people want to give off favorable impressions: they downplay or omit what they perceive as negatives and they accentuate their so-called positives. This happened during the interviews, probably to a greater extent than I can imagine. Still, the use of such variable and complementary data strategies in so many different locations and over such a long period of time likely shores up the story's reliability.

Notes

CHAPTER 1

1. ROAR is an acronym for Ravers Organized Against the Rave Act. Once active in protesting the social control of raves and the EDM scene, it has since been disbanded.

2. The mid- to late 1990s (1996–1999) is generally considered the peak of raves in the United States and England (Hill 2002; Reynolds 1999).

3. *Generation X* typically refers to the U.S. cohort of individuals born after the Baby Boom, or between the years of 1965 and 1980—see Ulrich and Harris 2003.

4. The word *establishment* refers to both government and corporate entities or interests.

5. Incidentally, Generation X also launched the grunge rock scene and sXe (Haenfler 2004a, 2004b, 2006). In addition, scholars (Kitwana 2002; Sharpley-Whiting 2007) have called white Gen X's black peers the Hip Hop Generation. A point to consider, then, is that this birth cohort launched numerous antiestablishment, youth-oriented music collectives.

6. These include academics and journalists as well as government institutions and the people who act on their behalf who either write about or attempt to control raves and the EDM scene.

7. See Bennett 2000, 2001; Hesmondhalgh 1998; Hill 2002; Hutson 2000; McRobbie 1994; Reynolds 1999.

8. For example, the Misuse of Drugs Act in 1987 and the Criminal Justice Public Order Act of 1994 in Britain and the Illicit Drugs and Anti-Proliferation Act of 2000 and 2003 in the United States. Each of these laws targeted entertainment events that were oriented around the rave scene.

9. See, for example, Kelly, Parsons, and Wells 2006; Schensul et al. 2005; and Yacoubian et al. 2004, 2006.

10. The term *club drugs* is commonly used to represent MDMA or ecstasy, Special K or ketamine, GHB, Rohypnol, and, at times, LSD. I discuss these drugs more in Chapters 3 and 4.

11. Melanie Takashi and Tim Olaveson (2003) do a nice job describing the diverse viewpoints on raves.

12. The article is titled "Raves: The End of an Era." www.raves.com.

13. See both Hill 2002 and Hutson 2000 for more discussion on this point. Also, Sylvan (2002, 2005) further discusses the drug-induced spirituality of raves and rave culture.

14. Kai Fikentscher (2000) claims that underground music is produced in an oppositional or antiestablishment fashion and its distribution occurs outside of conventional, commercialized industry and outlets, often in a DIY (do-it-yourself) sort of fashion.

15. Throughout this book, I use both real names and pseudonyms for people, venues, events, and locations (e.g., streets) depending on anonymity and confidentiality requests by those cited. My university Institutional Review Board (IRB) cleared the ability to use real names upon request. However, I do not indicate which names are real or fake in order to further protect privacy.

16. There is a substantial literature in ethnomusicology that focuses on the technological developments in EDM that helped originate the rave scene. See books by Andy Bennett, Barry Shank, and Jason Toynbee 2006; Sara Cohen 2007; and Fikentscher 2000. Since my study is a sociological study about the rave scene's alteration and decline, I do not adopt such an approach in my study.

17. See Fikentscher 2000; Hutson 2000; and Reynolds 1999 for more on this. In addition, many early rave anthems referred to the shaman or god-like qualities of the DJ, including "God is a DJ" by the U.K. group Faithless.

18. The virtual DJ key informants are not, however, included in the analysis reported in Chapters 2 through 5, because they were not part of the Philadelphia scene. They provided input on what was going on in their cities or more globally. Thus, their insights are included in Chapter 6, since it deals with comparisons between Philadelphia and other locations.

19. For example, local DJs working in other states and nations and event promoters who brought in outside talent to perform in the city.

20. Incidentally, both of these clubs have closed. Earlier Explosion! parties—like the one I described above—would likely have been held at one or the other. See Chapter 4 for more on formal social control and raves.

21. An explanation for this has to do with what Pierre Bourdieu (1984) and Herbert J. Gans (1999) have noted about how tastes for cultural products are related to demographics, or one's social class, race, and ethnicity.

22. This is an acronym for the Electronic Music Educational Defense Fund.

23. When I visited the site in the fall of 2006, the last article posted to it was from mid-2003. However, the page was still an active URL.

24. The term *scene* is very similar to Anselm Strauss's (1978) concept of the "social world."

25. The study of music scenes is popular not only within sociology but also in the fields of cultural studies, American studies, musicology, and various other humanities-based areas. Some have focused heavily on the production of music or its technical aspects. Consistent with Bennett and Straw, I believe that music scenes are collectives where people create identity, lifestyle, and fundamental elements of culture (e.g., ethos,

language, norms, and values) around the appreciation of music and its related activities. Given this, I treat music scenes as a type of cultural scene.

26. The concept of collective identity features firm boundaries for membership and clearly established political goals (Gamson 1991; Snow and McAdam 2001; Taylor and Whittier 1992). Scholars have historically addressed youth-based music scenes under the rubric of "deviant subcultures" (Sara Cohen 1972; Hebdige 1979), including raves, rather than as social movements, due to the relative absence of the clear political ambitions. A few exceptions to this can be found in the work of Ross Haenfler (2006) and J. Patrick Williams (2006). I present a nuanced discussion of the term *collective identity* in Chapter 3.

27. There is also a large literature on the role of music, and at times music scenes, in social movements. See Eyerman 2002 and Roscigno, Danaher, and Summers-Effler 2002 for excellent recent examples.

28. This debate is defined by Bennett (1999), Shane Blackman (2005), and Hesmondhalgh (2005).

29. The White Power movement commonly refers to a call for white supremacy by young skinheads.

CHAPTER 2

1. The Illicit Drug Anti-Proliferation Act of 2003 is a federal law that holds club and bar owners responsible for illicit drugs sold on their premises, particularly at raves or dance music parties. Please consult www.dea.gov for more information.

2. Branded parties are named events marketed as an independent cultural product. Through professionalized branding, promoters hope to establish the unique entertainment value of their event as well as enhance its economic prospects.

3. See Richard Peterson's study of country music, *Creating Country Music: Fabricating Authority* (Chicago: University of Chicago Press, 1997).

4. See David Grazian's 2003 study of the blues, *Blue Chicago* (Chicago: University of Chicago Press).

5. I want to reiterate that when I use the word *authentic* I am adopting the position that what people believe to be an authentic rave *is* one. My job as an ethnographer is to describe how they determine this.

6. For a comprehensive discussion of EDM-based club culture, please consult Thornton 1996.

7. Bennett (2000, 2001), Matthew Collin (1997), and Reynolds (1999) have mentioned this but have not directly addressed it in their work. This book attempts to fill that gap.

8. *PLUR* is a native term (i.e., used by scene participants) of the rave scene in the United States. Although the acronym is unique to the U.S. scene, the general sentiments of PLUR have been described as prominent in the UK scene as well. See Hutson 2000, D. Moore 1995, Reynolds 1999, Takashi and Olaveson 2003, and Sylvan 2002 for more on this.

9. A cuddle puddle is a group of ravers who sit on the ground or floor at a rave to talk with each other and listen to music. It is one way solidarity is displayed at raves.

10. See below for more on fashion-based identity markers of raves and current EDM parties.

11. See Collin 1997 and Hill 2002 for more on this point.

12. Hill 2002; Measham et al. 2001; and Redhead 1993.

13. See, for example, Malbon 1999; Redhead 1993; and Reynolds 1999, to name a few.

14. I am referring here to many of the U.S. public health–oriented scholars mentioned previously and in Chapter 1. See also Tammy L. Anderson and Philip R. Kavanaugh 2007 for more examples.

15. See Kavanaugh and Anderson 2008 for an analysis of this matter.

16. Visible in the "DJ Night" section of the *Philadelphia City Paper*, which is compiled weekly by Sean O'Neal, a Philadelphia-based DJ and music journalist, with national and international exposure. O'Neal's column is one of the leading sources of entertainment happenings of all kinds in the city.

17. This follows the methods of autoethnography.

18. EDM scenesters, like homeless people pursuing housing, squat or occupy/take over an abandoned house or building and use it as a site for unlicensed, illegal parties. See Chapter 6.

19. The events I call corporate raves are sometimes called "massives" by attendees or other academics (Hunt and Evans 2008; Hunt et al. 2005; Hunt, Evans, and Kares, 2007).

20. One of the first tasks we complete during direct observation is a canvassing of the event for its demographic makeup. To the extent that we can, we also note social class, sexual identity, alcohol, and drug consumption markers as well. We repeat this several times over the course of the night.

21. Incidentally, the roughly forty-five DJs were all white males except for one white female, one black female, and two black males.

22. Candy kids are rave enthusiasts—usually very young—who sport many of the scene's traditional identity markers, including wearing baggy, parachute, or track pants; antiestablishment t-shirts; and neon bracelets and necklaces.

23. See Chapter 6 for a discussion of those in London and Ibiza, Spain.

24. In addition, there are few promotion groups within the city that put on "corporate raves," making them very similar to each other.

25. The Creamfields festival is one of the very few festivals that travel to several locations.

26. In 2005, Starscape was about $60, while Ultra was $85.

27. I have, however, attended the Ultra Music Festival in Miami on two separate occasions, but do not include it in Table 2.1 because it was not within Philadelphia's city limits.

28. *Rolling* refers to being high or intoxicated on ecstasy.

29. Members of a crew encircle one of their comrades as he or she dances. They trade off dancing in the circle, one at a time, by tagging each other. This usually happens in the middle of the dance floor and attracts and entertains onlookers. Incidentally, two forms of rave-era dancing, Liquid and Digitz, were created in Philadelphia by Digital Hybrid Experiment. Digitz involves rolling finger and hand movements that one can perform sitting down or standing up. Liquid combines the rolling finger and hand movements with a form of body gliding, similar to moonwalking and the pop-n-lock (moving arms and shoulders in a robotic and nonsexualized fashion).

30. This is another example where the concepts of scene and tribe work well together.

31. Decks are turntables that play vinyl records.

32. Both locations have been credited with defining the house music style and the early rave scene. See Collin 1997 and Reynolds 1999 for a discussion.

33. See Chapter 3 for a description of a loyalist. Loyalists are one type of scene insider I found.

34. The Winter Music Conference is the leading worldwide professional and social gathering for industry stakeholders and fans in the contemporary dance music scene.

35. In the three years of my study, I found very few female DJs with their own weekly party. In general, I found the professional side of the EDM scene extremely male-dominated (see McRobbie 1994 for a good discussion of gender, raves, and EDM).

36. To give some examples, I have learned that at some of the one-offs I have attended, superstar DJs were paid between $10,000 and $20,000 to spin for three to six hours. Opening DJs, on the other hand, were often paid nothing or very little. However, the lower-paid DJs could always boast about opening for so-and-so. In addition to the DJ's fee, many superstars now have elaborate contracts that stipulate coverage of other costly items (e.g., equipment, hotels, and limousines). In short, the once-equalized DJ system of the rave era seems to have given way to a star system like in the pop music industry.

37. For example, Red Bull, Absolut, and Sobe beverage companies often sponsor superstar one-offs and, at times, corporate raves and music festivals. At the 2004 and 2005 Winter Music Conferences, corporate sponsorship of events was a popular topic.

CHAPTER 3

1. Pacha's capacity is roughly 3,000 to 4,000 people.

2. This expression describes a DJ on fire, one playing hot music that amazes and moves the audience.

3. This is the standard beat pattern to most dance music, which includes eight beats per measure, based on a four-four combination.

4. See also trance and psytrance communities discussed by Greener and Hollands (2006) and Lynch and Badger (2006).

5. See Denisoff and Peterson 1972. This stellar collection of essays describes how many music scenes in the Civil Rights era inspired collective identity and social and political action toward change.

6. See Frith 1981.

7. See Eyerman 2002.

8. See Gamson 1991; Snow and McAdam 2001; and Taylor and Whittier 1992.

9. Some musical genres have more lyrical content than others. Consider, for example, hip hop and rap versus trance or classical.

10. Most other rave-era studies concur with this. See those previously cited.

11. See Fikentscher 2000 for a good discussion of dancing, solidarity, and collective identity, as well as Futrell et al. 2006 and Kavanaugh and Anderson 2008.

12. Musicians often sing us their stories in English, and their content is heavily influenced by western commercialism. Thus, if a scene crosses national boundaries in scope and membership, then the placement of a language in music—its core cultural element—will be divisive to some, thus undermining one of the fundamental rave and EDM values: unity.

13. See Futrell, Simi, and Gottschalk 2006: 277.

14. This is not to say that all dance music is without lyrics. In fact, some genres—vocal house—have more lyrics than others—trance and techno. However, it is usually the case that lyrics do not drive any type of dance music. They are simply not a priority.

15. The Reagan-Bush and Thatcher-Major regimes of the 1980s.

16. See Bennett 2000; Malbon 1999; and Redhead 1993.

17. Sarah Thornton (1996) also discussed this point, but not in the detail offered here.

18. The reasons for this are the subject of the next chapter.

19. One exception to this is Bennett's (2000) discussion of dance, bhangra, and hip hop music. He discusses how people use music as a local race- and ethnicity-related identity resource, yet he does not delve into more personal motivations for such identity quests.

20. See Anderson and Kavanaugh 2007 for a review of this literature.

21. I discuss the link between understanding drug-related identity for improved social policy in T. Anderson 1993, 1994, and 1998.

22. Again, a good example here is Bennett's stellar work, including his 2000 monograph and his more recent 2001 book on music and popular culture.

23. Respondents are the twenty-seven people I conducted biographical, in-depth interviews with. The primary purpose was to secure information about their personal involvement in the EDM scene over time.

24. The twenty-two key informants I interviewed are people with considerable experience in the EDM scene who were asked to provide expert testimony on the behind-the-scenes workings of the past and present EDM scenes. Little personal biographical information was elicited from them. Moreover, interviews or conversations and communications (e-mails, text messages, or phone calls) were frequent and informal and highly variable in content, depending on the informant's expertise.

25. Because there were no significant differences between respondents and key informants regarding demographic background, and in order to simplify discussion, I collapsed these two categories.

26. Collin 1997; Measham et al. 2001; Reynolds 1999.

27. Thornton's 1996 book *Club Cultures: Music, Media, and Subcultural Capital* is one of the best treatments of this issue in the United Kingdom.

28. Reynolds 1999.

29. See Bennett 2000 and Collin 1997.

30. I separate producers from DJs since there is such distinction within the scene, although all producers are DJs. What separates them is that producers create original music.

31. The approach I used in this study did not call for a random sample. Furthermore, there is no "official directory" of EDM clubbers or stakeholders, so ascertaining equitable demographic representation is impossible. However, I made an effort to secure as diverse a population as I could in order to give voice to those who might otherwise be missed or underrepresented and to secure a great range in opinions and experiences.

32. Recall Jason and Stephanie from my description of the weekly in Chapter 2.

33. EDM chat rooms are also places where social issues and politics are discussed, as well as routine experiences.

34. I have not found any published analysis about why males dominate the EDM industry, which is something McRobbie (1994) pointed out earlier. There have been some recent developments in the EDM industry, however, to increase the amount and visibility of female DJs. For example, Lainie Capicotto of Aurelia Entertainment spearheaded the first women-oriented DJ panel at the 2005 Miami Winter Music Conference (and it was replicated in 2006) and groups like Shejay, a women's DJ collective started by DJ Kellilicious in London (www.shejay.com), are gaining international exposure. The topic of gender equity in the EDM scene is, however, worth further investigation.

35. Some of these include record labels or distribution companies, bars, lounges, and clubs in the entertainment industry, government officials for permits, and so on.

36. Kurt is referring to China's one-child-per-family rule.

37. This refers to people who practice the art of DJ-ing at home or in a private location without an audience or pay, as either a hobby or practice for later paid gigs.

38. During my research, I learned about two types of scene politics. The first pertained to the society and culture. I described these largely left-wing ideas in Chapter 2. The second and perhaps more dominating set, especially for insiders, was scene politics. People told me over and over again how important it was to attend other events in order to shore up their own scene clout and reap important benefits. This is another example of the status system that has developed over time with the scene's transformation.

39. Mash-up is a style of club music where the DJ mixes records from very different genres, for example, house music, reggae, pop, hip hop, and rock or vacillates between these genres from song to song. I discuss this scene more so in Chapter 7.

40. This is one thing that outraged stakeholders, club owners and managers, and others about the Rave Act. They protested the unreasonableness of the new law to hold them responsible for illegal drug use or sales taking place at their events.

41. The pathbreaking study of ecstasy sellers in San Francisco by Sheigla Murphy and colleagues (2005) substantiates this pattern in the dance scene.

42. The involvement with illegal activity decreases as one's stakes in the scene increase. Like any other profession, the more they have to lose, the less likely people are to risk doing so.

43. If I had to estimate, I would put this at about 10 percent of all the events I attended over the course of my study. Thus, I want to make it clear that while drug dealing happens at EDM events, it is not as dominant as people tend to believe. Moreover, I have also spent lots of time in other scenes—gay clubs, hip hop events, and pop and rock concerts—and have noticed illegal drug use in them as well.

44. Thornton's (1996) book eloquently elaborates on the notion of clubbing capital, and Adorno (1991) also wrote about how some people bought tickets to the symphony or opera simply to boast about being there.

45. Many, but certainly not all, of the corporate raves I attended or learned about had "opening" parties on Fridays and "closing" parties on Sundays. In this scenario, the main event is usually held Saturday night, stretching into the early morning hours on Sunday. "After"-parties happen immediately at the end of the main event and typically from 6:00 A.M. until noon or so on Sunday. Thus, "closing" parties often start at 6:00 to 8:00 P.M. Sunday night and end at midnight or 2:00 A.M. Monday morning.

46. Epstein's (1998) edited volume offers a useful discussion of these types as they pertain to youth, especially Generation Xers. In addition, I (Anderson 1994, 1998) have also discussed versions of them previously when describing the identity change processes of drug abusers.

47. Karl Marx and Émile Durkheim were among the first to describe this form.

48. See T. Anderson 1998 for more on this topic.

49. Epstein's (1998) collection on identity and youth.

CHAPTER 4

1. See Anderson and Kavanaugh 2007 for more on this debate.

2. Another dilemma to settle, one the rave scene and many other music scenes have had to face over time, is about how a cultural collective—a music scene—fares when its music expands (successfully or not so successfully) beyond it. Today, hip hop is a huge commercial success, enjoying a hegemonic-like presence in the U.S. pop music

mainstream. Its commercial success has also left behind its Old School scene that championed resistance to white society's oppression. One could ask the same questions about the state of the underground hip hop scene.

3. For example, see Tim Lawrence's (2003) book on disco, Collin's (1997) book on raves, and Jim Fricke and Charlie Ahearn's (2002) book on hip hop.

4. See also Irwin's (1977) book on cohorts as a force of scene stagnation.

5. See Ulrich and Harris 2003.

6. See Mattson 1999: 58–63. Also relevant are works by others, including Harris and Ulrich (2003) and Doug Coupland (1991).

7. Since Generation Xers were born between 1965 and 1981, they were teenagers (thirteen to nineteen years old) by the late 1980s and early 1990s. Thus, a sixteen-year-old in 1992 (a popular year for raves) would have been born in 1978. The twenty-one-year-old who raved at Epic or The Lighthouse in 1998 would have been born in 1977.

8. I provided evidence of this at the individual level in Chapter 3, but this notion has received sociological support over time, including in a recent piece by Robert T. Wood (2000).

9. See Eyerman and Jamison 1998 for a fuller discussion of Generation X, Kurt Cobain, and the grunge rock scene of the 1990s.

10. There have been many reports documenting the dominance of hip hop music among teenagers and young adults in the latter twentieth century and early twenty-first century United States. One of the leading scholars, Bakari Kitwana, has published many articles and books on hip hop. See his book *The Hip Hop Generation* (2002). Also important is Nelson George's *Hip Hop America* (1998).

11. See Barbara Walters's 2002 report on *20/20* and Peter Jennings's "Ecstasy Rising," *ABC News*, April 1, 2004.

12. The television show *90210* was very popular with youth and young adults in the 1990s.

13. Data on these youth trends is available at http://www.nida.nih.gov/Infofacts/HSYouthtrends.html.

14. DiMaggio and Mukhtar 2004.

15. David Looseley's (2003) book on popular music in France directly addresses the issue of authenticity.

16. Two major theoretical statements on this process can be found in Adorno 1991 and Gans 1999. Adorno's is specific to music, while Gans's refers to many cultural forms.

17. Also, refer back to Adam's statement in Chapter 3 about the competition between the raves he put on and local nightclubs' events.

18. This point is discussed by many, including Collin (1997), Fikentscher (2000), Lawrence (2003), and Reynolds (1999).

19. Antonio Melechi (1993: 37) commented earlier that one of the major attractions of acid house was "the emergence of a scene without stars, spectacle, gaze and identification."

20. Becker (1963) also wrote about this dilemma in his classic study of jazz musicians.

21. Paoletta 2000a: 49.

22. *Courtesy stigma* was coined by sociologist Erving Goffman (1963). It refers to how allies of deviants might be labeled deviant themselves, even if they do not engage in the deviant behaviors or acts themselves. In other words, if you hang out with deviants, people may consider you one.

23. I mean attract newcomers, people who are not insiders, so that the number of people attending events increases. Many insiders regularly attend EDM events, with or without superstar DJs, because they are committed to the scene and all of the people involved, including local DJs.

24. Incidentally, six years after Mike Paoletta declared DJs to be the new "pop stars," the more commercialized EDM scene is struggling, not only in cities like Philadelphia but also in larger ones as well. On the other hand, Philadelphia's mash-up scene—where DJs charge $300 to $500 per event, perhaps because they are not yet superstars—is flourishing.

25. While some people are motivated to hear superstar DJs because of their musical selection and mixing skills, many others go simply to brag about seeing them. I noted this pattern among scene outsiders—on which superstar one-offs are dependent—in Chapter 3.

26. For an excellent discussion of branded parties and other commodities in leisure industries, see Chatterton and Hollands 2003.

27. Fisher 2005.

28. See also Hill 2002; McRobbie 1994; Redhead 1993; and Reynolds 1999 for more on this point.

29. XLR8R magazine deemed the rave style of dress one of the worst of all times in its year-end review issue, December 2006. This is remarkable since XLR8R has always been central to rave and EDM culture.

30. See Thornton 1996 and Malbon 1999 for more on this.

31. For some of the people I spoke with, the distaste for drugs was conflated by their aging out of rave culture and into professional life as more conventional adults. For others, antidrug attitudes were a direct repudiation of a core element of rave culture.

32. See also Reynolds 1999 and Collin 1997 for similar reports.

33. More specifically, 90 percent of the respondents reported drug use at some time in their life. Among these, the average age of first drug use was eighteen (range of thirteen to twenty-five). Marijuana and ecstasy were commonly the first drugs used. Regarding current drug use, the respondents reported using marijuana, alcohol, ecstasy, cocaine, mushrooms, ketamine, and crystal methamphetamine (meth). Levels of use were varied. Twenty-seven percent reported having quit all substance use or reported casual alcohol use only. Current use of cocaine, ecstasy, mushrooms, ketamine, and meth was reported among 59 percent of respondents and was reported as occasional or infrequent (yearly, semiyearly) or not elaborated on. Cocaine use, however, was reported as monthly or semimonthly. Regular (daily, semiweekly) marijuana use was reported among 22 percent of the respondents, all males.

34. See Cole et al. 2002; Green et al. 2003; Maxwell 2005; and Schilder et al. 2005.

35. For a comprehensive review of research on the side effects or consequences of ecstasy use, please consult Baylen and Rosenberg 2006.

36. See Alexander 2004 for the replacement of cultural elements as cultural collectives expand.

37. Skater culture commonly refers to the lifestyle that has emerged among many young people who ride skateboards.

38. This viewpoint on deviance is fundamental to the Birmingham Centre for Contemporary Cultural Studies and is articulated in classic work by Mike Brake (1985), Stuart Hall and Tony Jefferson (1976), Dick Hebdige (1979), McRobbie (1994), and Paul Willis (1977), to name a few.

39. I have no definite information on the cause of her illness. It could be from many things, ranging from drugs to alcohol or some combination of them.

40. On a personal note, I felt terrible about this situation. Should I have alerted security? I still do not know. I watched the couple leave, and I wondered how they were going to cope and if they would be okay. I went back inside to observe the event, but the incident, and perhaps my complication of it, spoiled my stay and I left shortly thereafter. I never ran into the couple again, and my respect for the club, and the U.S. war on drugs, declined significantly afterward.

41. In 1982, well-known criminologists James Q. Wilson and George L. Kelling coined the phrase *broken windows* to refer to a policing strategy that maintains routine order on American streets through the enforcement of various anti-loitering and vandalism laws. Wilson and Kelling theorized that such order maintenance would deter more serious crime.

42. Bennett (2000, 2001), Collin (1997), Redhead (1997), and Reynolds (1999) document this point.

43. Several rave-related drug laws were also passed in the United Kingdom, albeit prior to those passed in the United States.

44. Harrison et al. (in progress).

45. Office of National Drug Control Policy, available at www.whitehousedrugpolicy .gov; SubstanceAbuse and Mental Health Services Administration, available at www .samsha.gov; Monitoring the Future Study, available at www.monitoringthefuture.org; and Project Cork, available at www.projectcork.org.

46. Information about local and national ecstasy markets is available at www.dea .gov, and information about the global trade and nation comparisons is available at www.unodc.org/world_drug_report.html.

47. Please consult Gouzoulis-Mayfrank and Daumann 2006 for a current review of this debate.

48. The Crack House law is U.S. Code 21, Section 856 (see http://caselaw.lp.find-law.com/scripts/ts_search.pl?title=21&sec=856). It was crafted by Biden and signed by President George W. Bush in order to curtail the growing epidemic of crack use in the United States.

49. See Eliscu 2001.

50. Comer 2001.

51. For an encyclopedic account of electronica and the hundreds of genres that it comprises, see Bogdanov et al. 2001.

52. Goldberg 2003. Incidentally, there are some similarities between the reasons Goldberg gives for the demise of the Workers Alliance movement and the five forces of change offered here. This suggests some utility for the forces of change model outside of music scenes and into more politically and socially conscious cultural collectives.

53. Other sociologists have written about this process as well, including Alexander (2004) and Anselm Strauss (1978).

54. See Bourdieu 1984.

55. Herbert Gans (1999) wrote about dilemmas between divergent taste publics (people) and taste cultures.

56. For example, many told us drugs like ecstasy, with its empathic-inducing qualities, facilitated PLUR, while stimulants like cocaine and crystal methamphetamine worked against it, causing aggression and hostility instead (see Kavanaugh and Anderson 2008).

57. Incidentally, break dancing initially also took place in unconventional settings and was a unique art form, much like raves and the dancing style embodied at them.

CHAPTER 5

1. This is a 2005 CD title from the U.K.-based group *Everything But the Girl*.

2. Josh Wink is a Philadelphia native who currently enjoys international fame as one of the best house and techno DJs and producers in the world. The 2004 issue of *BPM* magazine ranked him fifty-second. Wink's record label, Ovum, is also internationally recognized. Josh has remixed tracks for countless artists, released X mix CDs, and XX artist albums. In any given month, his calendar is cluttered with DJ gigs on eighteen or more days in countries across the world.

3. I was quite nervous about meeting Wink, since he is a local hero and the first "superstar" DJ I met face-to-face.

4. Again, this is social change in the nontraditional sense described in Chapters 1 and 3. It is geared toward a lifestyle and a unique culture that exists within a scene. It is not expressly political or targeted toward the larger society.

5. Bielby 2004.

6. For example, PLUR ethos, grassroots organization, illegal venues, all-night dancing, illegal drug use, and so on—the cultural elements of raves discussed in Chapter 2.

7. Jason was the music scene pessimist I met at a popular weekly. He was critical of the DJ, the music, and the overall event, claiming nothing measured up to raves from the past.

8. See Grazian 2003; Looseley 2003; and Peterson 1997.

9. See Chapter 4 for respondent testimony on this point.

10. For example, the event might be held to benefit a liberal-leaning cause: tsunami relief, pro-environment, pro-human and animal rights, and antiwar and antiterrorism. People might also adopt interaction patterns that are highly congenial and nonconfrontational.

11. For example, Fisher claims Roland released a virtual version of its 303 synthesizer machine. The Roland 303 synthesizer was often used to produce the acid house sound.

12. "The Politics of Dancing: Turning Up the Underground" (2005).

13. These parties are similar in form and content to the underground parties on the rave–club culture continuum in Chapter 2.

14. For example, New York City has a solid underground EDM scene due largely to grassroots groups like Blackkat.org and UndergroundNYC.org that promote events and serve the scene in still other ways (e.g., maintaining mailing lists and newsletters). See also Fikentscher's (2000) book on the underground dance music scene in New York City.

15. A club manager told me how many students attended the party.

16. I saw three women throwing up at the party and several others doubled over or disoriented over the course of the evening.

17. A resident DJ is one who has a regular, paid gig at the club. Residents are the club's DJs who spin on multiple days of the week at a particular venue. In other words, they work for the club or bar. They do not "contract" with the venue to put on a night or party. Thus, residents can be said to engage in less grassroots cultural work than DJs who create, promote, and organize their own events.

18. See, e.g., Bennett 2000; Ross Haenfler 2004b; Hesmondhalgh 1998; Looseley 2003; and Thornton 1996.

19. At both the 2004 and 2005 conferences, I heard scene heavyweights endorsing the hip hop image and style as something EDM needed to emulate.

20. A cursory look through any of the major EDM magazines—BPM, Mixmag, M8, DJ, and others—will reveal advertisements for these designers and photos of clubbers dressed accordingly.

CHAPTER 6

1. I met people from more than twenty different nations while conducting fieldwork in London and Ibiza. The EDM scenes there were multinational, multiethnic, yet mostly white.

2. See Anderson and Kavanaugh 2007 for a review of work on raves.

3. See Collin 1997 and Reynolds 1999 for discussion about raves' origins.

4. "White Isle" is a nickname for Ibiza, Spain—the third largest of the Balearic Islands.

5. For example, the December 2006 listing of New Year's Eve parties at timeout. com/london listed forty-six house, techno, and electro, of which four had "secret locations." In contrast, there were only ten hip hop, R & B, and drum and bass (part of the EDM scene) parties listed and thirteen rock ones. Clearly, these three genres of EDM dominated London's 2006 New Year's Eve parties.

6. See Bennett 2000; Collin 1997; Malbon 1999; and Redhead 1993.

7. Club research in the United Kingdom has also found this (for example, Measham et al. 2001 and Riley et al. 2001).

8. For example, I was a relative outsider to the London scene and did not have sufficient time to achieve insider status as I did in Philadelphia. Moreover, my recruitment had to be expedited since I had only two months to complete the London and Ibiza fieldwork. Thus, I began contacting potential respondents via a key informant I met on www.clubradio.net and recruited others live at clubs or on a house music chat room. The early interviews and direct observations at clubs eventually broadened the pool of respondents.

9. In 2004, the U.S./U.K. exchange rate was about 1.96. Thus, a reported annual salary of 12,000 pounds is about $23,520 and 80,000 pounds is $156,000.

10. *Timeout London* magazine is a weekly directory of all kinds of leisure activities in London. The London version's music section lists DJ-ed events by genre for each night of the week. It provides the same kind of information as Sean O'Neal's "DJ Nights" column of the *Philadelphia City Paper*. Thus, the two publications are comparable.

11. During my seven weeks in London, I attended eight EDM parties for a total of 40 hours or about 5 hours each. There was some exception to this. Two were early evening parties and I was there for 2 to 3 hours each. The others were much longer and I typically stayed at them between 5 and 6.5 hours each. However, the undergraduate students accompanied me to some of the eight parties and then branched out on their own to two other parties. So, I have field notes on direct observations of ten separate events.

12. The distinction between underground *clubs* and underground *parties* is important in London and the rest of the United Kingdom. Underground *clubs* refers to less commercial venues, whereas underground *parties* refers to those that are illegal, that is, held in violation of local ordinances.

13. Several DJs I spoke with kept citing a figure of 60,000 DJs working in London alone. While I could never find a source to verify this statistic, the sheer number of parties and the numbers of DJs made me think they were not exaggerating.

14. The Cyberdog clothing line, worn by the corporate raver in Figure 6.1, is available for sale in the Covent Garden and Camden Town neighborhoods. Such attire is not, however, prevalent among clubbers at most London parties.

15. There were also plenty of local DJs, who were not superstars, who put on weeklies and monthlies just as the Philadelphia DJs.

16. I did not observe a squat or boat party during my time in London. My description follows from respondents' testimony, *Timeout London*, and local flyers and fanzines.

17. There is big debate about what was the original rave culture. Was it ever grassroots and working class, or was it middle class and entrepreneurial? See Measham et al. 2001 for more on this point.

18. There is some debate that the PLUR aspect of raves was a U.S. phenomenon. Please see Kavanaugh and Anderson 2008 for a discussion of this.

19. "On the pull" is an English phrase for actively seeking sexual contact while clubbing.

20. *Bloke* is an English slang term for males. *Bird* is its female counterpart.

21. Of course, this is an exaggeration, which the respondent confirmed in the interview when I asked him about it.

22. The androgynous and asexual vibes of raves and the EDM scene have been previously cited as motivations for involvement. See McRobbie 1994 and Takashi and Olaveson 2003.

23. According to Drugscope (available at www.drugscope.org.uk), a drug awareness group and clearinghouse in the United Kingdom, this amendment "makes it a criminal offence for people to knowingly allow premises they own, manage, or have responsibility for, to be used by any other person for: (1) the administration or use of any controlled drugs which are unlawfully in that person's possession, (2) the supply of any controlled drug, or (3) the production or cultivation of controlled drugs. Professionals can be prosecuted if they knowingly allow any of these things to occur on work premises. The same legal obligations apply to people with regard to their own homes. The law requires that if staff is aware of the use or supply of illicit drugs on their premises, they must take reasonable action to prevent it from continuing."

24. See Adorno 1991 and Negus 1999.

25. In fact, I learned that some of the clubs I attended had twenty-four-hour licenses to remain open and serve alcohol. No such licenses are available in Philadelphia.

26. She is referring to the 1994 Criminal Justice and Public Order Act, a law believed to have altered England's rave scene in similar ways as did the 2003 U.S. Rave Act. Such acts were rarely enforced, but they exacted symbolic obstacles to raves. Like in the United States, such laws pushed raves indoors to avoid prosecution, but also at a time when people began to tire of driving around the countryside and dancing in muddy fields (see Measham 2006a and Measham et al. 2001).

27. This might be due to the failure to enact the 2001 Section 8 legislation.

28. Official crime statistics in the United Kingdom are collected by the Home Office and are available at http://www.homeoffice.gov.uk/drugs. See also Michael Shiner 2003 for a discussion of British drug use and drug policy. See also the 2005 report by *Focal Point* for current rates of ecstasy use among Brits. They report, for example, that ecstasy is the second most commonly used drug in the United Kingdom. The rate of

ecstasy use among young adults in the United Kingdom is more than twice that of the comparable U.S. group. The *Focal Point* (2005) report shows signs of ecstasy use stabilizing in the United Kingdom, while the overdose rate has dropped recently. Ecstasy use rates are higher among those who had attended a disco or club recently. Such data are also substantiated in Riley et al. (2001) and Measham et al. (2001).

29. There remains debate about whether raves are completely over in the United Kingdom. While the discussion gets back to what defines a rave, few disagree that raves have significantly declined since their peak in either the United States or United Kingdom.

30. There is some sense that the terms *Generation X* and *Generation Y* carry less currency in the United Kingdom. Even so, the break between an older cohort that launched raves and the younger cohort that followed remains a valid point about a generational schism impact on raves.

31. See International Center for Alcohol Policies 2002.

32. The finding of age- and class-based subscenes in London, but not in Philadelphia, calls into question the utility of tribes in understanding matters of lifestyle and identity in music scenes. For example, tribes are claimed to be heterogeneous and fluid, whereas the principle of homophily, found to motivate subscene development, is more rigid and premised on sameness. Reconciling this tension may be an important matter for future research. See Riley et al. 2001 and Measham, Aldridge, and Parker 2001.

33. This phenomenon is consistent with ideas put forth by Goldberg (2003) and Alexander (2004) about the growth of cultural entities and their eventual fragmentation. Also relevant here are M. McPherson, L. Smith-Lovin, and J. Cook's (2001) points about homophily and Bourdieu's (1984) conceptions of taste and distinction.

34. See Anderson and Kavanaugh 2007 for a review of this literature.

35. This matter is addressed directly and thoroughly in Kavanaugh and Anderson 2008.

36. See the Chatterton and Hollands (2003) book for a discussion of leisure in the United Kingdom.

37. Parker et al. (1998) note that U.K. youth may be the most drug experienced in Europe, accounting for what they call "normalization."

38. Measham, Aldridge, and Parker (2001) and Measham (2006a, 2006b) reported comparable rates.

39. Measham, Aldridge, and Parker (2001) documented that U.K. clubbers were, in fact, thinner than other U.K. residents.

40. To reiterate, the *Focal Point* (2005) report on drug use in the United Kingdom substantiates these drug use patterns and consequences that I observed and learned about in London.

41. The more medical approach to drug use in the United Kingdom is well documented and is supported by all kinds of government actors, including law enforcement, who recently called for a reclassification of ecstasy as less serious than its current listing (see www.drugscope.org.uk). See also Shiner 2003 and the 2005 *Focal Point* report for discussion of the United Kingdom's harm reduction approach.

42. Remember that Section 8 of the Misuse of Drugs Act (2001) was passed by the House of Commons, but it was never enacted, thus reducing the likelihood of police interference in club-based parties.

43. Social Responsibility Standards in the United Kingdom (Deputy Minister for Health and Community Care 2007) established firm guidelines for protections against such injuries in retail establishments that served alcohol.

44. The Balearic Islands include Mallorca, Menorca, Ibiza, and Formentera. They are located in the Mediterranean Sea, southeast from the Spanish mainland.

45. The close relationship between EDM clubbing in the United Kingdom and in Ibiza was also noted by Bellis, Anderson, and Hughes (2003); by Hughes, Bellis, and McVeigh (2004); and, historically, by Collin (1997) in the antecedents of acid house and raves.

46. During my summer 2005 trip, a longtime Ibiza resident and one of the founders of the Ibiza dance scene, Alfredo, told me that most tourists were from the United Kingdom. After our interview, I checked tourism data on www.eivissaweb.com and learned that 3.8 million tourists had already visited the island in the first half of 2005 and 77 percent of them were British and German.

47. In 2004, the Big 8 clubs were Pacha, Space, Amnesia, Privilege, Eden, DC10, Es Paradise, and El Divino.

48. I learned from stakeholders in 2005 that billboards like this cost 6,000 to 8,000 euros, or up to $10,000 for the summer season. Prices like that made it difficult for new or smaller parties to advertise and attract sufficient clubbers.

49. Bora Bora is a popular EDM beach party in Playa en Bossa with a worldwide reputation. Unlike other parties on the island, it is free and hosted by local resident DJs, who are not international DJ superstars but who are extremely talented regional heroes. The Bora Bora party starts at noon and runs until about 10:00 P.M. Thus, it is considered both an after-party and a pre-party spot.

50. Interestingly, the Manumission party officially ended after the 2005 season.

51. Again, I was drug- and alcohol-free during all three years of my research for both personal and professional reasons. At times, this made me somewhat of an outsider and damaged my credibility among scene insiders and even other academics. In sort of essentialist standpoint position, many of them believed you had to "roll"—be high on ecstasy—in order to fully understand rave culture and the EDM scene. This was not my experience, and others felt the same or supported me or anyone else who abstained from illegal substances.

52. Ibiza's history as a music colony dates back to the 1970s, when American hippies gravitated to the island to carve out a lifestyle embedded in leisure and hedonism. The so-called Summer of Love that originated in San Francisco in 1967 spread to Ibiza via American hippies. The hippie period inspired raves' "Second Summer of Love" in Britain and on the island in the late 1980s (Collin 1997; Reynolds 1999). Today, several hippies remain on Ibiza and attempt to showcase their culture via the infamous "hippie market" along the island's northwest coast.

53. The Ibiza summer season runs from about mid-June to mid-October. By the end of October, most of the clubs have closed, stakeholders have left on holiday or to work elsewhere, and U.K. and European clubbers have stopped boarding planes to the White Isle. The island does have permanent year-round residents, but the clubbing industry does not provide much work for them during the off-season. Thus, most people must earn their annual income in four short months.

54. These include a Municipal Guard (local Ibiza law enforcement), Regions Balearic (governing body of all four Balearic Islands), and the Spanish mainland.

55. Several of my informants have told me, however, that since my visits to Ibiza in 2004 and 2005, several major clubs have been closed down due to drug use, indicating what could be a globalization of clubbing social control.

56. Please see the article by Bulent Diken and Carsten Bagge Laustsen (2004) for a nice discussion of the Ibizan ideal about pleasure, holidays, and hedonism.

57. These patterns were also discovered by Bellis, Anderson, and Hughes (2003) and Hughes, Bellis, and McVeigh (2004).

CHAPTER 7

1. As indicated in previous chapters, this is also a question Mickey Hess considers in his 2007 book *Is Hip Hop Dead?*

2. Serwer 2006.

3. The relationship between music technologies and scene culture is often a topic in ethnomusicology studies. Scholars in that field claim that technologies advance music's production and distribution more often toward commercial adaptation rather than restoration. See Bennett, Shank, and Toynbee 2006 and Brown, O'Connor, and Cohen 2000 for good discussions of this matter.

4. The desire for a return to Old School or at least a noncommercialized form of hip hop proved to be a prominent theme in my research on the hip hop scene, especially among insiders, no matter what their race or gender.

5. Dave Chappelle, "Mitsubishi Eclipse Remix Commerical," television show skit on the "Chappelle Show," Season 1. Air date: January 22, 2003, on *Comedy Central.*

6. Dirty Vegas are very popular, and well-respected, EDM producers.

7. A few years ago, superstar DJs Deep Dish used a rock-like guitar lick in a remake of the title tune from the classic movie *Flashdance.* It sailed to the top of the charts and earmarked a new rock guitar sound in EDM. Soon afterward, the term *new rave* was being tossed around to refer to a fusion of rock and dance music. Was Deep Dish's musical innovation and the subsequent labeling "new rave" an attempted rebirth of rave culture or simply a new sound or style of music? Matt Annis, the editor of *XLR8R* magazine, warned in his December 2006 issue that the rock/EDM "new rave" sounds' "only link to the original rave movement appears to be the drug habits of the bands involved" (p. 4).

8. Van Dyk is consistently ranked as one of the top three DJs every year by the leading EDM magazines.

9. See Lawrence 2003 for an excellent history of disco.

10. See Green 2003; Mattison et al. 2001; and Westhaver 2005 for divergent analyses of the gay male circuit scene and debates about health-related risk.

11. Hollartronix is a two-person DJ mash-up team founded by Diplo and Low Budget. Please see www.hollartronix.com for more information.

12. Again, this is one of the central topics in ethnomusicology research.

13. The EDM DJ-producer Elite Force offered this quote in a recent issue of *I-DJ* magazine, in a November 2006 article written by Dave Jenkins (p. 41).

14. Perhaps this is because of copyright issues that complicate royalty payments to producers.

15. In fact, it may be that by the time this book is published the iPod will have lost its market share and appeal to newer electronic devices, such as Apple's own iPhone. However, downloading "everything" will likely continue and media such as albums and CDs will increasingly become a thing of the past.

APPENDIX

1. To reiterate an earlier point, Phil Kavanaugh came on late in the project and helped with direct observation at a few events.

2. These included *BPM, XLR8R, DJ Mag, International DJ*, and *MixMag.*

3. Other topics usually discussed in methods sections—that is, how sociologists study what they are writing about—are described throughout the book. For example, my interest in and entry to this project were described in Chapter 1, details regarding the types and number of events I witnessed are presented in Chapter 2 and important background characteristics of the people I spoke with are reported in Chapter 3. Comparable information on respondents I spoke with and events I attended in London and Ibiza is discussed in Chapter 6.

4. The people I spoke with in Ibiza or interacted with at club events are a transient population; most were not permanent residents of the island or even of Spain. Most are tourists from the United Kingdom or Europe, and many others are migrant workers from all over the world, mostly Europe. In contrast, my respondents in London tended to be residents of of that city. Thus, what made my data collection in Ibiza—and even London—so valuable was that I got information on a lot of different local scenes in addition to people's perceptions on other scenes.

5. I used basically the same interview guide in Philadelphia and London. The open-ended nature of the interview allowed respondents to report uniqueness.

6. I interviewed five key informants in London in 2004 and ten in Ibiza in 2005.

7. These were little flip pads from the Dollar Store by my house that could fit into my back pocket. I filled lots of them. Typically, I wrote down just what I saw or heard in them.

8. Usually I ducked behind a speaker or into a corner or bathroom to record them.

9. A grounded theory approach builds concepts and ideas from the data themselves rather than applying preexisting ideas from prior research.

References

Adams, Josh, and Vincent J. Roscigno. 2005. White supremacists, oppositional culture, and the World Wide Web. *Social Forces* 84 (2): 759–778.

Adler, Patricia A., and Peter Adler. 1987. *Membership roles in field research.* Newbury Park, Calif.: Sage.

Adorno, Theodor. 1991. *The culture industry.* London: Routledge.

Alexander, Jeffrey. 2004. Cultural pragmatics: Social performance between ritual and strategy. *Sociological Theory* 22 (4): 527–573.

Anderson, Leon. 2006. Analytic auto-ethnography. *Journal of Contemporary Ethnography* 35 (4): 373–395.

Anderson, Tammy L. 1993. Types of identity transformation in drug using and recovery careers. *Sociological Focus* 26 (2): 133–145.

———. 1994. Drug abuse and identity: Linking micro and macro factors. *Sociological Quarterly* 35 (1): 159–174.

———. 1998. A cultural identity theory of drug abuse. *The Sociology of Crime, Law, and Deviance* 1:233–262.

Anderson, Tammy L., and Philip R. Kavanaugh. 2007. A rave review: Conceptual interests and analytical shifts in research on rave culture. *Sociology Compass* 1:10.1111/j.1751-9020.2007.00034.x.

Anderson, Tammy L., Philip R. Kavanaugh, Ronet Bachman, and Lana D. Harrison. 2007. *Exploring the drugs-crime connection within the electronic dance and hip-hop nightclub scenes, final report* (NIJ Grant # 2004-IJ-CX-0040). Washington, D.C.: U.S. Department of Justice. NCJRS #219381.

Anderson, Zara, Karen Hughes, and Mark Bellis. 2007. *Exploration of young people's experiences and perceptions of violence in Liverpool's nightlife.* Liverpool, U.K.: Government Office for the North West (GONW).

Anthias, Floya. 2002. Where do I belong? *Ethnicities* 2 (4): 491–514.

Barrett, H. C. 2001. On the functional origins of essentialism. *Mind and Society* 3 (2): 1–30.

Barrett, Sean P., Samantha R. Gross, Isabelle Garand, and Robert O. Pihl. 2005. Patterns of simultaneous polysubstance use in Canadian rave attendees. *Substance Use and Misuse* 40:1525–1537.

Baulch, Emma. 2002. Creating a scene: Balinese punk's beginnings. *International Journal of Cultural Studies* 5, no. 2 (June): 153–177.

Baylen, C. A., and H. Rosenberg. 2006. A review of the acute subjective effects of MDMA/ecstasy. *Addiction* 101 (7): 933–947.

Becker, Howard S. 1963. *Outsiders: Studies in the sociology of deviance.* New York: Free Press.

———. 1982. *Art worlds.* Berkeley: University of California Press.

Bellis, Mark, Zara Anderson, and Karen Hughes. 2006. Effects of alcohol misuse enforcement campaigns and Licensing Act of 2003 on violence. Northwest Regional Alcohol Strategic Group, United Kingdom. http://www.cph.org.uk/showPublication.aspx?pubid=275.

Bellis, Mark, et al. 2003. The role of an international nightlife resort in the proliferation of recreational drugs. *Addiction* 98 (12): 1713–1721.

Bennett, Andy. 1999. Subcultures or neo-tribes? Rethinking the relationship between youth, style, and musical taste. *Sociology* 33:599–617.

———. 2000. *Popular music and youth culture.* New York: Palgrave.

———. 2001. Contemporary dance music and club cultures. In *Cultures of popular music.* Ed. Andy Bennett, 118–135. Philadelphia: Open University.

———. 2002. Researching youth culture and popular music: A methodological critique. *British Journal of Sociology* 53:451–466.

———. 2006. Punk's not dead: The continuing significance of punk rock for an older generation of fans. *Sociology* 40 (2): 219–245.

Bennett, Andy, and Richard A. Peterson, eds. 2004. *Music scenes.* Nashville, Tenn.: Vanderbilt University Press.

Bennett, Andy, Barry Shank, and Jason Toynbee, eds. 2006. *The popular music studies reader.* London: Routledge.

Best, Joel. 2004. *Deviance: Career of a concept.* Belmont, Calif.: Wadsworth Publishing.

Bielby, William T. 2004. Rock in a hard place: Grassroots cultural production in a post-Elvis era. *American Sociological Review* 69 (1): 1–13.

Blackman, Shane. 2005. Youth subcultural theory: A critical engagement with the concept, its origins and politics, from the Chicago school to post-modernism. *Journal of Youth Studies* 8 (1): 1–20.

Bogdanov, Vladimir, Chris Woodstra, Stephen Thomas Erlewine, and John Bush. 2001. *All music guide to electronica.* San Francisco: Backbeat Books.

Bolla, Karen I., Una D. McCann, and George A. Ricaurte. 1998. Memory impairment in abstinent MDMA ("ecstasy") users. *Neurology* 51:1532–1537.

Bourdieu, Pierre. 1984. *Distinctions: A social critique of the judgement of taste.* Cambridge, Mass.: Harvard University Press.

Boyd, Robert L. 2005. Black musicians in northern US cities during the early 20th century: A test of the critical mass hypothesis of urban sub-culture theory. *Urban Studies* 42 (13): 2363–2370.

Boys, Annabel, Simon Lenton, and Kathy Norcross. 1997. Polydrug use at raves by a western Australian sample. *Drug and Alcohol Review* 16:227–234.

Brake, Mike. 1985. *Comparative youth culture: The sociology of youth cultures and youth subcultures in America, Britain and Canada.* New York: Routledge.

Brandel, Lars. 2002. ADE debates the deterioration of the live dance music scene. *Billboard* 44 (November 11): 38.

Brown, Adam, Justin O'Connor, and Sara Cohen. 2000. Local music policies within a global music industry: Cultural quarters in Manchester and Sheffield. *Geoforum* 31:437–451.

Brown, E. R., D. R. Jarvie, and D. Simpson. 1995. Use of drugs at "raves." *Scottish Medical Journal* 40:168–171.

Camarotti, Ana Clara, and Ana Lia Kornblit. 2005. Social representations and practices of the consumption of ecstasy. *Convergencia* 12:313.

Camilleri, Andrew M., and David Caldicott. 2005. Underground pill testing, down under. *Forensic Science International* 151:53–58.

Carlson, Robert G., Russel S. Falck, Jill A. McCaughan, and Harvey A. Siegal. 2004. MDMA/Ecstasy use among young people in Ohio: Perceived risk and barriers to intervention. *Journal of Psychoactive Drugs* 36:181–189.

Cerulo, Karen. 1997. Identity construction: New issues, new directions. *Annual Review of Sociology* 23:385–409.

Chasteen, Amy L., and Thomas Shriver. 1998. Rap and resistance: A social movement analysis of the Wu-Tang Clan. *Challenge: A Journal of Research on African American Men* 9:1–24.

Chatterton, Paul, and Robert Hollands. 2003. *Urban nightscapes.* New York: Routledge.

Cheren, Mel, Gabriel Rotello, and Brent Nicholson Earle. 2000. *My life at the Paradise Garage.* New York: 24 Hours for Life.

Cherney, David Z. I., Mogamat R. Davids, and Mitchell L. Halperin. 2002. Acute hyponatraemia and "ecstasy": Insights from a quantitative and integrative analysis. *QJM: An International Journal of Medicine* 95:475–483.

Cohen, Sara. 2007. *Decline, renewal and the city in popular music culture: Beyond the Beatles.* Aldershot, U.K.: Ashgate.

Cohen, Stanley. 1972. *Folk devils and moral panics.* London: MacGibbon and Kee.

Cole, Jon, Harry R. Sumnall, and Charles S. Grob. 2002. Sorted: Ecstasy facts and fiction. *Psychologist* 15:464–467.

Collin, Matthew. 1997. *Altered state: The story of ecstasy culture and Acid House.* London: Serpents Tail.

Comer, M. Tye. 2001. Words get in the way: Understanding dance music's dewey decimal system. *CMJ New Music Monthly* 92 (April): 89.

Connell, John, and Chris Gibson. 2004. World music: Deterritorializing place and identity. *Progress in Human Geography* 28, no. 3 (June): 342–361.

Coupland, Doug. 1991. *Generation X: Tales for an accelerated culture.* New York: St. Martin's.

Critcher, Chas. 2000. "Still raving": Social reaction to ecstasy. *Leisure Studies* 19:145–162.

Damesin, Renaud, and Jean-Michel Denis. 2005. SUD trade unions: The new organizations trying to conquer the French trade union scene. *Capital and Class* 86:17–37.

Davis, Joanna R. 2006. Growing up punk: Negotiating aging identity in a local music scene. *Symbolic Interaction* 29 (1): 63–69.

Degenhardt, Louisa, Paul Dillon, Cameron Duff, and Joanne Ross. 2006. Driving, drug use behaviour and risk perceptions of nightclub attendees in Victoria, Australia. *International Journal of Drug Policy* 17:41–46.

Dennisoff, R. Serge, and Richard A. Peterson, eds. 1972. *The sounds of social change: Studies in popular culture*. Chicago: Rand McNally.

Deputy Minister for Health and Community Care. 2007. *Social responsibility standards for the production and sale of alcoholic drinks*. www.wsta.co.uk/images/stories/social _responsibility.pdf.

Diken, Bulent, and Carsten Bagge Laustsen. 2004. Sea, sun, sex, and the discontents of pleasure. *Tourist Studies* 4 (2): 99–114.

DiMaggio, Paul, and Toqir Mukhtar. 2004. Arts participation as cultural capital in the U.S. 1982–2002: Signs of decline? *Poetics* 32:161–194.

Dowd, Timothy. 2004a. The embeddedness of cultural industries. *Poetics* 32:1–3.

———. 2004b. Production perspectives in the sociology of music. *Poetics* 32:235–246.

Dudrah, Rajinder. 2002. Drum'n'dhol: British bhangra music in diasporic South Asian identity formation. *European Journal of Cultural Studies* 5 (3): 363–383.

Duff, Cameron, and Bosco Rowland. 2006. "Rushing behind the wheel": Investigating the prevalence of "drug driving" among club and rave patrons in Melbourne, Australia. *Drugs: Education, Prevention and Policy* 13:299–312.

Dundes, Lauren. 2003. DanceSafe and ecstasy: Protection or promotion? *Journal of Health and Social Policy* 17:19–37.

Durkheim, Émile. 1915. *The elementary forms of religious life*. New York: Free Press.

———. 1933. *The division of labor in society*, trans. George Simpson. New York: Free Press.

Egan, Danielle. 2004. Eyeing the scene: The uses and (RE)uses of surveillance cameras in an exotic strip club. *Critical Sociology* 30 (2): 299–319.

Eliscu, Jenny. 2001. The war on raves. *Rolling Stone* 869:21–22.

Epstein, Jonathan S. 1998. *Youth culture: Identity in a postmodern world*. Malden, Mass.: Blackwell.

Erikson, Kai T. 1966. *Wayward puritans: A study in the sociology of deviance*. Boston: Allyn and Bacon.

Eyerman, Ron. 2002. Music in movement: Cultural politics and old and new social movements. *Qualitative Sociology* 25 (3): 443–458.

Eyerman, Ron, and Andrew Jamison. 1998. *Music and social movements*. Cambridge: Cambridge University Press.

Eyre, Stephen, Rebecca Guzman, Amy A. Donovan, and Calvin Boissiere. 2004. Hormones are not magic wands: Ethnography of a transgender scene in Oakland, California. *Ethnography* 5 (2): 147–172.

Fidler, Helen, Amar Dhillon, David Gertner, and Andrew Burroughs. 1996. Chronic ecstasy (3,4-methylenedioxymetamphetamine) abuse: A recurrent and unpredictable cause of severe acute hepatitis. *Journal of Hepatology* 25:563–566.

Fikentscher, Kai. 2000. *You better work! Underground dance music in New York City*. Hanover, N.H.: Wesleyan University Press.

Fine, Gary A. 2003. Towards a peopled ethnography: Developing a theory from group life. *Ethnography* 4 (1): 41–60.

Fisher, Cristina. 2005. The politics of dancing: Turning up the underground. *BPM* 62 (April): 89–91.

Focal Point. 2005. *United Kingdom drug situation*, 2005 ed. London: Department of Health.

Forsyth, Alasair J. M. 1996. Are raves drug supermarkets? *International Journal of Drug Policy* 7:105–110.

Fricke, Jim, and Charlie Ahearn. 2002. *Yes yes y'all: Oral history of hip hop's first decade.* Cambridge, Mass.: Da Capo.

Frith, Simon. 1981. *Sound effects: Youth, leisure, and the politics of rock 'n' roll.* New York: Pantheon.

Furr-Holden, Debra, Robert B. Voas, Tara Kelley-Baker, and Brenda Miller. 2006. Drug and alcohol-impaired driving among electronic music dance event attendees. *Drug and Alcohol Dependence* 85:83–86.

Futrell, Robert, Pete Simi, and Simon Gottschalk. 2006. Understanding music in movements: The white power music scene. *Sociological Quarterly* 47:275–304.

Gaillot, Michel. 2001. Raves, a "cursed part" of contemporary societies. *Societies* 2:45–55.

Gamson, William A. 1991. Commitment and agency in social movements. *Sociological Forum* 6:27–50.

Gans, Herbert J. 1999. *Popular culture and high culture.* New York: Basic Books.

Garcia-Repetto, R. E., T. Soriano Moreno, C. Jurado, M. P. Gimenez, and M. Menendez. 2003. Tissue concentrations of MDMA and its metabolite MDA in three fatal cases of overdose. *Forensic Science International* 135:110–114.

George, Nelson. 1998. *Hip hop America.* London: Penguin Books.

Gill, James R., Jonathan A. Hayes, Ian S. De Souza, Elizabeth Marker, and Marina Stajic. 2002. Ecstasy (MDMA) deaths in New York City: A case series and review of the literature. *Journal of Forensic Sciences* 47:121–126.

Glaser, Barney G., and Anselm L. Strauss. 1967. *The discovery of grounded theory.* Chicago: Aldine.

Glover, Troy D. 2003. Regulating the rave scene: Exploring the policy alternatives of government. *Leisure Sciences* 25:307–325.

Goffman, Erving. 1963. *Stigma: Notes on the management of spoiled identity.* New York: Simon and Schuster.

Goldberg, Chad Allen. 2003. Haunted by the specter of communism: Collective identity and the resource mobilization in the demise of the Workers Alliance of America. *Theory and Society* 32:725–773.

Goode, Eric, and Nachman Ben-Yehuda. 1994. Moral panics: Culture, politics, and social construction. *Annual Review of Sociology* 20:149–171.

Gottschalk, Simon. 1993. Uncomfortably numb: Counter-cultural impulses in the postmodern era. *Symbolic Interaction* 16:351–378.

Goulding, Christina, and Avi Shankar. 2004. Age is just a number: Rave culture and the cognitively young "thirty something." *European Journal of Marketing* 38:641–658.

Gouzoulis-Mayfrank, E., and J. Daumann. 2006. Neurotoxicity of methylenedioxyamphetamines (MDMA; ecstasy) in humans: How strong is the evidence for persistent brain damage? *Addiction* 101 (3): 348–361.

Grazian, David. 2003. *Blue Chicago.* Chicago: University of Chicago Press.

Green, Adam Isaiah. 2003. Chem-friendly: The institutional basis of "club drug" use in a sample of urban gay men. *Deviant Behavior* 24 (5): 427–447.

Green, A. Richard, Annis O. Mechan, J. Martin Elliott, Esther O'Shea, and M. Isabel Colado. 2003. The pharmacology and clinical pharmacology of methylenedioxymethamphetamine (MDMA, "ecstasy"). *Pharmacological Reviews* 55:463–508.

Greener, Tracey, and Robert Hollands. 2006. Beyond subculture and post-subculture? The case of virtual psytrance. *Journal of Youth Studies* 9 (4): 393–418.

Hadfield, Philip. 2006. *Bar wars.* Oxford: Oxford University Press.

Haenfler, Ross. 2004a. Collective identity in the straightedge movement: How diffuse movements foster commitment, encourage individualized participation, and promote cultural change." *Sociological Quarterly* 45:785–805.

———. 2004b. Rethinking subcultural resistance: Core values of the straightedge movement. *Journal of Contemporary Ethnography* 33:406–436.

———. 2006. *Straight EDGE*. New Brunswick, N.J.: Rutgers University Press.

Hall, Stuart, and Tony Jefferson. 1976. *Resistance through rituals: Youth subcultures in post-war Britain*. London: Routledge.

Halnon, Karen Bettez. 2004. Inside shock music carnival: Spectacle as contested terrain. *Critical Sociology* 30 (3): 743–779.

———. 2005. Alienation incorporated: "F*** the mainstream music" in the mainstream. *Current Sociology* 53, no. 3 (May): 441–464.

Hammersley, Richard, Jason Ditton, and Ian Smith. 1999. Patterns of ecstasy use by drug users. *British Journal of Criminology* 39:625–647.

Harcourt, Bernard. 2001. *Illusion of order: The false promise of broken windows policing*. Cambridge, Mass.: Harvard University Press.

Harrison, L., T. Anderson, S. Martin, and C. Robbins (under contract and in progress). *Drug and alcohol abuse in social context*. Belmont, Calif.: Wadsworth.

Hebdige, Dick. 1979. *Subculture: The meaning of style*. New York: Methuen.

Heckathorn, Douglas. 1997. Respondent-driven sampling: A new approach to the study of hidden populations. *Social Problems* 44, no. 2 (May): 174–199.

Herman, Bill. 2006. Scratching out authorship: Representations of the electronic dance music DJ at the turn of the 21st century. *Popular Communication* 4 (1): 21–38.

Hesmondhalgh, David. 1998. The British dance music industry: A case study of independent cultural production. *British Journal of Sociology* 49 (2): 234–251.

———. 2005. Subculture, scenes, or tribes? None of the above. *Journal of Youth Studies* 8 (1): 21–40.

Hess, Mickey. 2007. *Is hip hop dead? The past, present, and future of America's most wanted music*. Westport, Conn.: Praeger.

Hier, Sean P. 2002. Raves, risks and the ecstasy panic: A case study in the subversive nature of moral regulation. *Canadian Journal of Sociology* 27:33–57.

Hill, Andrew. 2002. Acid House and Thatcherism: Noise, the mob, and the English countryside. *British Journal of Sociology* 53:89–105.

Hitzler, Ronald. 2002. Pill kick: The pursuit of "ecstasy" at techno events. *Journal of Drug Issues* 32:459–466.

Hitzler, Ronald, and Michaela Pfadenhauer. 2002. Existential strategies: The making of community and politics in the techno / rave scene. In *Postmodern existential sociology*. Ed. Joseph A. Kotarba and John M. Johnson, 87–101. Walnut Creek, Calif.: AltaMira.

Hollands, Robert. 2002. Divisions in the dark: Youth cultures, transitions and segmented consumption spaces in the night-time economy. *Journal of Youth Studies* 5:153–171.

Holstein, James A., and Jaber Gubrium. 2003. *Inside interviewing*. Thousand Oaks, Calif.: Sage.

Hughes, Karen, Mark Bellis, and Jim McVeigh. 2004. A potent cocktail. *Nursing Standard* 18 (47): 14–17.

Huizink, Anja C., Robert F. Ferdinand, Jan van der Ende, and Frank C. Verhulst. 2006. Symptoms of anxiety and depression in childhood and use of MDMA: Prospective, population based study. *British Medical Journal* 332:825–828.

Hunt, G., and K. Evans. 2004. Dancing and drugs: A cross-national perspective. *Journal of Contemporary Drug Problems* 30 (4): 779–814.

———. 2008. "The great unmentionable": Exploring the pleasures and benefits of ecstasy from the perspectives of drug users. *Drugs: Education, Prevention and Policy* 15 (4): 329–349.

Hunt, G., K. Evans, and F. Kares. 2007. Drug use and the meanings of risk and pleasure. *Journal of Youth Studies* 10 (1): 73–96.

Hunt, Geoffrey, Kristin Evans, Eileen Wu, and Alicia Reyes. 2005. Asian American youth, the dance scene, and club drugs. *Journal of Drug Issues* 35:695–731.

Hunter, James. 2002. Lifestyles of the rhythm: Dance music accesses an unseparatist pop sensibility. *Village Voice* 47 (26): 73.

Huq, Rupa. 2003. From margins to mainstream? Representations of British Asian youth musical cultural expression from bhangra to Asian underground music. *Nordic Journal of Youth Research* 11 (1): 29–48.

Hutson, Scott. 2000. The rave: Spiritual healing in modern Western subcultures. *Anthropological Quarterly* 73:35–49.

International Center for Alcohol Policies. 2002. *Drinking age limits*. ICAP Reports 4. Washington, D.C.

Irvine, Rodney J., Michael Keane, Peter Felgate Una, D. McCann, Paul D. Callaghan, and Jason M. White. 2006. Plasma drug concentrations and physiological measures in "dance party" participants. *Neuropsychopharmacology* 31:424–430.

Irwin, John. 1977. *Scenes*. Beverly Hills, Calif.: Sage.

Johnson, Matt. 2001. Successful rave operations. *Law and Order* 49:184–188.

Johnston, L. D., P. M. O'Malley, and J. G. Bachman. 2003. *Monitoring the Future national survey results on drug use, 1975–2002*. Volume I: Secondary school students (NIH Publication No. 03-5375). Bethesda, Md.: National Institute on Drug Abuse.

Kahn-Harris, Keith. 2004. The "failure" of youth culture: Reflexivity, music and politics in the black metal scene. *European Journal of Cultural Studies* 7 (1): 95–111.

Karlovšek, Majda Zorec, Armin Alibegović, and Jože Balažic. 2005. Our experiences with fatal ecstasy abuse (two case reports). *Forensic Science International* 147:S77–80.

Kavanaugh, Philip, and Tammy L. Anderson. 2008. Drug use and solidarity in the electronic dance music scene. *Sociological Quarterly* 49 (1): 181–208.

Kelly, Brian C. 2005. Conceptions of risk in the lives of club drug using youth. *Substance Use and Misuse* 40:1443–1459.

Kelly, Brian C., Jeffrey T. Parsons, and Brooke E. Wells. 2006. Prevalence and predictors of club drug use among club-going young adults in New York City. *Journal of Urban Health* 83:884–895.

Kirby, Alan. 2006. The death of postmodernism and beyond. *Philosophy Now* (November/December): 34–37.

Kitwana, Bakari. 2002. *The hip hop generation*. New York: Basic Civitas Books.

Knutagard, Hans. 1996. New trends in European youth and drug cultures. *Youth Studies Australia* 15:37–42.

Kosmicki, Guillaume. 2001. Musical meaning in today's free-parties: Between ideology and utopia. *Societies* 2:35–44.

Krebbs, Christopher P., and Danielle M. Steffey. 2005. Club drug use among delinquent youth. *Substance Use and Misuse* 40:1363–1379.

Laidler, Karen Joe. 2005. The rise of club drugs in a heroin society: The case of Hong Kong. *Substance Use and Misuse* 40:249–266.

Lawrence, Tim. 2003. *Love saves the day: A history of dance music culture, 1970–1979*. Durham, N.C.: Duke University Press.

LeBlanc, Lauraine. 1999. *Pretty in punk: Girl's gender resistance in a boy's subculture*. New Brunswick, N.J.: Rutgers University Press.

Levy, Kira B., Kevin E. O'Grady, Eric D. Wish, and Amelia M. Arria. 2005. An in-depth qualitative examination of the ecstasy experience: Results of a focus group with ecstasy-using college students. *Substance Use and Misuse* 40:1427–1441.

Looseley, David L. 2003. *Popular music in contemporary France*. New York: Berg.

Lua, Ahai C., Huei R. Lin, Yong T. Tseng, An R. Hu, and Pei C. Yeh. 2003. Profiles of urine samples from participants at rave party in Taiwan: Prevalence of ketamine and MDMA abuse. *Forensic Science International* 136:47–51.

Luckman, Susan. 1998. Rave cultures and the academy. *Social Alternatives* 17:45–49.

Lynch, Gordon, and Emily Badger. 2006. The mainstream post-rave club scene as a secondary institution: A British perspective. *Culture and Religion* 7 (1): 27–40.

MacLeod, Kembrew. 1999. Authenticity within hip hop and other cultures threatened with assimilation. *Journal of Communication* (Autumn): 134–150.

Maffesoli, Michel. 1996. *The time of tribes: The decline of individualism in mass society*. London: Sage.

Malam, Linda. 2004. Performing masculinity on the Thai beach. *Tourism Geographies* 6 (4): 455–471.

Malbon, Ben. 1999. *Clubbing: Dancing, ecstasy and vitality*. New York: Routledge.

Marshall, Donnie R. 2000. Ecstasy and other club drugs: What chiefs can do to stop their spread. *Police Chief* 67:61–67.

Mattison, Andrew M., M. W. Ross, T. Wolfson, D. Franklin, and HNRC Group. 2001. Circuit party attendance, club drug use, and unsafe sex in gay men. *Journal of Substance Abuse* 13:119–126.

Mattson, Kevin. 1999. Talking about my generation (and the left). *Dissent* (Fall): 58–63.

Maxwell, J. C. 2005. Party drugs: Properties, prevalence, patterns, and problems. *Substance Use and Misuse* 40 (9–10): 1203–1240.

McCaughan, Jill A., Robert G. Carlson, Russel S. Falck, and Harvey A. Siegal. 2005. "From "candy kids" to "chemi-kids": A typology of young adults who attend raves in the midwestern United States. *Substance Use and Misuse* 40:1503–1523.

McDowell, David M. 2005. Marijuana, hallucinogens, and club drugs. *Clinical Textbook of Addictive Disorders*, 3d ed. 3:157–183.

McElrath, Karen. 2005. MDMA and sexual behavior: Ecstasy users' perceptions about sexuality and sexual risk. *Substance Use and Misuse* 40:1399–1407.

McLoone, Martin. 2004. Punk music in Northern Ireland: The political power of "what might have been." *Irish Studies Review* 12 (1): 29–28.

McPherson, M., L. Smith-Lovin, and J. Cook. 2001. Birds of a feather: Homophily in social networks. *Annual Review of Sociology* 27:415–444.

McRobbie, Angela. 1994. Shut up and dance: Youth culture and changing modes of femininity. In *Postmodernism and popular culture*. Ed. Angela McRobbie, 155–176. New York: Routledge.

Measham, F. 2006a. The new policy mix: Alcohol, harm minimisation and determined drunkenness in contemporary society. *International Journal of Drug Policy*, Special edition: Harm reduction and alcohol policy 17:258–268.

———. 2006b. Cultures of intoxication, local leisure "scenes" and the new wave of criminalization. British Society of Criminology annual conference, Glasgow, July. Unpublished conference paper.

Measham, Fiona, Judith Aldridge, and Howard Parker. 2001. *Dancing and drugs: Risk, health, and hedonism in the British club scene.* London: Free Association.

Measham, Fiona, and Philip Hadfield. 2008. Your name's not down: Fragmentation, gentrification, and criminalisation in English clubland. Paper presented at the 2008 Club Health Conference, Ibiza, Spain.

Measham, Fiona, and Karenza Moore. 2008. The criminalization of intoxication. Unpublished manuscript submitted to Home Office, U.K.

Mejias, Sandrine, M. Rossignol, D. Debatisse, E. Streel, L. Servais, J. M. Guérit, P. Philippot, and Salvatore Campanella. 2005. Event-related potentials (ERPs) in ecstasy (MDMA) users during a visual oddball task. *Biological Psychology* 69:333–352.

Melechi, Antonio. 1993. The ecstasy of disappearance. In *Rave off: Politics and deviance in contemporary youth culture.* Ed. Steve Redhead, 29–40. Burlington, Vt.: Avebury.

Merton, R. K. 1988. Some thoughts on the concept of sociological autobiography. In *Sociological lives.* Ed. M. W. Riley, 78–99. Newbury Park, Calif.: Sage.

Miller, Brenda A., Debra Furr-Holden, Robert Voas, and Kristin Bright. 2005. Emerging adults' substance use and risky behaviors in club settings. *Journal of Drug Issues* 35:357–378.

Miller, Timothy. 1999. *The 60s communes: Hippies and beyond.* Syracuse, N.Y.: Syracuse University Press.

Moore, David. 1995. Raves and the bohemian search for self and community: A contribution to the anthropology of public events. *Anthropological Forum* 7:193–214.

Moore, Dawn, and Mariana Valverde. 2000. Maidens at risk: "Date rape drugs" and the formation of hybrid risk knowledges. *Economy and Society* 29:514–531.

Moore, Karenza, and Steven Miles. 2004. Young people, dance, and the sub-cultural consumption of drugs. *Addiction Theory and Research* 12:507–523.

Moore, Robin D. 2006. *Music and revolution: Cultural change in socialist Cuba.* Berkeley: University of California Press.

Moore, Ryan. 2005. Alternative to what? Subcultural capital and the commercialization of a music scene. *Deviant Behavior* 26:229–252.

Morel, Natalie. 1999. Recreational drug use and the club scene. In *Illegal drug use in the United Kingdom: Prevention, treatment and enforcement.* Ed. Cameron Stark, Brian A. Kidd, and Roger Sykes, 153–167. Aldershot, U.K.: Ashgate.

Morleo, Michela. 2008. Assessing the implementation and development of the new licensing legislation. Paper presented at the 2008 Club Health Conference, Ibiza, Spain.

Mosler, Damon. 2001. Club drugs. *Law Enforcement Quarterly* 30:5–10.

Muggleton, David. 2002. *Inside subculture: The postmodern meaning of style (dress, body, culture).* Oxford: Berg.

Murphy, Sheigla, Paloma Sales, Micheline Duterte, and Camille Jacinto. 2005. *A qualitative study of ecstasy sellers in the San Francisco Bay area, final report* (NIJ Grant # 2002IJ-CX 0018). Washington, D.C.: U.S. Department of Justice.

Negus, Keith. 1999. The music business and rap: Between the street and the executive suite. *Cultural Studies* 13 (3): 488–508.

Nencini, Paolo. 2002. The shaman and the rave party: Social pharmacology of ecstasy. *Substance Use and Misuse* 37:923–939.

Novoa, Roberto, Danielle Ompad, Yingfeng Wu, David Vlahov, and Sandro Galea. 2005. Ecstasy use and its association with sexual behaviors among drug users in New York City. *Journal of Community Health* 30:331–343.

ONDCP (Office of National Drug Control Policy). 2004a. Club drugs: Facts and figures. Washington, D.C.: whitehousedrugpolicy.gov.

———. 2004b. Cocaine. Washington, D.C.: whitehousedrugpolicy.gov.

Paoletta, Michael. 2000a. Dance: Getting into the groove—the mainstream is giving dance music more air time, but there's still room to grow. *Billboard* (July 22): 49–50.

———. 2000b. U.K. club culture wins devotees across the U.S. *Billboard* (October 21): 1–2.

Parker, H., J. Aldridge, and F. Measham. 1998. *Illegal leisure: The normalization of adolescent recreational drug use*. London: Routledge.

Parks, Kathleen A., and Cheryl L. Kennedy. 2004. Club drugs: Reasons for and consequences of use. *Journal of Psychoactive Drugs* 36:295–302.

Parrott, Andy C. 2004. MDMA (3,4-methylenedioxymethamphetamine) or ecstasy: The neuropsychobiological implications of taking it at dances and raves. *Neuropsychobiology* 50:329–335.

Parrott, Andy C., J. Rodgers, T. Buchanan, J. Ling, T. Heffernan, and A. B. Scholey. 2006. Dancing hot on ecstasy: Physical activity and thermal comfort ratings are associated with the memory and other psychobiological problems reported by recreational MDMA users. *Human Psychopharmacology: Clinical and Experimental* 21:285–298.

Partridge, Christopher. 2006. The spiritual and the revolutionary: Alternative spirituality, British free festivals, and the emergence of rave culture. *Culture and Religion* 7:41–60.

Perrone, Dina. 2006. New York City club kids: A contextual understanding of club drug use. In *Drugs, clubs and young people: Sociological and public health perspectives*. Ed. Bill Sanders, 26–49. Burlington, Vt.: Ashgate.

———. 2007. Clubbing, culture, consumption, capital, and control: Drug use among the club kids. Ph.D. diss., Rutgers University.

Peterson, Richard A. 1997. *Creating country music: Fabricating authenticity*. Chicago: University of Chicago Press.

Peterson, Richard, and N. Anand. 2004. The production of culture perspective. *Annual Review of Sociology* 30:311–334.

Pini, Maria. 1997. Women in the early British rave scene. In *Back to reality? Social experience and cultural studies*. Ed. Angela McRobbie, 152–169. Manchester, U.K.: Manchester University Press.

Pourtau, Lionel. 2002. Risk as stimulant: The example of rave parties. *Societies* 3:69–81.

Redhead, Steve. 1990. *The end-of-the-century party: Youth and pop towards 2000*. Manchester, U.K.: Manchester University Press.

———. 1995. *The end-of-the-century party: Youth and pop towards 2000*. Manchester, U.K.: Manchester University Press.

———. 1997. *Subculture to club culture*. Malden, Mass.: Blackwell.

———, ed. 1993. *Rave-off: Politics and deviance in contemporary youth culture*. Brookfield, Vt.: Avebury.

———, ed. 1998. *The club cultures reader*. Malden, Mass.: Blackwell.

Reynolds, Simon. 1999. *Generation ecstasy: Into the world of techno and rave culture*. New York: Routledge.

———. 2006. *Rip it up and start again: Postpunk 1978–1984*. New York: Penguin.

Ricaurte, George A., and Una D. McCann. 2005. Recognition and management of complications of new recreational drug use. *Lancet* 365:2137–2145.

Rietveld, Hillegonda. 1993. Living the dream. In *Rave off: Politics and deviance in contemporary youth culture*. Ed. Steve Redhead, 41–78. Brookfield, Vt.: Avebury.

Riley, Sarah C. E., Charlotte James, Danielle Gregory, Henry Dingle, and Mike Cadger. 2001. Patterns of recreational drug use at dance events in Edinburgh, Scotland. *Addiction* 96:1035–1047.

Roach, Ronald. 2004. Decoding hip-hop's cultural impact: Scholars are poised to take a close look at the influence of hip-hop on the social identity, values of today's youth (questions about hip-hop). *Black Issues in Higher Education* 21, no. 3 (April 24): 3.

Rome, Ellen S. 2001. It's a rave new world: Rave culture and illicit drug use in the young. *Cleveland Clinic Journal of Medicine* 68:541–550.

Roscigno, Vincent J., William F. Danaher, and Erika Summers-Effler. 2002. Music, culture, and social movements: Song and southern textile worker mobilization, 1929–1934. *International Journal of Sociology and Social Policy* 22 (1–3): 141–173.

Sachdev, Michael V. 2004. The party's over: Why the Illicit Drug Anti-Proliferation Act abridges economic liberties. *Columbia Journal of Law and Social Problems* 37:585–625.

Salasuo, Mikko, and Paulina Seppälä. 2004. Drug use within the Finnish club culture as marks of distinction. *Contemporary Drug Problems* 31:213–229.

Sanders, Bill. 2005. In the club: Ecstasy use and supply in a London nightclub. *Sociology* 39:241–258.

Sarabia, Daniel, and Thomas E. Schriver. 2004. Maintaining collective identity in a hostile environment: Confronting negative public perception and factional divisions within the skinhead subculture. *Sociological Spectrum* 24:267–294.

Schensul, Jean J., Sarah Diamond, William Disch, Rey Bermudez, and Julie Eiserman. 2005. The diffusion of ecstasy through urban youth networks. *Journal of Ethnicity in Substance Abuse* 4:39–71.

Schilder, A. J., T. M. Lampinen, M. L. Miller, and R. S. Hogg. 2005. Crystal methamphetamine and ecstasy differ in relation to unsafe sex among young gay men. *Canadian Journal of Public Health* 96 (5): 340–343.

Serwer, Jesse. 2006. New York state of rhyme. *Timeout New York* (December 28–January 3, 2007): 28–30.

Shank, Barry. 1994. *Dissonant identities: The rock and roll scene in Austin, Texas.* Hanover, N.H.: Wesleyan University Press.

Sharpley-Whiting, T. Deanan. 2007. *Pimps up, ho's down: Hip hop's hold on young black women.* New York: New York University Press.

Sherlock, Kellie, and Mark Conner. 1999. Patterns of ecstasy use amongst club-goers on the UK "dance scene." *International Journal of Drug Policy* 10:117–129.

Shiner, Michael. 2003. Out of harm's way? Illicit drug use, medicalization, and the law. *British Journal of Criminology* 43:772–796.

Silverstone, D., D. Hobbs, and G. Pearson. In press. *Nightclubbing.* Cullompton, U.K.: Willan.

Siokou, Christine. 2002. Seeking the VIBE: The Melbourne rave scene. *Youth Studies Australia* 21:11–18.

Snow, David A. 2001. Collective identity and expressive forms. *Center for the Study of Democracy.* Irvine: University of California.

Snow, David A., and Doug McAdam. 2001. Identity work processes in the context of social movements: Clarifying identity/movement nexus. In *Self, identity, and social movements.* Ed. Sheldon Stryker, Timothy J. Owens, and Robert W. White, 41–67. Minneapolis: University of Minnesota Press.

Snow, David A., Calvin Morrill, and Leon Anderson. 2003. Elaborating analytic ethnography: Linking fieldwork and theory, *Ethnography* 4 (2): 181–200.

Soellner, Renate. 2005. Club drug use in Germany. *Substance Use and Misuse* 40:1279–1293.

Spring, Ken. 2004. Behind the rave: Structure and agency in a rave scene. In *Music scenes*. Ed. Andy Bennett and Richard A. Peterson, 48–63. Nashville, Tenn.: Vanderbilt University Press.

Springhall, John. 1998. *Youth, popular culture and moral panics.* New York: St. Martin's.

Spunt, Barry. 2003. The current New York City heroin scene. *Substance Use and Misuse* 38 (10): 1539–1549.

Sterk, Claire E., Katherine P. Theall, and Kirk W. Elifson. 2006. Young adult ecstasy use patterns: Quantities and combinations. *Journal of Drug Issues* 36:201–228.

Strauss, Anselm. 1978. A social world perspective. *Studies in Symbolic Interaction* 1:119–128.

Straw, Will. 1991. Systems of articulation, logics of change: Communities and scenes in popular music. *Cultural Studies* 5:368–388.

———. 2004. Cultural scenes. *Society and Leisure* 27 (2): 411–422.

Sylvan, Robin. 2002. *Traces of the spirit.* New York: New York University Press.

———. 2005. *Trance formation.* New York: Routledge.

Tagg, Philip. 1994. From refrain to rave: The decline of figure and the rise of ground. *Popular Music* 13:209–222.

Takashi, Melanie, and Tim Olaveson. 2003. Music, dance and raving bodies: Raving as spirituality in the central Canadian rave scene. *Journal of Ritual Studies* 17:72–96.

Taylor, Verta, and Nancy E. Whittier. 1992. Collective identity in social movement communities: Lesbian feminist mobilization. In *Frontiers in social movement theory.* Ed. Aldon D. Morris and Carol McClurg Mueller, 104–129. New Haven, Conn.: Yale University Press.

ter Bogt, Tom, and Rutger Engels. 2005. "Partying" hard: Party style, motives for and effects of MDMA use at rave parties. *Substance Use and Misuse* 40:1479–1502.

ter Bogt, Tom, Rutger Engels, and Judith Semon Dubas. 2006. Party people: Personality and MDMA use of house party visitors. *Addictive Behaviors* 31 (7): 1240–1244.

ter Bogt, Tom, Rutger Engels, Belinsa Hibbel, Fritz van Wel, and Stijn Verhagen. 2002. Dancestasy: Dance and MDMA use in Dutch youth culture. *Contemporary Drug Problems* 29:157–181.

Thane, Katja. 2002. Crack cocaine use in Hamburg's open drug scene. *Journal of Drug Issues* 32 (2): 423–430.

Theall, Katherine P., Kirk W. Elifson, and Claire E. Sterk. 2006. Sex, touch, and HIV risk among ecstasy users. *AIDS and Behavior* 10:169–178.

Thomas, Helen. 1997. *Dance in the city.* London: MacMillan.

Thornton, Sarah. 1996. *Club cultures: Music, media, and subcultural capital.* London: Wesleyan University Press.

Tomlinson, Lori. 1998. This ain't no disco . . . or is it? Youth culture and the rave phenomenon. In *Youth culture: Identity in a postmodern world.* Ed. Jonathan S. Epstein, 195–211. Malden, Mass.: Blackwell.

Topp, Libby, Julie Hando, Paul Dillon, Ann Roche, and Nadia Solowij. 1999. Ecstasy use in Australia: Patterns of use and associated harm. *Drug and Alcohol Dependence* 55:105–115.

Trapp, Erin. 2005. The push and pull of hip hop. *American Behavioral Scientist* 48 (11): 1482–1495.

Ulrich, John M., and Andrea L. Harris, eds. 2003. *GenXegesis.* Madison: University of Wisconsin Press.

U.S. Census Bureau. 2000. United States census 2000. http://www.census.gov/main/www/cen2000.html.

U.S. Drug Enforcement Administration (DEA). 2000. DEA congressional testimony of John Andrejko before the Criminal Justice, Drug Policy and Human Resources subcommittee on September 18, 2000. http://www.usdoj.gov/dea/pubs/cngrtest/ct091800.htm.

Valdez, Al. 2002. Club drugs. *Police: The Law Enforcement Magazine* 26:74–77.

Valentin, Gill, and Tracey Sheffield. 2003. Finding oneself, losing oneself: The lesbian and gay "scene" as a paradoxical space. *International Journal of Urban and Regional Research* 27 (4): 849–866.

Van De Wijngaart, Govert F., Ruud Braam, Dick De Bruin, Maalste M. Fris, J. M. Nicole, and Hans T. Verbraeck. 1999. Ecstasy use at large-scale dance events in the Netherlands. *Journal of Drug Issues* 29:679–701.

Vannini, Philip. 2004. The meanings of a star: Interpreting music fans' reviews. *Symbolic Interaction* 27 (1): 47–69.

Verheyden, Suzanne L., Rachel Maidment, and H. Valerie Curran. 2003. Quitting ecstasy: An investigation of why people stop taking the drug and their subsequent mental health. *Journal of Psychopharmacology* 17:371–378.

Wacquant, Loic. 2003. Ethnografest: A progress report on the promise and practice of ethnography. *Ethnography* 4 (1): 5–14.

Watkins, S. Craig. 2005. *Hip hop matters: Politics, pop culture, and the struggle for the soul of a movement.* Boston: Beacon.

Weber, Max. 1994. *Max Weber: Sociological writings.* New York: Continuum.

Wedenoja, William. 1990. Ritual trance and catharsis: A psychobiological and evolutionary perspective. In *Personality and the cultural construction of society: Papers in honor of Melford E. Spiro.* Ed. David K. Jordan and Marc J. Swartz, 275–307. Tuscaloosa: University of Alabama Press.

Weimer, Mark. 2003. Rave clubs: The Kissimmee approach. *Police Chief* 70:32–34.

Westhaver, Russell. 2005. Coming out of your skin: Circuit parties, pleasure and the subject. *Sexualities* 8 (3): 347–374.

Whyte, William. 1979. Themes in chemical prohibition. In *Drugs in perspective*, xx. Rockville, Md.: National Institute on Drug Abuse.

Williams, J. Patrick. 2006. Authentic identities: Straightedge subculture, music, and the Internet. *Journal of Contemporary Ethnography* 35:173–200.

Willis, Paul. 1977. *Learning to labour: How working class kids get working class jobs.* Farnborough, U.K.: Saxon House.

Wilson, James Q., and George L. Kelling. 1982. Broken windows. *Atlantic Monthly* 249 (3): 29–38.

Wolfinger, Nicholas H. 2002. On writing fieldnotes: Collection strategies and background expectancies. *Qualitative Research* 2:85–95.

Wood, Robert T. 2000. Threat transcendence, ideological articulation, and frame reference reconstruction: Preliminary concepts for a theory of subcultural schism. *Deviant Behavior* 21:23–45.

Yacoubian, George S., Jr., Cynthia Boyle, Christine A. Harding, and Elizabeth A. Loftus. 2003. It's a rave new world: Estimating the prevalence and perceived harm of ecstasy and other drug use among club rave attendees. *Journal of Drug Education* 33:187–196.

Yacoubian, George S., Jr., Julia K. Deutsch, and Elizabeth J. Schumacher. 2004. Estimating the prevalence of ecstasy use among club rave attendees. *Contemporary Drug Problems* 31:163–177.

Yacoubian, George S., Jr., Sarah Miller, Selwyn Pianim, Michael Kunz, Erin Orrick, Tanja Link, Wilson R. Palacios, and Ronald J. Peters. 2004. Toward an ecstasy and other club drug (EOCD) prevention intervention for rave attendees. *Journal of Drug Education* 34:41–59.

Yacoubian, George S., Jr., and Eric D. Wish. 2006. Exploring the validity of self-reported ecstasy use among club rave attendees. *Journal of Psychoactive Drugs* 38:31–34.

Zhao, Huiru, Rudolf Brenneisen, Andre Scholer, A. J. McNally, Mahmound A. ElSohly, Timothy P. Murphy, and Salvatore J. Salamone. 2001. Profiles of urine samples taken from ecstasy users at rave parties: Analysis by immunoassays, HPLC, and GC–MS. *Journal of Analytical Toxicology* 25:258–269.

Index

Tammy L. Anderson is Associate Professor in the Department of Sociology and Criminal Justice at the University of Delaware. She is also the editor of *Neither Villain nor Victim: Empowerment and Agency among Women Substance Abusers.* For more information about her work, visit www.udel.edu/soc/tammya.